the lost art
of silence

the lost art of silence

RECONNECTING TO THE POWER
AND BEAUTY OF QUIET

SARAH ANDERSON

SHAMBHALA

Shambhala Publications, Inc.
2129 13th Street
Boulder, Colorado 80302
www.shambhala.com

Copyright and permission to reprint from "The Walnut Tree" thanks to
David Tas, whose earlier work appears in *Poems from a Marriage*.

Cover art: "Cloud Shadow after the Disturbance Period. (Midday)—Jena,
September 10th 1887," from *Studies on Twilight Phenomena, after Krakatoa*
Cover design: Katrina Noble
Interior design: Katrina Noble

9 8 7 6 5 4 3 2 1

First Edition
Printed in the United States of America

Shambhala Publications makes every effort to print on acid-free, recycled
paper.
Shambhala Publications is distributed worldwide by Penguin Random
House, Inc., and its subsidiaries.

LIBRARY OF CONGRESS CATALOGING-IN-PUBLICATION DATA
Names: Anderson, Sarah, 1947– author.
Title: The lost art of silence: reconnecting to the power and beauty of
    quiet / Sarah Anderson.
Description: First edition. | Boulder, Colorado: Shambhala, [2023] |
    Includes bibliographical references and index.
Identifiers: LCCN 2023027932 | ISBN 9781645472162 (trade paperback)
Subjects: LCSH: Silence. | Mindfulness (Psychology)
Classification: LCC BJ1499.S5 A525 2023 | DDC 158.1—dc23/eng/20230802
LC record available at https://lccn.loc.gov/2023027932

DEDICATION

To all those who have helped me in my quest

CONTENTS

ACKNOWLEDGMENTS

Firstly, huge thanks to both Robert McCrum and Alan Samson who not only read early drafts but were also extremely encouraging. I would also like to thank the following for their suggestions and help—with apologies to those I have omitted: Camilla Anderson, Liz Anderson, Marie-Laure Aris, Anne Baring, Bella Bathurst, Caroline Baum, Caroline Blunden, Lavinia Byrne, Mark Cazalet, Kate Chisholm, William Chubb, Liz Claridge, Artemis Cooper, Marilyn Curran, Caroline Dawnay, Janine di Giovanni, Maggie Fergusson, Victoria Finlay, Clare Ford-Wille, Bill Forse, David Fraser Jenkins, Martin Goodman, Aidan Hart, Anthony Holden, Heather Holden-Brown, Clare Hornsby, William Howard, Lucy Hughes-Hallett, Tim Husband, Teresa Keswick, Alan McClue, Sarah Miller, Adam Munthe, Nelly Munthe, Emma Parsons, Nicholas Pearson, Robert Perkins, Richard Philp, Sarah Quill, Simon Richey, Sophy Roberts, Johanna Roeber, Kate Sapara, Peter Sawbridge, Jean Schooling, Rupert Sheldrake, Sarah Spankie, Peter Stanford, Philip Stevens, Sean Swallow, David Tas, Sara Wheeler, Andrew Willson; and to my editor, Breanna Locke, and all at Shambhala, The Literary Consultancy (TLC), The London Library, and The Society of Authors.

INTRODUCTION

There is a Taoist saying that claims "those who know, do not speak; those who speak, do not know,"[1] and I wanted to find out if this was still relevant today and if we do indeed need silence to help solve the world's problems. All of humanity shares this secret silent interior, whether they know it or not, and the ways of discovering that interior are diverse and exciting. By examining the many facets of silence, this book will invite you to develop and embrace periods of silence in your life by means you had previously possibly not thought about. I'll consider my own relationship with silence—which is far from straightforward—and I suspect my own yearnings for silence, as well as my doubts and fears, will chime with those of many others. Nothing about silence is clear-cut. So although I believe that silence is essential, sometimes I find its pursuit a struggle. Silence can force you to confront yourself, which is why many people do everything they can to try to avoid it—often filling their world with vacuous sound. Silence can be transformative—when it snows, the landscape becomes hushed; when machines stop operating, a quietness descends. But silence inevitably also has a dark side, and the exploration of that leads into murky places.

Is silence just the absence of sound? Or does it have a deeper, more profound meaning? Does silence ever really exist? Silence comes before sound—it is not just the cessation of sound; it is there already. The word comes from the Latin *silentium*, meaning "to abstain, to forbear from speech." The first use of the word *silence* in an English text and as an English word dates from 1225 and appears in the text *Ancrene Riwle*, written at the request of three noble anchoresses: "In silence and in hope shall be our strength."[2] The dictionary states that it is "the fact of abstaining or forbearing from speech or utterance; the state or condition resulting from this; muteness, reticence, taciturnity."[3] This initial meaning seems to put rather a negative gloss on the word, but it continues: "The state or condition when nothing is audible; complete quietness or stillness; noiselessness," which is more appealing.

Where is this boundary between the visible world and the audible world? And if there is a boundary, what and where is it? You can close your eyes and become part of the audible world, leaving the visible behind, but how much harder it is to block out the world of sound. If we think about sound, it is an imposition and, as the British writer Robert Macfarlane points out in *Underland*, "We cannot see behind ourselves, but we can hear behind ourselves. From all directions, sound flows in."[4] We're all so wordy today that just sitting in silence with another person can feel awkward. In the nineteenth century, the philosopher and theologian Søren Kierkegaard wrote that if he were a physician and he had just one thing to prescribe for all the world's problems, it would be silence: "And even if it were blazoned forth with all the panoply of noise so that it could be heard in the midst of all the other noise, then it would no longer be the Word of God. Therefore, create silence!"[5]

But why is it that we crave silence? Or what is it in us that needs silence? Silence certainly enhances our powers of attention, and it is a break and rest from the stimuli of the external world. Of course, noise and silence are inextricably linked—the yin and the yang—but do we really only appreciate silence as an absence of sound? I don't think so. I think it's far more important than that; as Mahatma Gandhi noted, "It has often occurred to me that a seeker after truth has to be silent."[6] This makes total sense to me—for how can we possibly grow in depth if we are being constantly distracted by external noise? Silence can stop a rush to judgment. As the philosopher Ludwig Wittgenstein said in the last sentence of his *Tractatus Logico-Philosophicus*: "Whereof one cannot speak, thereof one should be silent."[7] To discover a unity and connection with all creation, one has to experience being alone and isolated. By learning to appreciate silence and its benefits, one also learns to truly listen—and when one is truly listening, one begins to hear. The more one can listen, the more one really begins to hear others with compassion and kindness. Often if somebody is grieving or has had bad news, all the person requires is a listener. Words seem, and are, mostly inadequate, and a solution at the time is the last thing needed; it is listening that is important.

Doing mundane tasks in silence can be an anchor to being in the present. As the psychologist and spiritual leader Ram Dass is quoted, "The quieter we become, the more we hear."[8]

Finding silence is never easy, as we are having to compete with not only exterior sounds but also an almost constant interior dialogue that judges, analyzes, compares, and questions. But if we can get past this barrage, there is a quiet place definitely worth the search.

HOW THIS BOOK CAME TO BE

Silence has always been, and remains, an elusive subject—some people are naturally drawn to it, whereas others fight it. Some places feel silent and peaceful, whereas others don't have that quality however quiet they are. That kind of quiet seemed to be becoming rarer and rarer—until the pandemic lockdown in the spring of 2020. Suddenly with the absence of planes in the sky and many fewer cars on the road, silence, even in London, became more and more of a reality. I felt that we had been given time to value it, and as a result we could perhaps start thinking of it not as an absence but as a presence. Of course, that period quickly ended, but the possibility of a more silent city was there.

There could not have been a better time for me to fully plunge into writing my book on silence than during lockdown, although the actuality of lockdown for me was fairly typical of any day I spend at my desk, only quieter. Many people found it difficult to concentrate at this time, suddenly realizing how important it is to have even silent interaction, such as eye contact, with strangers. It's difficult to know whether our personal behavior changes in the absence of company. I suspect that we all change when we're on our own; and with the enforced isolation and solitude of the lockdown, I think I've become more hermit-like and antisocial. I've been lucky in that I was able to write, read, and paint throughout—it could have become all too easy to fritter away whole days reading jokes, watching Netflix, and having meetings on Zoom.

Whatever the way, I will show the benefits—physical, psychological, and practical—of awakening silence and including it more consciously in our lives. One of the things I aim to do is to inspire people to think about silence in ways that they haven't done before. I have talked to musicians, read about hermits, been on retreats, experienced silence in the desert, and looked at paintings and at the works of artists that I think give one a profound feeling of silence. Of course, this is my choice and a very limited choice with which some might disagree.

I live in London, a noisy city, but over the last fifty years I have been lucky enough to travel widely. During those years of travel, I observed the customs and rituals of many cultures. Running the Travel Bookshop for over thirty years also gave me the opportunity to meet and talk to a wide range of travelers and writers and learn about the traditions of places I hadn't yet been to. While I was running the shop full-time, I had little opportunity for travel, but after a few years I was able to take off, and it was then that I started painting seriously. I find the solitary act of painting a wonderful way of immersing myself in silence—nothing that's going on around me matters; it's just me and the painting and the landscape.

Rather than being negative about noise, perhaps we should start becoming more positive about silence. As the Greek philosopher Socrates pointed out, the secret of happiness is not to be found in seeking more but in developing the capacity to enjoy less.[9] Our short lives are bookmarked by silence—we come from a silence and with death we go to another silence.

WHO NEEDS SILENCE?

Who needs silence? We all do. Noise is tiring, and constant noise is exhausting. Living in a city, one is surrounded by noise. But on top of regular city din, we are now subjected to smartphones and social media full-time. For those unfamiliar with silence, this book shows its advantages and how it can be found in the most unlikely places. For those already pursuing a spiritual journey, there might be some unexpected and unusual suggestions in the search for silence. And for those who found the isolation of lockdown overwhelming, I hope there might be some useful advice about how to turn negative isolation and loneliness into positive solitude.

OVERVIEW OF THE BOOK

Silence is increasingly rare—and that should frighten us. All imaginative creation needs a degree of silence, and as the world gets noisier, it seems that we may be in danger of losing this precious yet free commodity. We need to start thinking seriously about what we stand to lose if we ignore the need for silence. Looking back into the past, we can tell that it has *always* been important, but never more so than now in this increasingly frantic noise-driven world in which we live. For our sanity I believe that silence needs to reclaim its position in our lives by examining and reconnecting to this "lost art."

The book is organized into six main parts. "Lived Experiences" introduces the role that silence has played in my personal life as well as notable figures who have decided to embark on silent quests of their own. "The Concept of Place" looks at silence from the perspective of setting—our relationship with nature, the majesty of the desert, and even humanmade structures such as historic buildings and ruins that can amplify or inspire quiet. In "Spirituality" we look at the relationship between silence and a range of different spiritual traditions, religions, and practices throughout history. "The Arts" shows how writers, artists, and creators have been inspired by and used silence in their work. "Darker Sides of Silence" acknowledges silence's presence in wartimes and how it can be used for punitive measures. Finally, "Going Forward" concludes by offering final food for thought around experiencing and embracing silence in life, embracing curiosity, and being mindful to both the quieter and noisy moments in life.

LIVED EXPERIENCES

1

My Silence

AS A CHILD, I refused to talk at times. My decision not to talk was very temporary and was not mutism, but my silence was unsuccessful in that it didn't achieve what I wanted. I found the parties that I had to go to during the school holidays in my early teens excruciating. However, my mother was adamant that I should attend, and it became something of a ritual before going to each of them that I would lock myself in the bathroom and scream and scream that I didn't want to go. So my protest wasn't a silent protest, but in retrospect the screams seemed silent, as they weren't heeded. In adolescence, awareness of self is intensified anyway, and I didn't want to go to these parties because I didn't want my lack of arm to be noticed, and I certainly didn't want to answer questions about what had happened. I thought that if I kept the fact of having one arm to myself and to my family, it somehow wouldn't be real in the outside world. On the whole, this silence and denial served me well.

I had had cancer—synovial sarcoma of the soft tissue round my elbow—when I was ten, and 1957 being the dark ages in terms of cancer treatment, it had necessitated having my left arm amputated. I was so loathe to have anyone mention anything to do with my arm that I didn't even know I'd had cancer until I was in my late teens. I still recall the car journey during which I made myself ask what had happened to my arm. Before the end of the journey, I remember digging my nails into my palm and forcing myself to break the silence to ask what had occurred. As we got closer and closer to home, I blurted out, "What happened to my arm?" Of course I knew that I'd had to have my arm amputated, but since no one in my family or at school ever referred to it, I didn't know why. My mother's response was how surprised she was that I hadn't asked before. When she started telling me everything about that year when I was ten, I wanted her to go on and on.

Back to the teenage parties where none of my protestations from the bathroom had helped: After I would exhaust myself with crying and get cajoled out, I would be forced into going to the dreaded event. On arrival, I would wait by the wall at the edge of the dance area, with a tear-stained face, for my parents to come to collect me and take me home. I stood there determinedly wearing a white cardigan and white ankle socks, dreading being asked to dance yet hating looking as conspicuous as I did by not dancing. The question I most dreaded was people asking why I didn't take my cardigan off. I hoped that by wearing it I could disguise the fact that I only had one arm, and I also hoped that the white ankle socks would prevent me from looking grown up. I wanted to remain safely in childhood, and I did not want to embark on what seemed the terrifying and long journey to adulthood.

In addition to the horror of being among a whole lot of strangers who might ask me about my arm, there were also boys at parties. I had no idea what boys talked about. Admittedly I did have a brother, but he was five years younger than me, so he was of no use as a conversational model. To me, males were beings from another planet, and there was always the fear that perhaps these aliens would mention my arm. I have just discovered from someone who used to be at those parties that his mother had alerted him to my arm and had told him to be especially nice to me. "Being nice" to me meant asking me to dance, along with two other girls she had picked out for his special treatment—the hostess and the largest girl in the room. Had I known this was why I was being asked to dance, I don't think anything would have ever gotten me out of that bathroom.

My silence regarding my arm continued all through my teens and during my years at boarding school. I felt that the silence was protecting me, and it worked. During my five years at school, no one asked me a single question about my arm. So silence became my ally. Whether this was a healthy approach is debatable, but it worked for me. I only began to question the silent approach when I went to America for the first time at age twenty-two. In the States, it seemed natural for people to ask in an unembarrassed way what had happened to my arm, with none of the English reserve. Maybe it was because it was simply the right time to talk about it, but for whatever reason, it was a huge relief. Silence around this issue was over.

Families can have taboo subjects, things that are never talked about—for example, the death of a child. The fact that the topic is never mentioned means that by wrapping the forbidden matter in silence, it becomes like a parcel that can never be opened, a terrible secret. As a result, the silence around the subject becomes toxic—an unpunctured canker. The longer that the topic is left unaddressed and in silence, the harder it becomes to broach it as a subject. In my own case, the fact that I couldn't talk or ask about having one arm for nearly ten years, until I was nearly twenty, meant that for me the topic grew out of proportion and I felt that I just couldn't ask what had happened. However, the reality was that I felt silence was my ally. I could pretend that since no one commented on my lack of arm, they probably hadn't noticed it.

Silence as avoidance is just one kind of silence—a silence that worked well for me for a time. But of course there are many other varieties. It is these different types that I want to explore in this book.

5

POWERFUL MOMENTS OF NOISELESSNESS

For years, if anyone asked me where I most wanted to go in the world, I would always say Antarctica, and in March 2005, I was lucky enough to go. It was the blues and turquoises in the icebergs that, as a painter, had first enticed me, but I came away with something else: silence. Silence with a deep sound. The Antarctic can be incredibly noisy; icebergs are constantly calving, and boat engines are loud. Although the noise isn't necessarily something that you are aware of at the time, when it stops, you notice its sudden absence: a wonderful all-embracing silence.

It was there in the Antarctic that I experienced the most profound silence of my life. A few passengers had left the Russian icebreaker and climbed into inflatable dinghies to weave in and out of multi-blued icebergs. At some point, all the engines were turned off; we were totally still and totally quiet, and then it began to snow. There was a real feeling of completeness. Many years later I can still conjure up that feeling of connection and wholeness—it was one of the most profound moments of my life. I think these experiences are often referred to as "peak experiences," a term that makes me feel slightly uneasy. Maybe that's because the letdown can be brutal. My experience in the Antarctic was something that just happened, though. Yes, I had to be open to it, but there was no anticipation and therefore no letdown afterward. Indeed, the aftermath brought a feeling of deep peace.

It would probably be impossible to re-create those particular circumstances. Even if I had the time, energy, and money to go back to the Antarctic, the chances of it beginning to snow at exactly the right time would be remote. The memory, though, is a wonderful thing to have. I think this is true of most silence. We are so used to noise around us most of the time—especially if we live in a city—that it is often only when it suddenly isn't there that we take notice. Even the countryside can be noisy with farm machinery, cars, and animals—and, of course, the ubiquitous airplanes. After the eruption of the Icelandic volcano Eyjafjallajokull in 2010, when due to the ash cloud there were no planes flying overhead at all, many people remarked on how wonderfully quiet it was. Sadly, this kind of blanket quietness is not repeatable.

Another memory of snow-quiet stands out to me—this time I was in a city. I arrived in New York for the first time in January 1969. Soon afterward, there was a big snowstorm and the city more or less came to a complete halt. There was no traffic, and to get anywhere you had to walk—and all with a muffled hush. I couldn't believe that this could happen in a city of the size and importance of New York. I remember walking through the silent city in the snow, carrying my party shoes to a party at the famous El Morocco nightclub. Of course the silence didn't last for long—and there were police sirens in the background—but while the snow was still falling, it was silent.

PURSUITS SUITED TO SILENCE

Until the nineteenth century, walking was for many the only way of getting around—to work, to school, errands. It was also a way of escaping from often overcrowded living conditions. During the COVID-19 lockdown, walking regained popularity. It became a regular and necessary escape from monotony as one of the few activities one was allowed to do. Walking is now often treated as a leisure pursuit, and there are many organizations devoted to rambling, trekking, hiking, and walking.

But walking can still be an escape. When I walk alone, I don't have to connect to anyone else; I can be solitary and silent. The British academic G. M. Trevelyan insisted that for a walking tour to be properly enjoyed, it should be done alone since by being alone, you can go at your own pace and be free to stop where and when you want. Talking to someone while walking might disturb the "harmony of body, mind and soul,"[1] wrote Trevelyan. For the poet John Clare, solitary walking enabled a better appreciation of the beauty of the natural surroundings. Clare would often take a book with him on his walks, something that walkers often did; they went to read in solitary locations. Finding a secluded place to read outside in the middle of London can be challenging, but its cemeteries—Kensal Green, Highgate, Brompton, and Margravine—are fairly reliable sources of silence and good places to visit for both reading and walking. Although there is no cemetery in Battersea Park, I am extremely lucky to live nearby this two-hundred-acre green space in the heart of London as it is always possible to find quiet corners. The British historian David Olusoga visits cemeteries to find the grave of the person he is going to write about so that he can first commune with them in silence.

The leisurely speed at which one walks is ideal for reflection; it can help to clear the mind and provide a good ground for creativity. "I'm just taking the dog for a walk" must have been used many times as an excuse to get out of the house and be on one's own. A dog is a wonderful companion—and a mostly silent one. Walking is also very good for one's health—in *The Songlines*, the great traveler and writer Bruce Chatwin referred to the Pintupi of Australia valuing strong legs.[2]

I also swim regularly—easy to do in silence. There are those who see swimming as a social activity, but I avoid this and practice swimming as a solitary sport. Of course there might be noise around, but it's easy enough to shut off anything extraneous. Having a moment of quiet contemplation in water can be inspiring—for instance, *Waterlog*, the late Roger Deakin's wonderful book about swimming through Britain, was an idea that came to him while he was swimming in his moat, eyeballing frogs.[3]

Sailing and fishing are solitary pursuits too. In *The Compleat Angler*, Izaak Walton describes fishing as an occupation in total contrast to that of a lawyer or statesman. A fisherman can sit on "cowslip banks, hear the Birds sing and possesse our selves with as much quietnesse as these silver streams which we now see glide by us."[4] Though I am not someone who actually fishes, I appreciate sitting quietly on a riverbank absorbing the surroundings. In 2017, a friend of mine rented a large house in Sutherland to celebrate his seventy-fifth birthday. Alongside his three children, their partners, and his six grandchildren there were three nonfamily members, myself included. Fishing was the main purpose of the holiday, but as a nonfisher, I was extremely content to sit and draw silently on the riverbank.

I once did a weeklong icon-painting course at West Dean College of Arts and Conservation in Sussex. I had never thought of doing icon painting before, but I happened to see it in the West Dean brochure and it leaped out at me. It ended up being one of the most rewarding things I have ever done. There were only six of us students, and we were extremely lucky to have the distinguished icon painter Aidan Hart as our teacher. He had never taught at West Dean before, and never did again. For six years, Hart had lived as a hermit in Shropshire, feeling that the more he entered prayer, the more he entered silence; and the deeper into himself he journeyed, the more he felt that he was entering into the mystery of God: "As a hermit I would sit for about two hours twice a day trying to pray in silence. For most of the time in the early years I would come face to face not with God but with myself, in all my noisiness, fragmentation, distractions, facades . . . Then a light began to shine." Painting an icon is a meditation. In Hart's words, "As an icon painter, I paint faces. I am not painting a philosophical system but people. So my work is to do with persons looking at persons, with contemplation and therefore, in a sense, with silence. Words then have their meaning as a means of communion, not as space fillers. For me the content of silence is therefore relationship."[5]

This course only lasted five days, so we skimmed the surface of what it is to be an icon painter. A first-year student will only brush the floor; in the second year, he or she will progress to painting eyebrows (this also lasts for a year). We crammed everything into a few days. I found the week, much of it spent in silence, a profoundly meditative experience. It was something to do with the total concentration that was necessary—a glimpse into the immersive life of a committed icon painter. I have an icon painted on a piece of driftwood made by a present-day monk from Mount Athos. When I look at it, it gives me an intense sense of continuity, a link to an ancient tradition.

While writing this book, I have often thought about how I could try to paint silence—it's something I would really like to do, but I find the reality intimidating. So one of the things I have started to do is to copy paintings I consider silent, and by doing so, to immerse myself in the world of the painter.

I have always been fascinated by books on mountaineering—climbing is not something I have ever even remotely wanted to do, but I find the accounts written by mountaineers compelling; and I find reading silently about mountaineering, while in a safe place, totally absorbing. Sailing can also be a solitary sport—one person alone with the elements. Strangely, most long-distance sailors are not given to much introspection—with Bernard Moitessier, who abhorred the commercialization of long-distance sailing, being an exception. His book *The Long Way* treats the actual voyage as a spiritual journey.[6] Even if you do not climb or sail, you may embrace the silent spirit of such activities secondhand through reading, a solitary experience in itself, as I do.

Another silent pursuit is, of course, the practice of meditation. In June 2019, I went on a silent Buddhist retreat in Spain called "Loving Awareness," led by Jack Kornfield, a Buddhist teacher in American Theravada Buddhism, and his wife, the dharma teacher Trudy

Goodman. There were about thirty of us, an unusually small number for one of Jack's popular retreats. The first thing that Jack asked us was "How do you individually navigate the world?" He pointed out that every ancient and wise culture has set aside time—sometimes in the desert, others in the forest—to just stop. He posited that we need to find that sacred time in order to live wisely, and Trudy added that in a spiritual life, silence is your best friend. Ironically the room we were in was never completely silent. Either the air-conditioning unit was roaring away or the windows were open and outside sounds filtered in—some good, such as the chime of bells and birdsong; some, such as traffic or people's voices, more distracting.

There is a very different feeling when meditating in a group; the quality of the silence feels thicker and more rounded. Jack trained as a monk in Thailand, Burma, and India before cofounding the Insight Meditation Society in Barre, Massachusetts, in 1975 and the Spirit Rock Meditation Center in Woodacre, California, in 1987. The "Loving Awareness" retreat was held at Santa Maria de Montserrat Abbey in Catalonia, about an hour from Barcelona in Spain. The abbey is famous for its Black Madonna, the patron saint of Catalonia. She sits high up above the altar in the monastery with long queues of people waiting to see her. About sixty monks in residence contend with busloads of tourists until about 5 p.m. every day. When the hoards leave, the monastery returns to a sense of peace. Benedictine chanting takes place in the cathedral regularly throughout the day. Although the present cathedral was built in the nineteenth century, there have been monks on this site since the eleventh century. Despite its destruction by Napoleon's troops in the Peninsula War and its suppression during the Spanish Civil War, there seems to be a feeling of spiritual continuity in the monastery. During Franco's time in the mid-1900s, it even became a refuge for artists and writers.

The retreat in Spain was also one of my first experiences of silent eating. We were encouraged not to communicate with our hands while eating. However, I have to confess that there were a few glances exchanged in the restaurant, since the food—rice and salad—was monotonously the same every day. I have often read that people on silent retreats feel they get to know their fellow participants through the shared silence, and this connection through silence becomes the shared link that is so bonding. Those raised eyebrows, perhaps not exactly in the true spirit of a silent retreat, were very unifying! Eating food in silence is meant to make you more aware and more appreciative of what you are eating, but in my case, I wanted to leave the restaurant as soon as decently possible. Conversation, by distracting, would certainly have made the tasteless food more palatable. Most evenings, after those bland and silent suppers, I went to the bar for a glass of red wine, which I sat and drank by myself. I felt like a naughty schoolgirl, as it seemed everyone was staring at me on the way to their rooms. Although I wasn't breaking the silence, maybe I was breaking the spirit of the retreat? Did I mind this? It certainly made me wonder whether I belonged there, and I began to resent being made to feel guilty for having a glass of wine. Was I doing it as an act of rebellion or was I turning into an alcoholic unable to spend an evening without a glass of red wine? Whatever the reason, I was annoyed!

There is no question that within the silence, bonds and connections with fellow participants are formed, although it was only on the way home when we were drinking beer at the Barcelona airport (what a relief to discover that I wasn't the only drinker!) that we discovered one another's names. Connecting in silence in retreats is universal. Although in most monasteries monks ate in silence, they were often read to during mealtimes. Could this have been to distract them from their probably rather monotonous food? The Canadian-born Ronald Rolheiser, OMI (Missionary Oblates of Mary Immaculate), was on a thirty-day Ignatian retreat, conducted in total silence, with about sixty other participants. At the end of the thirty days, the participants all had the feeling that they knew one another more deeply than they would have done had they been talking to one another. The silence, he wrote, "was a powerful language, stronger than words."[7]

PRACTICING SILENCE

In the last few years, I have sought out unusual practitioners of silence for the purpose of writing this book. One such occasion was in October 2018. I arrived at St. James's Church in Piccadilly, London, an hour before the scheduled start of a sell-out appearance by Braco, the Croatian "Gazer." The queues were already snaking around the courtyard, and members of his team were filming. People had come from as far as Australia and America as well as from France, Germany, Hungary, and Ireland. When everyone was seated in the church, a rather hysterical sounding woman told us how Braco had changed her life and the lives of many others. After this talk, we were meant to watch a film about Braco called *The Power of Silence*. However, there was something wrong with the technology, and it took a long time before the film started. When it finally began, the sound was unfortunately very distorted. Before the film addressed the subject of Braco himself, it had about twenty minutes of people, including the model Naomi Campbell, talking on screen; they had seen the film being made and were saying how wonderful it was. The film follows the silent Braco around the world—we see him walking along the beach, by rivers, and along pavements, as well as in front of large audiences. His mother is interviewed, alongside many others, and we see photographs of his wife and family.

Twenty-two years ago, the film explained, Braco discovered that he had a power to help people. He does this by standing on a podium and gazing at the audience in silence. Many of those being stared at feel a sense of deep peace and a release of stress, and they often claim to be healed. Braco does not call himself a healer and does not offer any specific theory, philosophy, or message. He has not spoken publicly since 2004 and has never given an interview to the media. In 2012 in New York, Braco was given a Peace Pole, the most prominent international symbol and monument to peace, distributed by the World Peace Prayer Society, bearing the message "May Peace Prevail On Earth." Other special recipients of the Peace Pole symbol include Mother Teresa, the Dalai Lama, and Pope John Paul II.

When he finally appeared on the podium, people surged forward and I found myself forced fairly far back. I obviously lacked a devotee's pushiness. However, I was able to see his eyes, and yes, I did feel he was looking directly at me but I didn't feel any flow of peace or well-being. There's no doubt that when he is standing on a podium, he can look at people without flinching for about ten minutes. And maybe it is because we are so deprived of human contact that just to have somebody looking at us fulfills a little of that human need. After ten minutes, he left the stage and I left the church. At the exit, I was given, along with everyone else, a single white de-thorned rose, which survived the bus journey home, and unlike many shop-bought roses, it opened the following day.

Another time, I sought out silence by spending four days on a training seminar called Presence in Stillness with a group of therapists in the Sussex countryside. This was a totally new experience for me. Most were craniosacral practitioners who were refreshing their skills and topping up their hours of supervision. Among the twenty-one women and three men there, only four of us weren't therapists of any kind. I was slightly anxious about this to begin with, and as I looked around the room at all these serious and committed people, I wondered if I really belonged there. But the distinguished facilitator, the late Mike Boxhall, assured me that I was as human as anyone else, which was reassuring. The sessions took place in Cowdray Hall, with Mike starting each day with meditation followed by a short talk, before then telling us to find a partner. One person would lie on a couch, fully clothed, and the other would act as the practitioner; this lasted about fifty minutes. Afterward, the person on the couch would share their experience of how it had felt to be held with a light touch by someone who was completely present for them. Sometimes the practitioner would stay at someone's feet for the entire session and at others they might move to the head or shoulders. We were practicing craniosacral therapy, something that takes place in almost total silence, although if something feels uncomfortable, it is perfectly permissible to say something. Over four days we had three complete sessions with different partners, and the feeling—for me, anyway—while acting as both practitioner and patient was one of deep silence. Stillness is not something we *do*—it is that point at our center that is in all of us. It is something that T. S. Eliot captured in the *Four Quartets* when he refers to the unmoving part of the world being where the action is.[8]

Certainly there were times during the weekend when I felt a stillness and sense of unity with the universe, but for me they were fleeting moments. This not-doing to achieve something seems counter to everything that's happening in today's busy and noisy world. I fall right into this too. I find it extremely difficult to sit and do nothing, mostly because there are so many things I want to do. Having four days at this workshop, with long hours during which seemingly nothing much happened, was difficult for me. Wasn't this taking away from time that could be spent on writing my book, painting, reading, or going for a walk? But maybe, as my friend Richard Philp wrote, "You need silence to think deeply and meaningfully. . . . The state of silence becomes a springboard for creativity. . . It is not sterile, it's not a vacuum, it's not black outer space—it's a position of clearing out the unnecessary, of wiping the slate clean so that you are then able and free to respond to sounds that have personal meaning for you."[9]

It all makes so much sense—going into that deep silent space and using it as a springboard for creativity, finding the still point and letting the dance emerge. So why do we find it so difficult; rather, why do *I* find it so difficult? I think the older I get, the more I am aware of the speed of passing time—and of course I won't be able to do everything I want before I die. I won't have time to read a fraction of the books I'd like to, or paint the paintings, or write the books, or visit the countries, or learn the languages—so perhaps my lesson should be an acceptance of that and more of an attempt to appreciate the now. Certainly times like the Stillness weekend in Sussex help push me in that direction.

As the Stillness website says, "The main thrust of the work is to encourage a stillness and space in the practitioner in which the patient trusts herself to be heard. In this being heard lies the healing. Intelligence knows, the intellect can only ever know partially . . . much will be gained from reference to other ancient traditions and to modern science."[10]

Many years ago, I taught an adult-education course on travel writing at City University, part of the University of London. I did it for a year, and different students enrolled each term. I felt that the first term was successful—there was a very good interaction between the participants, and if I asked a question, many hands shot up. I enjoyed it; I felt that I was achieving a good rapport with the students and that they were learning something. However, when the second term began with entirely new students, I couldn't get anyone to speak. I felt like a total failure. Had this been my first term, I don't think I would have gone back. It was like trying to squeeze water out of a stone; it was a nightmare. This silence from the students made me feel acutely uncomfortable—it was not the kind of silence worth pursuing! I took a couple bottles of wine in for the last session and that loosened them up, but by then it was too late. The silences in that classroom felt negative and awkward. I have always been intrigued by group dynamics, and this was a classic example of a group dynamic at work, so I did learn something. From memory, the third term worked okay, but it was the contrast between the first and second terms that have stuck with me.

Ninfa, located southeast of Rome, has been described as the most romantic garden in the world. The site, which contains Roman and medieval ruins, was initially deserted due to the spread of surrounding marshes and consequently malaria, but it was rescued by the half-English Gelasio Caetani in 1921. He began to plant many different plant species from his travels abroad, including roses and other climbing plants, which grow over the ruins. The river Ninfa, fed by many small springs, flows through the garden, and I can attest to the coldness of the water—I swam in the icy river—as I am lucky enough to have stayed at Ninfa for a few days with the Howard family who has access to a house on the property. A foundation administers the garden now, but the Howard family—Hubert Howard married Lelia Caetani—are still very involved at Ninfa. The Victorian writer Augustus Hare, who would have seen Ninfa before the restoration of the gardens, described it as "an incredibly silent place and there is something supernatural about it which invades and fills all your senses . . . an unspeakably quiet scene of sylvan beauty."[11] Visitors are very restricted, and so it is still possible to enjoy the "silent place" with the only sound being that of flowing water and birds. I think that all of this has taught me that however elusive silence might be, the reality is that it's everywhere—waiting to be discovered.

2

Seeking Elusive Silence

THERE IS A LONG HISTORY of people who have tried to purge their environments of noise. The computer pioneer Charles Babbage conducted a war against street musicians. Thomas Carlyle, the author of a three-volume work on the French Revolution, tried and failed to build a totally silent room at the top of his house in Cheyne Row in the Chelsea area of London. The philosopher Arthur Schopenhauer identified noise as a threat to health; and Joseph Pulitzer, he of the prizes, had silent rooms built in all his properties.

RESISTANCE TO NOISE

To some extent, with progress in society also came noise. The painter J. M. W. Turner was aware of new noises arriving with the Industrial Revolution. In his 1844 painting *Rain, Steam and Speed— the Great Western Railway*, a train hurtles toward you like a dark and terrifying monster. Trains were a new invention in the nineteenth century, and the noises they emitted must have seemed shattering to farmers and others who had been used to a tranquil countryside. On the right side of the painting, Turner has painted a farmer as if to emphasize the contrast between the old rural and the new industrialized England.

In his essay "On Noise," Arthur Schopenhauer identified noise as the biggest spoiler of the capacity for concentration. He was particularly averse to the cracking of whips. He called noise the most impertinent of all interruptions, especially for "intellectual people." He wrote that the same people who were not sensitive to noise could not appreciate the humanities, as they are "insensitive to reasons, thoughts, poetry, and works of art." In the essay written in early 1851, he wrote, "Eminent minds have always abhorred every kind of disturbance."[1]

If sound can seem horrendous to a seeing person, how much worse it might be for someone who is blind, when every sound intensifies. The French author Jacques Lusseyran, who became blind as a small child, wrote about how important it is to defend blind children against shouting, background music, and other hideous assaults, as sound can be so intense that its presence is like a body blow passing through.[2]

In the mid-1970s, Jenny James established the Atlantis Foundation, a commune for primal screaming in County Donegal in Ireland. As well as practicing primal screaming in a group, the residents yelled at one another throughout the day; all this was in total contrast to the usual quietness of Donegal and inevitably upset many of the neighbors. The locals made so many objections to the noisy way of life that in 1980, after they had received bomb threats, the thirty participants, also known as the Screamers, moved to the uninhabited Innisfree. In 1989 they left Europe and moved to Colombia, where some of them were captured and murdered by Revolutionary Armed Forces of Columbia (FARC) rebels. The daughter of a couple who lived at Atlantis now teaches meditation and talks of the damaging effect that too much noise had, saying, "We all have silence within us."[3]

While people have long complained of noise in urban areas around the world, London is a great example of a place where individuals have consistently tried to resist noise. Charles Babbage waged war on street musicians who used to play so loudly outside fashionable establishments as a ploy that they would be paid to leave. This presumably only succeeded in encouraging more players to try their luck. In 1864 Babbage published *A Chapter on Street Nuisances* extracted from *Passages in the Life of a Philosopher* in which he summarizes his numerous court appearances; on one occasion he produced a list of 165 interruptions that he'd endured over a period of eighty days. His list of "instruments of torture" permitted by the government included organs, brass bands, hurdy-gurdies, drums, bagpipes, trumpets, and the human voice. He blamed tavern keepers, gin shops, and ladies of doubtful virtue for encouraging street noise. Babbage was considered elitist and was not popular, possibly because he said what he was doing was on behalf of the intellectual worker. Unfortunately for him, his efforts to suppress noise worked against him, leading one set of neighbors to hire musicians to play outside his house, another neighbor to blow a tin whistle for half an hour every day for months on end, and others to arrange for him to be followed by a mob of jeering children and get his windows broken. None of this put him off his mission. He went on writing letters to *The Times* and even had the support of the English writer Charles Dickens, who wrote that he was "daily interrupted, harassed, worried, wearied, (and) driven nearly mad, by street musicians."[4] Eventually a law, known as Bass's Act, was passed in 1864 banning street musicians from residential neighborhoods, but it did not come into effect quickly enough to prevent an organ grinder from playing outside Babbage's house as he was dying.

The Victorian artist John Leech, who was a friend of Charles Dickens and illustrated several of his books, was also driven nearly mad by the incessant noise of London's streets: "Rather . . . than continue to be tormented in this way, I would prefer to go to the grave, where there is no noise."[5] An editorial in *The Times* in 1856 referred to London noise as having a "noisy, dizzy, scatterbrained atmosphere." So although people might complain about the noise in London today, and although the kind of sounds might be different, it is evident that London has always been extremely noisy.

In a letter that Thomas Carlyle wrote to Geraldine E. Jewsbury, a popular English novelist and intimate friend of Carlyle's wife Jane Carlyle, his violent feelings about noise are evident: "SILENCE, SILENCE: in a thousand senses I proclaim the indispensable worth of Silence, our only safe dwelling-place. . . . This shallow generation knows nothing of Silence."[6] For many years, Carlyle worked in the front room of his house in Cheyne Row in Chelsea, but the noise from the street eventually increased to the point where he could no longer work: "Chelsea, as London generally, grows every year noisier and the swelling out as if it were mad! It is astonishing how many cocks, parrots, dogs, dustcarts, and dandy carriages do announce themselves."[7] His street was also dug up several times, and around fifteen thousand visitors a day visited the nearby Cremorne Gardens between the King's Road and the Thames, which flourished in the mid-1800s. In these gardens, people could enjoy a maze, a gypsy grotto, theater, medieval jousting, a brass band, and—most popular of all—the Grand Chinese Pagoda with a fifty-piece orchestra and up to four thousand dancers. But the noisiest entertainment of all was the Spectacular Naval Tournament, which had boats attacking a fortress on the Thames, with cannons firing back in defense and an old steamer packed with explosives being blown up—and all of this accompanied by fireworks.

The combination of the noise from his street and from the gardens drove Carlyle nearly mad and led him to take drastic measures in search of quiet.

Carlyle decided to build another room at the top of the house to seek the silence he craved. He wrote to his sister Jean: "After deep deliberation, I have decided to have a top storey put upon the house, with double walls, lighted from above artfully ventilated, into which no sound may come! Jane encouraged and urged me."[8] He was very certain of what he wanted, and in August 1853 he instructed a builder to take off the existing roof and put on a new roof to form a new room with a skylight. He specified that he wanted the roof to be made from slate from Bangor and that the room should have small double windows. The builder told him that it could all be done within six weeks; in fact, it ended up taking nine months and was inevitably far more expensive than he'd bargained for. To make matters worse, Jane Carlyle wrote that this proposed silent room was actually very noisy, with Carlyle describing it in a letter to his brother James as "a room that was to be silent, inaccessible to sound, it is a most perfect *failure*, one of the undeniablest *misses* ever made! So that all my labour and suffering, and £200 or more of ready money has been quite thrown away."[9] To compound Carlyle's unhappiness, during the building work, his maid Fanny ran off with one of the workmen.

In its heyday, the twelve acres of Cremorne Gardens lay between Chelsea Harbour and the Kings Road, but today the only remaining part is a narrow strip at the bottom of Cheyne Row where there is, ironically, a statue of Carlyle. He sits forever over a pile of books in the remains of the pleasure gardens that so thoroughly tormented him. I often walk past Carlyle's house on my way to the Catholic Church of Our Most Holy Redeemer and St. Thomas More in Cheyne Row, built after Carlyle's day in 1894. No doubt he would have objected to the noise of people gathering outside after a service. It is hard to imagine pleasure gardens in what is now a quiet residential part of London, but living just far enough away, I think they could have been rather fun!

This part of London is much quieter now than it was in Carlyle's day. His silent room at the very top of the house, now run by the National Trust, does seem quiet; you don't even really hear the traffic thundering along the Chelsea Embankment. One of the reasons that Carlyle had cofounded The London Library, London's first lending library, in 1841, was because he considered the British Library too noisy, complaining that people in the British Library gave him "museum headache." The London Library originated in Pall Mall in 1841, but in 1845 it was moved to its present site in St. James's Square. Its open shelves and the fact that it is a lending library make it unique. In 1944, the library lost around sixteen thousand volumes to bomb damage, but apart from selling much of its incunabula in 1970, very little was disposed of, and the library now has over a million items. There is meant to be silence in the Reading Room, and it is pretty quiet and a good place to work, but like many others, I have often had whispered conversations there. There are areas of the library where laptops and electronic devices are banned, but there are plenty of other areas where you can use them.

Joseph Pulitzer, who is best known today for the Pulitzer Prizes established in his memory in 1917, is another noted individual who tried to construct silence. He lived just off Fifth Avenue in New York and designed two rooms, his study and his bedroom, as places that were intended to be completely silent. He also had "silent vaults" built in his house in Bar Harbor, Maine, and on his yacht, *Liberty*. The rooms in New York were meant to be isolated from all vibrations, but unfortunately the reverse ended up being true and the soundproofed walls accentuated the plumbing noises that gurgled throughout the house. There was nothing new about having noises run through pipes: The fifth-century mathematician and architect Anthemius, who helped rebuild Hagia Sophia, lost a lawsuit brought about by his upstairs neighbor Zeno. In revenge, he simulated an earthquake with a steam line that he ran into Zeno's apartment, and he also managed to make noises that mimicked thunderstorms. However, some people actively encourage noise in their houses. When the Russian novelist Ivan Turgenev was living with the singer Pauline Viardot and her husband in Paris, he had an acoustic tube specially installed between rooms so that he could hear the singing lessons that were in progress.[10]

People went to great lengths in pursuit of silence. Theodor Lessing, the German Jewish philosopher who was assassinated by Nazi sympathizers in 1933, was the first person to lead a public campaign for noise abatement in Germany in 1907. In 1906, Julia Barnett Rice, known as the "Queen of Silence" in America, founded the Society for the Suppression of Unnecessary Noise.[11] Her first objective was to track down the hooting tugs on the Hudson River, and in 1907 she helped pass New York's first anti-noise law, a precursor to New York's Operation Silent Night of 2002. Yet nowadays, once again, according to the US Census Bureau, noise is the number one reported neighborhood complaint. The *New York Times* has written that "excessive noise pollution is not just hard on the ears, but is also linked to higher levels of stress, hypertension and heart disease."[12] Ironically, Rice's house in Manhattan is now a Jewish elementary school, no doubt full of screaming children.

Octavia Hill, one of the founders of the National Trust in 1894, felt that there was a universal need for silence, space, and art: "That sense of quiet which whispers of better things to come to us gently."[13] Initially the Trust was primarily concerned with protecting open spaces and endangered buildings of historic interest.

Silence can also be used diplomatically. When people feel that they have to fill a gap caused by silence, they are often so overcome by the anxiety of the moment that they divulge their innermost secrets. In the sixteenth century, the Dutch William of Orange, also known as William the Silent, got his name after a diplomatic coup. By saying very little during a conversation with the King of France, William managed to get the king to reveal state secrets and learned of French policy that the king assumed he must already know. Gaps in conversation can often force an anxious person to fill a silence, frequently with inane words, but sometimes with much bigger consequences. By keeping silent, much is often revealed. A journalist friend of mine who had a very bad stammer told me that this often worked to his advantage when he was interviewing people. The interviewee would get so embarrassed by his inability to formulate the question that they would often blurt out some of their deepest secrets.

HERMITAGES

Although a silent way of living is usually associated with a religion, it certainly wasn't only the religious who decided to devote themselves to a life of silence. In 1570, the French philosopher Michel de Montaigne devoted himself to a life of solitude, living and writing in a tower (which still exists) close to Bordeaux. The author and teacher Stephen Batchelor was lucky enough to be able to spend a morning alone in the tower. When he was there, he sat in the library and organized and edited his selection of Montaigne's thoughts on solitude for his own recent book on solitude, *The Art of Solitude*.[14]

Almost a century later, in the seventeenth century, the French philosopher and mathematician Blaise Pascal found the idea of silence in space frightening. In his *Pensées*, he wrote that when he thought about the brevity of his life and his insignificance compared to infinity of space, he was terrified. This was the same man who wrote, "All of man's misfortunes come from one thing, which is not knowing how to sit quietly in a room."[15] A vast area of silence terrified him, but he saw salvation in the silence and solitude of a small room. Pascal's terror was later captured by the French painter Odilon Redon, who did an engraving based on Pascal called *The Eternal Silence of These Infinite Spaces Frightens Me* in which a solitary man, who seems to have just climbed a mountain, looks out onto a bleak landscape with no living thing in sight.

The people who live solitary hermetic lives are mostly thought to be eccentric, but maybe this is because, for many people, the thought of being alone, even for a day, is terrifying. People who live alone are often thought of as selfish, but then anyone who leads a different kind of lifestyle from the norm can often be viewed as a threat. The author Sara Maitland, who lives alone, relates in her book *A Book of Silence* that her mother, who as a widow felt unbearably lonely, called her daughter selfish as she could not countenance the fact that she was enjoying her solitude.[16]

Hermitages are often located in beautiful places. Although they fell out of favor in the United Kingdom in the sixteenth century, they came back into favor in the eighteenth century when they were often built and used by the owners of large estates as places of refuge. In the second half of the eighteenth century, many large estates had their own hermits living on their grounds in specially built hermitages. Today there are English hermits living in Northumberland and in caves in Shropshire. My friend Bill Forse had a hermit named Brother John Mercer living in one of his converted farm buildings in West Sussex. He died in 2020, and according to Bill, he wasn't that silent and enjoyed the odd whisky. There are also still hermitages at Kedleston in Derbyshire, Badminton in Gloucestershire, Stowe in Buckinghamshire, Warkworth Castle in Northumberland, St. Robert's Cave in North Yorkshire, Painshill in Surrey, Ossian's Hall in Dunkeld, Perthshire and St. Nicholas's Church in Surrey. The difference between hermits and anchorites, both of whom withdraw from secular society for religious reasons, is that hermits could leave their cells, whereas anchorites were permanently attached to theirs.

I came across a woman in Provence who lived a solitary life in a remote cottage, but like many hermits, she wasn't protected from curious visitors—myself included. Hermits seem to grow in compassion and are polite to their unannounced visitors.

In 2017 the film director Mike Hannon made *The Cloud of Unknowing*, a documentary about Rodney Thompson, who lived thirty years as a hermit—away from the mainstream without electricity or running water—in pursuit of solitude, silence, and prayer in an isolated cottage in Connemara on the west coast of Ireland, in the tradition of the Desert Fathers. The documentary was short-listed as one of the nominees at the thirty-eighth annual London Film Critics' Circle, a demonstration of how intrigued people are by lives so different from their own. Hannon said that when he met Thompson, he was struck by his graceful calm and benevolence—throughout his time in the west of Ireland, he had always welcomed visitors. Hannon described Thompson's life as a relief from the escalating speed of life today. At one point in the film, Thompson walks toward the camera over wild Connemara country, remarking that the world today is too garrulous; he then admits that he too tends to be garrulous and that it takes discipline not to be. This is a man who obviously knows himself well.

In northern Thailand, hermits are associated with forests.[17] The Thai Forest tradition is a lineage of Theravada Buddhist monasticism that started around 1900. In Russia, hermits are also associated with forests; some families of Old Believers, Eastern Orthodox Christians who maintained the liturgy and rituals of the Russian Orthodox Church in existence before the reforms of the seventeenth century, fled to Siberia to escape Stalin's Russia and to this day are still living remotely. One hermit named Viktor has lived in the forests of Siberia for sixteen years, saying that he prefers trees to people.

As a young man, Mircea Eliade, a Romanian historian and writer, spent time in a cave in the pinewoods of the Himalayas. He became an expert on shamans and ended up being a professor at the University of Chicago.

Henry David Thoreau famously relished the opportunity to be alone for much of the time and is full of wise sayings about silence, linking it to many things in nature. When he was walking, he felt that "all sound is nearly akin to Silence; it is a bubble on her surface which straightway bursts . . . it is a faint utterance of Silence, and then only agreeable to our auditory nerves when it contrasts itself with the former."[18] He experienced it as harmony and melody and went on to suppose that "Silence alone is worthy to be heard. Silence is the various depth and fertility, like soil."[19] I shall never look at mosses in quite the same way again, after reading Thoreau and discovering that he contemplated their silent and unambitious nature. Many people have written about the silence that comes with walking; the American novelist Jack Kerouac found the silence so intense that "you can hear your own blood roar in your ears . . . a great Shhhh . . ."[20]

For most of us today, silence can be ended at any time by simply switching on the radio, television, computer, or smartphone—a big change from earlier times. If one had been alone in a quiet place before the advent of technology, there would have been no way to end the silence other than by talking or singing to oneself. There is no question that the sound of music, television, and podcasts can do much to dispel loneliness, but the ease of access means that the temptation to flip the switch to avoid being silently with oneself is huge.

UNUSUAL METHODS OF FINDING SILENCE

While deciding to have more silence in one's life should be a conscious decision, it perhaps need not be as radical as the route taken by the writer and broadcaster Anne D. LeClaire. Her method was to have silent Mondays, which is difficult if you're living in the same house as someone who is not in agreement with your plan. It wasn't only her husband who was annoyed but also many other people she encountered. They couldn't understand why she was being silent for a day a week, and it angered them. This made LeClaire feel guilty, but it's how she worked through these feelings that is interesting. When she first embarked on her silent journey, she heard a voice saying to her, "Sit in silence." This was repeated often, and it was through remembering this phrase that she managed to push on through the difficult times. And she found many difficult times. Everything that she had tried to push under the carpet emerged—all the unhappiness and unresolved family issues that had bubbled beneath the surface were suddenly exposed. "It is only when we drag our smallest, shabbiest parts into the light that we can move toward becoming whole."[21] After many years of her silent Mondays, Anne D. LeClaire was asked why she did it, and her reply was that she found her silences restful and restorative. She also found that she listened better, paid more attention, and that rather than automatically reacting, she reflected before speaking. She was adamant that her reasons were neither religious nor spiritual but ended up admitting that essentially of course they were: "It seems I was the last to know."

For many years, the actor Larry Hagman, who played J. R. Ewing in the television series *Dallas*, refused to speak on Sundays. He insisted that this was not for any religious reason, and he never explained why he was doing it, only that "you've got to try it to appreciate how nice it is."[22] Back in 2012, the journalist Alexander Chancellor agreed that there was something rather appealing about a day of silence each week, although he said he felt sorry for Hagman's wife. Chancellor thought that the silence should also involve an abstinence from emailing, texting, tweeting, and so forth—he realized early on that FOMO (Fear of Missing Out), a cause of the compulsion to engage with social media, was spreading like wildfire worldwide and should be combatted.[23]

People find many different and original ways of experiencing silence as an art. Karin Paish, an art student, stopped talking for the six months leading up to the millennium. At the time she was feeling "fractured" and overwhelmed by the destruction of the ozone layer and ocean pollution, and she envisaged silence as "a cocoon—a healing place." She planned it well in advance, telling her local shops that she would be using written notes to communicate, but she has said that if she were to do it again, she would not write notes, as the written word "contaminated" her silence. The relationship she was in at the start of her experiment inevitably broke up, and she found, predictably, that many people got angry when she didn't respond to them. Even if she had been able to explain what she was doing, which obviously she wasn't, when people don't understand why someone is doing something, they can become resentful and cross. But despite the setbacks, she found the experience enriching, extending it from an initial three months to six months. She felt that the experiment changed her, and she had the sense afterward of everything being more immediate and more connected.[24]

I recently came across a blog[25] written by a young woman who decided not to speak for a week. She had sat next to a man on a bus who had talked incessantly for thirty-five minutes when she'd just lost her job, smashed her phone, and was feeling very stressed. Having discovered that we each speak an average of twenty thousand words a day, she decided not to speak for a week, although she did continue to communicate important information through WhatsApp and by email. One of her initial discoveries, while sitting silently over supper opposite her boyfriend on the first evening, with him speaking, was an awareness that previously she hadn't really listened to what he had been saying. But now that she wasn't talking and was really listening, inevitably she found it hard not to reply. During her silent week, she met a friend who needed consoling after splitting from a boyfriend; at the end of their meeting the friend said, "That was a strange one-way conversation, but it was weirdly therapeutic." By the end of the week, she found herself desperate to start speaking again, but after her silent time, she definitely felt different, and one of the things she felt she'd learned was how to listen properly. She vowed that she was going to try to speak less and to make what she did say more meaningful. During her silence she hadn't been able to stop the conversations she'd had in her head—conversations that were largely negative; things that she had usually blocked with chatter. It only took a week for her to feel that she'd had an experience that completely changed her life.

THE CONCEPT
OF PLACE

3

Nature

AS FAR BACK as the fifth century B.C.E., Pythagoras was aware of the feeling of unity that can come over us when we contemplate mountains, rivers, or the sea in silence. He said, "Learn to be silent. Let your quiet mind listen and absorb the silence."[1] Over the intervening years, people have both loved and abhorred the silence of nature. The Italian painter Luigi Russolo, along with his fellow Futurists, hated silence and bemoaned the fact of a silent nature; he even wrote a manifesto called *The Art of Noises*, styled as a letter to his friend Francesco Balilla Pratella.[2] One wonders quite what he meant by "silent nature" and where he found it, since silence in nature is notoriously difficult to find. For nature can be incredibly noisy—earthquakes, thunderstorms, hurricanes, tornadoes, the roar of the sea, and wind are all often louder than any man-made noise. Despite the loud sounds of nature, however, nature can also be supremely silent—and unless we know what silence is and what we want from it, it can be hard to appreciate. But maybe we try too hard, and it would be easier to find silence if we could just forget what we're looking for.

"The eternal silence of infinite places frightens me,"[3] wrote the French philosopher Blaise Pascal. It is true that what many people find blissful can be terrifying to others. People have chosen to go into the wilderness and follow a life of silence for spiritual or religious reasons—for example, the Desert Fathers, described in chapter 4, during the third century C.E.—but others in the wilderness feel more forced to experience silence. Some learn to appreciate this, but others find it almost unbearable. This awareness of silence is peculiarly human; many animals live in a more or less silent world, without themselves making much sound, and most tend to run away from noise. We can learn a lot from watching animals, especially cats, leading their mostly silent lives. As the philosopher John Gray wrote, "Humans seek silence because they seek redemption from themselves; other animals live in silence because they do not need redeeming."[4]

In her collection of essays *Teaching a Stone to Talk*, Annie Dillard describes the silence of nature and how you have to get ready to listen by emptying yourself and being wholly attentive: "After a time you hear it: there is nothing there. . . . You feel the world's word as a tension, a hum, a single chorused note everywhere the same. This is it: this hum is the silence. . . . There is a vibrancy to the silence, a suppression, as if someone were gagging the world. . . . The silence is not actually suppression; instead, it is all there is."[5] Dillard suggests that you have to learn to listen to the silence of nature—it will be there, but it requires an effort. Once you are aware of it, it's all that there is.

Forests can give the impression of being silent and indeed are sometimes compared to cathedrals, with the Scottish-American naturalist John Muir considering the silence of sequoias as solitary, silent, and serene. In Olympic National Park in Washington State, the largest and best example of temperate virgin rain forest in the Western Hemisphere, a project originated in 2005 called "One Square Inch of Silence." Gordon Hempton, an acoustic ecologist, traveled across America with his recording equipment and eventually chose Olympic National Park as the quietest place in the United States. The motto of this independent research project is "Silence is not the absence of something but the presence of everything." People are encouraged to visit the spot but silently; after two hours' hike from the Visitor's Center in Hoh Rain Forest, you come to a moss-covered log surrounded by a collection of small, red-colored stones—the silent center. One of the theories is that just as noise impacts a large area, silence can do the same.[6] One Square Inch does indeed affect a sizeable stretch of forest. I have listened to a recording from this space, and although there is no human noise, the natural sounds of animals, birds, and water are fairly loud. So it seems that the project is less about seeking total silence and more to do with the absence of *human* sound. In 1984 there were twenty-one "quiet places" in Washington State, but they started disappearing fast. By the early 1990s, there were only three left, and there were fewer than ten in the whole of the United States; with people needing houses, natural wild spaces are being built on, and ironically, with more people wanting to experience nature, the "quiet places" lose their silence. Although One Square Inch maintains that it is the most silent place in the United States, a man-made anechoic chamber at Microsoft's HQ, also in Washington State, has sound-absorbent qualities that allow it to claim to be the quietest place on the planet.

Because we are all encouraged to get outside to exercise, one of the problems for national parks and public hiking trails is the sheer number of visitors. Though this is a real dilemma, an increasing number of organizations and activists are attempting to get special protection for the remaining quiet places. Quiet Parks International (QPI)—a movement comprising audio engineers, scientists, environmentalists, and musicians—works to establish certification for quiet places worldwide. So far, QPI has identified 262 sites that they believe could be preserved as natural quiet places. In Great Britain, the identified areas are the Brecon Beacons National Park, Snowdonia National Park, the Jurassic Coast, and Galloway Forest Park; in July 2022, Glacier National Park in Montana was the first to be awarded Quiet Park Status in the US while American Prairie Reserve, also in Montana, and Boundary Waters Canoe Area in Minnesota and Haleakala National Park in Hawaii are currently being evaluated. In 2002, the European Union approved an environmental noise directive whose aim was to determine noise levels across Europe and to create and protect quiet areas. Among the places chosen are Blessington Street Basin in Ireland, Lake Bäcksjön in Sweden, and Tondiloo Park in Estonia.

Some places even boast tourist-destination status due to their quiet. Because of its rural wooded landscape, Finland markets itself as one such silent tourist destination; there was even a marketing slogan—"Silence Please"—that was aimed at the Asian market to encourage tourists to come and experience the peace and quiet. But it is not only the landscape that is silent in Finland; small talk in Finland does not exist in the same way as it does in the US and UK. Finns do not feel the need to fill the gaps in conversation with inconsequential words, as the author Horatio Clare discovered on his journey to the Arctic on a Finnish icebreaker.[7] Research shows that this may be due to Finland's relatively late industrialization and urbanization—talking for the sake of it in such a comparatively rural environment was deemed unnecessary.

Sometimes even recording sensations in writing can interrupt the solitude and silence when it is better just to absorb them in the present moment. In 2001, Robert Kull spent a year on his own on a remote island off Patagonia. In his journal he wrote that writing something daily often felt like a breaking of his solitude: "The voice of solitude must, in some sense, remain silent."[8] In his book *The Last*

Wilderness, Neil Ansell, who spent several years living in isolation in various parts of Britain, wrote that his essential way of being was to be "quiet and still" and that the rest is distraction. He said that when you are on your own, observing things in nature, the feeling is very different from when you are with somebody else; when you are on your own, you can observe with pure sensation.[9]

HUMANS SURVIVING IN NATURE

The so-called North Pond hermit Christopher Knight spent twenty-seven years living undiscovered in the woods in Maine. He survived by stealing food and other necessities from local, mostly vacation homes; residents had been both exasperated and admiring of this hermit who avoided detection for so long. Knight grudgingly allowed the journalist Michael Finkel to visit him in prison when he was finally caught, and Finkel wrote about him in his book *The Stranger in the Woods*, which tells the extraordinary story of someone who felt so alienated by contemporary society that he believed the only way to survive was effectively to disappear. Knight honed his methods of walking through the woods without making a sound or leaving any tracks. This meant that in winter when there was snow on the ground, he couldn't leave his camp. He kept himself clean and tidy-looking and never stopped feeling guilty about stealing. When Finkel first visited his camp, which was extremely close to where other people lived, he described the silence: "It was the kind of total quiet that literally made my ears ring."[10]

Knight's life in his camp would have been the ideal environment for maximum brain function—he regularly stole books and, largely due to the silence around him, seemed to remember everything that he read. Global studies of the differences in brain function between subjects living in quiet places or around noise have concluded that noise and distraction are toxic.[11] It is almost impossible to ignore noise around us; we have evolved to react to it. Indeed, the word *noise* comes from the Latin *nausea* (seasickness) or maybe from the Latin *noxia* (hurting, injury, damage) or the Ionic Greek *nausea*—all of which have unpleasant associations.

A 2013 study on mice, published in the journal *Brain Structure and Function*, involved comparing the effects of ambient noise, white noise, pup calls, and silence on the rodents' brains. The researchers used silence as a control and found that two hours of daily silence led to the development of new cells in the hippocampus, a key region of the brain associated with learning, memory, and emotion.[12]

Some people are thrust into a silence they hadn't anticipated. In 1934, Rear Admiral Richard E. Byrd spent five months on his own at Bolling Advance Base, a meteorological station in Antarctica. As leader of the expedition, he had planned for three men to stay at the remote base, but for some reason this proved impossible. As he did not want just two men to go, feeling that they might have major disagreements, he volunteered to go on his own. I wonder whether he was already craving silence and solitude, since he wrote, "You might think that a man whose life carries him into remote places would have no special need for quietude. Whoever thinks that has little knowledge of expeditions."[13] The temperatures that Antarctic winter were unseasonably low—during July, twenty days were -60°F or colder; on six days it reached -76°F, with almost twenty-four hours of total darkness. Byrd had regular radio contact with the base called Little America, but gradually his unpredictable and often nonsensical broadcasts began to worry the men at base camp. It turned out that he was suffering from carbon monoxide poisoning. Luckily for him, the men from Little America realized that something was very wrong, and they managed to fight their way through the cold and darkness in order to reach him at Advance Base. Even when he was seriously ill, his overwhelming concern was for his men's safety, which is why he had refrained from telling them that he was struggling.

His book *Alone* was published four years later, at a time when it was unusual to put feelings into a narrative. Indeed, he writes in the preface that the experience had been so personal, and he was so worried about a loss of self-respect, that for four years he could not bring himself to write anything at all about his ordeal.[14] However, he was nagged by his friends to write the account of his time at the base, and the book is an extraordinary testament to the resilience and guts of one man. Before he got poisoned, he was able to appreciate some of the beauty and silence, seeing Venus in the west as an "an unblinking diamond," with her twinkling counterpart in the east, both set off in an exquisite sea of blue. "The colours were subdued and not numerous; the jewels few; the setting simple. . . . I paused to listen to the silence. . . . My frozen breath hung like a cloud overhead. The day was dying, the night being born—but with great peace. . . . Harmony, that was it!" He found a rhythm in the silence: "The strain of a perfect chord, the music of the spheres, perhaps." He found himself part of the rhythm: "In that instant I could feel no doubt of man's oneness with the universe." He believed that there had to be a purpose to the whole and that humankind had to be a part of it and was no accident: "It was a feeling that transcended reason; that went to the heart of man's despair and found it groundless. The universe was a cosmos, not a chaos; man was as rightfully a part of that cosmos as were the day and night."[15]

In the book he often refers to this harmony that he believed existed in the world, and it is this harmony that links the Tao, the music of the spheres, a term used by the astronomer Johannes Kepler in 1619 who suggested that the planets in the solar system generated harmonies as they orbited the sun. With harmony, no spoken language is needed to communicate; there can be a connection with others on a deep level, in silence. Before Byrd became ill, he found that his life had become largely a life of the mind, and he spent a lot of time thinking about humanity and our place in the cosmos:

"This whole concept is summed up in the word harmony. For those who seek it there is inexhaustible evidence of an all-pervading intelligence. The human race, my intuition tells me, is not outside the cosmic process and is not an accident. It is as much a part of the universe as the trees, the mountains, the aurora, and the stars. My reason approves this; and the findings of science, as I see them, point in the same direction."[16]

It was the silence and solitude that had led Byrd to these conclusions; the silence had proved positive for him. Twenty or so years earlier, Teddy Evans—Captain Robert Falcon Scott's second-in-command on the ill-fated 1910–13 Terra Nova Expedition to the South Pole—wrote about what was for him the disturbing nature of silence: "The silence now that we had no other party with us was ghastly, for beyond the sound of our own voices and the groaning of the sledge-runners there was no sound whatever to remind us of the outer world."[17] These two very different reactions to the silence of the Antarctic demonstrate two very different personality types—one reflective, the other not. Byrd had found a harmony in the silence, whereas Evans found it distressing. In a small way, I too experienced the silence and peace of the Antarctic, as described in chapter 1, and once you have had that feeling of harmony, when who you are merges into the greater whole, you are changed forever.

WILDLIFE

Owls can fly almost soundlessly because the unique formation of their wings and feathers suppresses sound waves. Their wings have a jagged leading edge, a fringe on the trailing edge, and a velvety plumage on top. With large wings in comparison to their body mass, owls can fly extremely slowly, enabling them to glide noiselessly, which is useful for hearing and hunting their prey. This could have huge and constructive implications for our noisy world—imagine the positive impact on many lives if airplanes were able to fly silently. Another extraordinary fact about owls is that if the hairs in the cochleas of their ears are damaged, they can grow new ones. Once the hairs in our cochleas are flattened, they are never replaced; we cannot grow new ones. This flattening of the hairs is the source of deafness caused by exposure to very loud music; the damage is permanent.[18] It is therefore important that to preserve our hearing, we shouldn't expose ourselves to very loud music.

I love the minuteness of the description by the writer and clergyman's son Llewelyn Powys, who wrote that the stillness of an evening was such that "the fur of a field mouse's jacket brushing against the stem of its grassy jungle would have been audible."[19] It's something I think the English writer and naturalist Beatrix Potter would have appreciated, since Old Brown, the owl in *The Tale of Squirrel Nutkin*, remains silent despite Nutkin's daily taunts.[20] Children's nursery rhymes always have a great deal of wisdom and truth in them—for example, a rhyme from 1875 that has a wise owl living in an oak tree, looking rather than speaking and as a result hearing more.[21]

I have been lucky enough to travel widely, certainly not in search of silence, although I have often encountered it. In May 2003, very early one morning, I walked through the Bialowieza Forest in eastern Poland on the Belarus border. This vast forest is all that remains of Europe's primeval forests and covers an area of over three thousand square kilometers. At one point, our Polish guide froze suddenly, and a great gray owl (*Strix nebulosa*) flew silently across the path just in front of us. It perched on the branch of a tree about twenty yards from us and stayed there for about ten minutes, a thrilling and extremely unusual sight. Our knowledgeable guide knew the forest well and had never seen one there before. The great gray can be up to thirty-three inches long with a wingspan of over five feet, thus making it one of the largest—if not the largest—owls. The bird had flown silently, and of course we watched it silently. I can recall the sensation vividly nearly twenty years later. What better place to observe such an owl than in this ancient forest where it is sometimes known as the Phantom of the North.

Another time I came face to face with extraordinary wildlife was in August 1991, when I left the comforts of Notting Hill to trek around the northwestern shores of Lake Baikal in eastern Siberia. For twelve long days I tramped with fifteen others around the shores of this beautiful and unspoiled lake—the oldest and deepest lake on the planet. Every evening I would swim in the lake, gulping water as I swam along—this drinking and swimming is a rare pleasure, since it isn't possible in swimming pools or the sea. Brushing my teeth in the lake, I reminded myself of how many things, such as running water, we take for granted. Throughout this whole trip I felt immersed in the silence of the forest. Yes, of course there were the other people on the trip—and bears—but there was always the space for silence.

Our trek group never saw anyone else, and it often felt as though we were walking where no one had been before. But we were on bear alert. Our Russian hosts issued us whistles and warned us not to run away if we encountered a bear, a thought that was simultaneously terrifying and exciting. As we walked, we saw many bear pawprints by the water's edge and once even a bear carcass, and the longer we walked, the more we wanted to see one of these huge living creatures.

On the last day of the trek, I joined a climb to an unnamed peak that was just visible from our camp. We set off at 6 a.m. and I finally reached the top at 5 p.m., long after the others, with our English guide Jim. The climb had been difficult, and I was exhausted, but when Jim shouted "Bear!" I momentarily forgot my tiredness. The carnivorous brown bears of the Siberian taiga weigh up to eight hundred pounds (360 kg) and can be aggressive. I ran around the bend, and there was a bear on its hind legs looking at us. It hesitated for a few minutes and then turned into the forest and sped through the trees, an extraordinary feat as this taiga was denser than any we had encountered.

MOUNTAINS

After the bear sighting, that night in Siberia also gave me a taste of a mountainous soundscape. As the light faded, we had to make about ten river crossings on what we thought was the way back to the camp. When it was completely dark, we got out our flashlights and made slow progress until my companion's flashlight, with brand-new Russian batteries, failed. Then while I was climbing over a fallen tree, I dropped my flashlight into the river; I can still remember that *clatter, clatter, splash* followed by silence. Realizing that it was too dangerous to continue moving—there was no moon, so it was pitch black—we found a relatively flat piece of ground, took off our soaking boots, and prepared to spend the night in the open. Our surroundings were anything but silent, and fortunately so—the loud roar of the river drowned out most of the night sounds, many of which would have been unwelcome. Even so, I was convinced that every slight movement was a bear. (They can attack unprovoked.) But we survived the night, despite the cold, and finished the remaining two hours of our journey at first light. We were told afterward that fingers in bear feces were the only remains of three foresters who were the last known people to have spent the night in the forest.

Though occasional avalanches can be noisy, and my overnight experience on a mountain had the noises of the river, mountains can also be supremely silent. When John Muir was climbing Mount Shasta in California and sleeping alone in the mountains on a calm night, he wrote about snowflakes: "To feel the touch of the first of these little silent messages from heaven is a memorable experience; no one could forget something so delicate."[22]

The author and poet Nan Shepherd shared her love of walking in the Cairngorms in her only nonfiction book, *The Living Mountain*. She trained herself to "listen to silence" in the Scottish mountain range, and by the practice of listening for it she realized how seldom it was there. Something always moved—maybe it was running water—"but now and then comes an hour when the silence is all but absolute, and listening to it one slips out of time."[23] That kind of silence is not just the absence of sound but something new and different—an entity of its own. These moments of silence can come in mist, in snow, on a summer's night, or in a September dawn: "In September dawns I hardly breathe—I am an image in a ball of glass. The world is suspended there, and I in it."[24]

SNOW AND FOG

The Japanese language has a word for the sound of snow falling: *shinshin*. *Shin* means the absence of sound where there was sound before, a deep silence, as the author and poet James Crowden writes: "Deep silence, deep snow and deep solitude"[25] Snow brings a muffled silence to everything. It was the silence I felt during that snowfall in the Antarctic I mentioned earlier, the trigger to writing this book. Snow affects the way sound travels; snowflakes accumulate as they fall with air between them, so that sound waves have less room to bounce off them. Physicists say that humans cannot hear snow falling—the sound it makes is too high-pitched—but wolves and bats can hear it. As snowflakes are full of air when they meet water, the noise is, apparently, unbearably loud for fish. So, something that is silent for us may not be silent for animals in the world around us, which leads me to think that the noise made by boats, ships, and everything else on the sea must be agonizingly loud and detrimental to the creatures that live in the ocean.

In *The World of Silence*, the twentieth-century Swiss writer Max Picard wrote about the silences of nature, which can be expressed in myriad ways: "In winter silence is visible; snow is silence become visible." Silence is also present in the quiet of the dawn, at nightfall, in moonlight "trickling down into the night like a rain of silence"[26]— all culminating in the silence of the soul shaped by the natural world of silence.

In his novel *A Love Story*, Émile Zola describes snow silently falling as Madame Rambaud visits her daughter's grave: "The endlessly shifting layers of whiteness grew thicker, like floating gauzes gradually unwinding. The snow fell . . . without the sound of a sigh . . . the flakes . . . alighted one by one, ceaselessly, in their millions, more silently than a flower sheds its petals; and this moving multitude, whose march through space could not be heard, brought an oblivion of earth and of life, a sense of sovereign peace."[27] The silence produced here by the snow feels tangible.

James Russell Lowell, an ardent abolitionist who taught at Harvard University and who was United States minister to England from 1880 to 1885, was also a poet. His first wife and three of his children died in 1853, and in his poem "The First Snowfall," he describes snow as "the noiseless work of the sky." The snowfall reminded him of the graves of his dead children, which had been hidden by the snowflakes:

Then, with eyes that saw not, I kissed her;
And she, kissing back, could not know
That my kiss was given to her sister,
Folded close under deepening snow.[28]

The explorer, painter, and writer Robert Perkins experienced a different kind of silence in the wilderness. On July 28, 2013, a young helicopter pilot flew him to the crash site of a small plane in the Aberdare Mountains in Kenya, in which his wife, stepdaughter, and the pilot had all been killed three days prior in bad weather. The helicopter pilot thought that it might help Perkins's grieving process to visit the last place on earth they had been. Perkins, like many of us, had experienced many different kinds of silence in life—Quaker services, meditation groups, the silence in paintings, music, death, stars; the silence after an argument and after lovemaking—but the silence he experienced in the Aberdares that day was unlike any other. "It was snowing. Snow has no sound. Standing on the wet ground staring at the broken plane, never to fly again, elided with the depth of uncomprehending grief inside me and created a complete and terrifying silence, a dark un-blunted nowhere." It requires courage to dig oneself out of this "un-blunted nowhere," but hope can emerge. Fast-flowing rivers are noisy, but a slow-flowing river can be silent, as Perkins observed: "The silence of a river moving past you, especially at night . . . indeed, the silence of night coming and night departing, the sun's colour appearing along the bottom of a cloud."[29]

Gontran de Poncins was a French aristocrat who started traveling when he became bored with business, eventually settling in the Canadian Arctic where he lived with the Inuit for a time. Initially he was disparaging about them, but he admired their way of life and considered that there was nowhere else in the world where the silence was so perfect. His book *Kabloona*[30] was first published in the United States in 1941. The reason for much of the silence he experienced was the emptiness of the landscape. Since there were no trees, there was no sound of wind rustling their branches; as the water was frozen, there was no sound of flowing water; and since the stones were buried under the snow, there were none to trip on. "Is there another country in the world in which the silence is so perfect? . . . And yet this world is far from dead: it is only that the beings which dwell in this solitude are noiseless and invisible."[31]

People are often astonished by the Inuits' ability to track prey in what seems like a featureless landscape, but this skill of theirs comes through sound. Hunters have to be absolutely silent. The Inuit Norman Hallendy thinks *inuinaqtuk* (the silent state of awareness) is more important than the vision quest and dreaming. Henry David Thoreau described an Indian hunter as "elastic, noiseless, and stealthy."[32] Although others might not hear how the wind blows, its strength, direction, and smell are the clues to tracking in this landscape. In the long winter darkness and in terrain in which the sky and land horizon merge, visual landmarks become irrelevant and sound is the hunter's guide.

Fog also has silencing properties. The French poet Stéphane Mallarmé wanted accumulating banks of fog to rise and build "a great and silent ceiling."[33] When foghorns at sea break through a thick blanket of silence with their eerie booming, the lack of visibility contributes to the loud effect. If I go for a walk in good, clear weather, it feels as though the air is full of noise, whereas when it is foggy or snowing the world feels far quieter. In snow, although you can hear the crunch of your footsteps, many other sounds are eliminated. A noise that springs out of the foggy silence and cushion of obscurity can often be startling in its suddenness and unexpectedness. It feels as if one is being hauled out of a silent reverie and dragged into the world of sound.

THE SEA

Many people assume that life under the sea is silent. Jacques Cousteau, one of the inventors of the Aqua-Lung diving apparatus, certainly did. He was keen to introduce his young sons to diving, and because they would not stop talking before their first dive, he lectured them on the theme that the sea was a silent world. Later, in his book *The Silent World*, he described the deep ocean environment as mostly silent, noting that undersea sounds are so rare that those that do exist are accorded great importance: "The old round of life and death passes silently, save among mammals—whales and porpoises . . . it is a silent jungle . . ."[34] This was written in the early 1950s. New research has shown that life under the sea is anything but silent: the oceans have always been naturally noisy, with cracking ice and earthquakes, typhoons and tsunamis, and sociable whales making three kinds of sound—clicks, whistles, and pulsed calls.

But it is the noise of shipping that seriously impinges on the world of the deep and has been found to be seriously detrimental to sea creatures. Both natural and artificial sounds permeate the vast depths of the Mariana Trench in the western Pacific, eleven thousand meters below sea level, but it is the artificial sounds of ships that now predominate. Evidence shows that newly hatched fish larvae cannot hear the call of their habitat because of so much man-made noise. At the beginning of 2020, when much of the world went into lockdown because of the COVID-19 pandemic and noise pollution was reduced by 20 percent, whales were seen in places they hadn't visited for years.

ISLANDS

Islands are another sort of wilderness. When the writer Adam Nicolson's father left him the Shiants, a group of largely uninhabited islands in the Outer Hebrides, off the northwest coast of Scotland, he wrote that more than anywhere else he knows, the past seemed to be very present there. In his book *Sea Room*, he explains, "Perhaps it is because the islands are so pristine in their silence."[35] He believes that the Shiants are removed from ordinary life, possessing a kind of innate silence, since the daily life and its habits are pared away by dint of crossing the sea in a boat. The silence here has something to do with a lack of communication with outsiders. The few islanders do not have other people as props, which would be alarming to some but enriching to others, and the silence feels far from empty.

Nicolson sometimes found the silence and the solitude of the Shiant Isles overwhelming, and at times he was frightened by the ghosts that he felt around him. Nevertheless, overall he appreciated the silence, and he felt embraced and nourished by the sun on his face and the rhythm of the waves. Reflecting that the grave of a Viking was nearby, he remembered W. H. Auden's poem "Look, Stranger," which recommends being silent.[36]

Nicolson writes that all solitaries inevitably live with crowds of infuriating internal people—taunters and seducers—as well as benign friends. There is no hiding from this crowd, and they can be relentless. One solution, chosen by Robinson Crusoe, the castaway who lived on a remote tropical island in Daniel Defoe's novel of the same name, was to keep endlessly busy, building and planting—anything to keep the silent taunters at bay. But of course, keeping endlessly busy is not the only solution.

The memories that linger in places are silent memories. Those memories we have of places become part of that place. They contribute to the "spirit of place." Places never forget—what happened in a particular place happened nowhere else.

4

Call of the Desert

DESERTS HAVE an everlasting allure. In *A Sand County Almanac*, the American author, philosopher, scientist, and environmentalist Aldo Leopold wrote, "To those devoid of imagination, a blank place on the map is a useless waste; to others, the most valuable part."[1] He is not actually saying that the areas are silent, but in places with no towns or villages and few people, they might well be. For if you examine a map with blank spaces on it, those parts seem silent in comparison to the urban sprawls that by their very presence seem busy. When I look at a blank place on a map, I have the feeling that I'm expanding and opening up—the possibilities within those blank areas seem endless. In that space, all kinds of fantasies, dreams, and flights of fancy seem possible. Is it a desert? Undiscovered territory? A Shangri-la? Somehow it's not important to know what is there; the very emptiness itself is inspiring. As my finger hovers over a blank space on a map, I feel a thrill of excitement—will I ever get there? Cartographers call these blank spaces on maps "sleeping beauties," confirming any number of exciting possibilities.

Deserts have often been associated with silence, but it is debatable as to whether there can be true and absolute silence in the desert. However, desert silences seem to have a quality not present elsewhere—the aforementioned quality of space. In 1970, on a visit to Egypt, I stood in front of the "trunkless legs of stone" and quoted the English poet Percy Bysshe Shelley's "Ozymandias":

> I met a traveller from an antique land,
> Who said—"Two vast and trunkless legs of stone
> Stand in the desert. . . . Near them, on the sand,
> Half sunk a shattered visage lies, whose frown,
> And wrinkled lip, and sneer of cold command,
> Tell that its sculptor well those passions read
> Which yet survive, stamped on these lifeless things,
> The hand that mocked them, and the heart that fed;
> And on the pedestal, these words appear:
> My name is Ozymandias, King of Kings;
> Look on my Works, ye Mighty, and despair!
> Nothing beside remains. Round the decay
> Of that colossal Wreck, boundless and bare
> The lone and level sands stretch far away."[2]

The silence and vastness of the desert are evoked, and there are no humans to break the silence apart from the traveler, in this instance myself—150 years after the poem was written. It was this kind of occasion—another was in the desert in Iran reading the explorer Robert Byron's *The Road to Oxiana*[3]—linking where I was with some book or poem, that eventually led me to found the Travel Bookshop in Notting Hill in 1979, in the belief that reading about somewhere makes you a better traveler. I still get a thrill when I find that there is a direct link between somewhere I am currently visiting and a writer from the past; a bond has been created. I believe that places evolve by what happens in them and what's written about them.

In his book *The Desert*, the American nature writer John Charles Van Dyke describes the silences that he found in the desert, silences with which many desert wanderers fall in love: "The weird solitude, the great silence, the grim desolation."[4] Van Dyke was clearly besotted by deserts and refers to the mystery and the absolute stillness that there can be in a desert, especially at night. He names and shames humans as the perpetrators of noise and also as being responsible for light pollution, and it is within the darkness that silence seems more possible.

The British author Aldous Huxley spent several years in a house in Llano in the Mojave Desert in California where he worked on his book *The Perennial Philosophy*. Llano del Rio was a commune that had been established in 1914 by Job Harriman but that had been abandoned in 1918, largely due to a lack of water. Huxley's study had a large window that looked over the desert, and according to his friends, he was happier, healthier, and more at peace there than he had been for a long time. He was very struck by the silence of the desert: "Silence is the cloudless heaven perceived by another sense . . . it is a natural symbol of the divine"[5]—the divine being something he compares to both space and emptiness, silence and emptiness traditionally being the symbols of divine immanence or God within.

While writing *The Perennial Philosophy*, mostly in the silence of the desert, Huxley immersed himself in reading and research. In mysticism he found a common ground among the world's religions. Although Huxley was a humanist, he had long associations with both Vedanta, a school of Hindu philosophy, and with the twentieth-century philosopher and mystic Jiddu Krishnamurti, with whom he entered into a long correspondence. But he told his Catholic sister-in-law Rose D'Haulleville that "if I had to choose a religion, I would choose Catholicism."[6]

Huxley believed that the emptiness and silence of the desert only revealed a spiritual meaning to those with some kind of psychological security. Deserts can provide the solitude that promotes self-reflection, but they can also do the reverse. So, although he was able to find comfort in the desert, he realized that not everyone would. For example, a gold seeker who took the southern route to California in 1849 had the following to say about the silence of the desert: "Until one has crossed a barren desert, without food or water, under a burning tropical sun, at three miles an hour, one can form no conception of what misery is."[7] Huxley knew that the desert had already entered the armament race, since there was the necessary empty space to explode atomic bombs: "The desert silence is still there; but so, ever more noisily, are the scientific irrelevancies . . . [and they will] succeed in abolishing the silence."[8] He understood that although in his day there was enough stillness and silence in the Mojave to absorb the brutal noise of jet planes, he rightly anticipated the future: between 1945 and 1962, 210 nuclear tests were carried out in the Mojave Desert.

The particular silence of the desert at night and the multitude of stars, and human's insignificance, struck many writers. "In the naked desert's night we were stained by dew, and shamed into pettiness by the innumerable silences of stars," wrote the archaeologist, army officer, and writer T. E. Lawrence in *Seven Pillars of Wisdom*.[9] Of course what may seem silent to us—like the world of those innumerable stars—is in fact not silent at all, but they are distant enough to give us the illusion of a serene and silent world. In *Wind, Sand and Stars*, the French writer Antoine de Saint-Exupéry comments that no amount of money "could buy the night flight with its hundred thousand stars, its serenity, its few hours of sovereignty. . . . Over the desert a vast silence as of a house in order reigns."[10]

In his essay "Baptism of Solitude," the American composer and author Paul Bowles captures the silence of the Sahara: "Immediately when you arrive in the Sahara, for the first or the tenth time, you notice the stillness. An incredible, absolute silence prevails outside the towns."[11] He felt that even in the markets there was a "hushed quality," conjecturing that the quiet had a strength about it that resented noise and was therefore immediately able to dissolve it. He was also struck by the sky: "Then there is the sky, compared to which all other skies seem fainthearted efforts. Solid and luminous, it is always the focal point of the landscape."[12] He continued by describing *le bapteme de la solitude*, "the baptism of solitude," a unique sensation that has nothing to do with loneliness and that can be addictive. Nothing and nowhere else can compete once you have been under the spell of the huge, luminous, and silent country: "No other surroundings can provide the supremely satisfying sensation of existing in the midst of something that is absolute." He wrote that after experiencing the absolute in the desert, the traveler will have a compulsion to return: "Whatever the cost in comfort and money, for the absolute has no price."[13]

In *Desert Divers*, the Swedish Sven Lindqvist writes that when he stopped and listened, every sound was magnified and that silence was rare. He observed, "A cricket, dark as a splinter of stone, chirps shrilly. The wind whistles in the six telephone wires, a thin, metallic note I haven't heard since childhood. And then silence, which is even rarer."[14]

But Eugène Fromentin, the French writer and painter, considered "the silence [of the desert] one of the most subtle charms of this solitary and empty land,"[15] because it was born of emptiness and acquired a density that encouraged a spiritual interpretation. Many other French writers—such as Francois-René de Chateaubriand, Alphonse Lamartine, Gérard de Nerval—have written about the silence of the desert. Barthélemy wrote of the desert, "Silence too is something Other."[16] The Swiss explorer Isabelle Eberhardt's desert experience was "to try once more to isolate myself for months on end in the total silence of the desert."[17]

The journalist Martin Buckley traveled all over the world in search of deserts. He and his wife-to-be, Penny, even decided to get married in a desert in Senegal. Unlike many desert travelers, Buckley did indeed find silence in the desert: "True silence requires the absence of friction of air upon object—the emptiness and stillness found only in the desert."[18] The desert can concentrate a sense of self, remote from the noise of cities where even if you switch off a computer or a radio, there always seems to be noise of some kind, whereas in the desert, "enormous" silence is a given and other senses are enhanced. "I remember a dawn in Death Valley," Buckley writes. "The air was dense, still, scented with sage musk released in the night."[19] Buckley is conscious of how most people deny solitude, finding it frightening, and as a result, many lives are filled with needless chatter: "We deny solitude, yet a preparation for it must be essential, because we have to die alone."[20] This solitude, and by definition silence, is of course what most religions emphasize.

Much of the reason for desert travel can be this search for solitude. In an increasingly crowded world, the lure of empty spaces intensifies, and if you are lucky enough to find a silent empty space, the memory of it can be incorporated into daily life. Buckley felt that he could "keep the image of a silent, spacious place."[21] But William Atkins, another contemporary writer, disagrees; he reckons that the desert isn't silent and that to achieve silence in the desert is hard work. He could never escape from his own bodily noises and had to "stop fidgeting, stop the gulping, the ceaseless tonguing and lipping, the clicking of your jaw, the blinking of your jellied eyes, the burbling of the nostrils and the boiling of the guts"[22]—in fact to almost stop breathing. He considers that one of the things that travelers are searching for are absolutes, and absolutes are hard to find—whether it be absolute darkness or absolute silence. But they are worth the search, for as Paul Bowles said, the "absolute has no price." While you can, of course, close your eyes and have the illusion of absolute darkness, it is much harder to get absolute silence, since as Atkins wrote, the quieter the surroundings, the more you can hear your own bodily sounds. James Crowden writes that "absolute silence, like absolute zero, is a state of mind."[23] But there is a deep association between darkness and silence. It's almost as if there is an expectation of silence in a dark place. Light can be a distraction, since light enables us to see, and when we are seeing, we are involving another one of our senses—something that makes it harder to absorb silence.

Uwe George is a documentary filmmaker who studied birds in the Sahara. In his book *In the Deserts of This Earth*, he describes the silence on a particular day when there was no wind and he became acutely conscious of the noises of his bodily functions, which, like William Atkins, suddenly seemed very loud: "I heard every heart-beat and even the coursing of the blood in my veins. A swallow from my canteen produced a loud gurgling noise as the water ran down my gullet into my stomach. This condition of oversensitivity rapidly mounted and became anxiety."[24] He felt totally alone and as if he were on a lifeless planet; at one point he panicked and thought he was lost until he found his own tracks in the sand, which he was then able to follow back to his camp. He began to think about the astronauts who had landed on the moon, and he thought that he understood why it was necessary that this kind of adventure should be undertaken in pairs.

George reckons that he found total silence and that the kind of silence he found is only achievable in the desert. In the desert you can no longer consider silence as the opposite of noise but rather some-thing that can be seen as a state in its own right that can introduce you to another dimension. A one-time silence that occurs in the desert can have a positive and lasting resonance for the rest of life. But as to whether George found total silence is debatable since he was so very aware of the sounds of his own body and his mind that was so full of words. But sometimes in that deep internal space to which we all have access, it is possible not to be conscious of any sound.

In Janette Turner Hospital's book *Oyster* there is a very poetic description of silence in the Australian outback. Silence is the link between now and the Ice Age: "Out here, silence is the dimension in which we float. It billows above us like the vast sails of galleon earth, ballooning into the outer geography of the Milky Way."[25] Later in the book, she writes that there are always our bodily sounds to contend with, but in the desert, "the vastness of the silence frightens all of us, I think."[26] She thinks that it was the fear of the silence that historically encouraged workers to congregate together in camps where they could be noisy together.

In *Tracks*,[27] Robyn Davidson relates how she took camels across Australia through some of the harshest deserts on earth. She scarcely mentions the silence of the desert, but then as we have seen, silence in the desert is not a given. If you are not looking for it, maybe it can pass you by? There is no doubt that the silence of the desert can be richly rewarding—but as has been shown, for some it can be deeply alarming.

DESERT FATHERS AND OTHER HERMITAGES

In addition to attracting writers, the silence of the desert also has ties to religion. Within three centuries of Christ's death, when Christianity was legalized by the Roman emperor Constantine, the religion became hierarchical and institutional—something that Jesus had spent his whole ministry opposing. And so in the third century C.E., in order to escape this institutionalization, ascetics took to the Egyptian desert to live in silence and contemplation. Contemplative prayer was central to the Desert Fathers (mostly men—Desert Mothers came later and were relatively few) as these early Christian hermits and monks became known, and later Christian monasticism was based on the lives that the Desert Fathers had led. John Cassian, one of the early Desert Fathers, understood the difficulties that many newcomers to the eremitic life faced: solitude made them feel "the many-winged folly of their souls . . . they find the perpetual silence intolerable."[28] But the majority of the Desert Fathers went to great lengths to remain silent. One of them, Abba Agathon, kept a stone in his mouth for three years to prevent himself from speaking, and certain Christian sects, although maybe not to that extreme, have followed a silent route for centuries.[29]

Although the word *hermit* derives from the latinization of the Greek word meaning "of the desert," the Greeks never had a hermit culture. Nevertheless, they worked out a philosophical justification for living alone: a philosophy of solitariness.[30] There were many different kinds of hermits. In the fifth century, St. Simeon and other hermits who lived on pillars were called *stylites*, and those who lived in trees were known as *dendrites*. When you see Simeon's column, north of Aleppo in Syria, it is hard to imagine how anyone could have survived a single night on it, let alone the thirty-seven years St. Simeon is reputed to have lived on the small platform he built himself at the top. When I saw it, I wondered how he had managed to get to the top in the first place. Such methods as living on a platform in the desert were certainly drastic, but as hermits, they were looking for a way to live wisely and did this by setting aside time to stop and reassess their lives.

St. Anthony of Egypt, also known as St. Anthony the Great, began to practice an ascetic life at the age of twenty, and after fifteen years of a moderately solitary life, he retreated into complete solitude and silence in the desert. It was here that he endured his legendary combats with the devil, portrayed in paintings by so many artists that it seems that it was almost a rite of passage for an artist to paint him. He was painted by, among others, Matthias Grünewald, Albrecht Dürer, Max Ernst, Odilon Redon, Giambattista Tiepolo, David Teniers, Hieronymus Bosch, Pieter Bruegel, Salvator Rosa,

Paul Cézanne, James Ensor, Stanley Spencer, and Salvador Dali; all portray him being tempted by the devil in his solitary and silent reclusiveness.[31]

After a misspent youth, the French explorer Charles de Foucauld heard the "call of silence" and became a missionary among the Tuareg. In 1904, he settled in Tamanrasset in Algeria. He was assassinated there in 1916, but not before he'd written much about the benefits of silence. He had found happiness "in the silence of the desert. This desert is for me deeply sweet . . . so it is hard for me to travel, to leave this solitude and this silence."[32]

PERSONAL PERCEPTIONS

My own experience of a night in the Wahiba Sands desert in Oman was neither tranquil nor silent. Two friends and I rode camels into the desert and were deposited near where we were meant to be meeting a guide with tents—"just over that sand dune," we were told as the camel driver left us. But there was no one where we were told he'd be, and "just over that sand dune" there was another sand dune and another and another . . . My feeling was of panic—as far from silent serenity as it's possible to be. All we could see in any direction was sand, sand, sand. We had no provisions, and as sunset approached, anxiety levels rose, and then it was dark and cold. Would we even survive one night in the desert with no tents, no food, no water? I was able to phone our friend in Muscat, but when he asked where we were, I despaired. The mere fact of being able to ring someone, of course, detracted from our intrepid status, but we weren't there to prove anything. Actually, why were we there? Just for the experience, I suppose. I certainly had no positive thoughts about our adventure until, with a huge feeling of relief, we saw the guide walking toward us. We then spent an extremely noisy night with howling wind and flying sand. We were told that the wind should drop at sunset, but it didn't, which made our eventual attempt at cooking almost impossible. My camp bed even collapsed in the middle of the night, consolidating my feeling that I wasn't meant to be a desert explorer.

An altogether more silent desert experience was when I arrived at sunset at the Makgadikgadi salt pan in Botswana, one of the largest salt flats in the world and all that remains of Lake Makgadikgadi (meaning "thirsty place"), which had once been the size of Switzerland before it dried up thousands of years ago. The guide encouraged me to experience this silence by walking off alone into the distance. Clutching my requisite sundowner, I walked toward the setting sun and experienced a time of total tranquility and silence. This silence was massive and all-enveloping.

There is an urban myth attached to the "Silence Zone," an area of desert patch located in northern Mexico. It is believed that radio waves cannot be transmitted normally there and that this is something to do with a test missile that crashed in the region in 1970 while carrying a radioactive element. During the US Air Force's rescue operation, "strange magnetic anomalies that prevented radio transmission" were thought to be present. The district also has a large number of meteorites and a large variety of endemic species, such as the desert tortoise, unique reptiles and hares, kangaroo mice, coyotes, and owls, as well as many obscure plant species. In 1974, a biosphere reserve was established in this very arid place. Radio transmissions are also limited near the Green Bank Telescope, in Green Bank, West Virginia, which is the world's largest fully steerable radio telescope located near the center of the United States National Radio Quiet Zone. This allows the telescope to detect faint radio frequency signals that might otherwise be imperceptible.

So although there is no guarantee that you will find silence in the desert, if approached in the right frame of mind, silence is there to be found.

5

Searching for Silent Buildings

SILENCE CAN BE FOUND in a variety of places, and it is often man-made structures, ruins, abandoned buildings and places of worship that resonate with peace and quietness.

THE HUSH OF RUINS

Ruins are an interesting source of silence, and I think this is something to do with the link that exists between us and the past. Although the buildings that are now lying in ruins might once have been busy and noisy, the fact that they have fallen into disrepair allows us to wonder and to contemplate their history silently. Wandering around an ancient ruin, made derelict by the elements or natural decay, can give one an overwhelming and silent connection to the past:

> There is a temple in ruin stands,
> Fashion'd by long forgotten hands:
> Two or three columns, and many a stone,
> Marble and granite, with grass o'ergrown![1]

Many travels are undertaken specifically with the goal to see ruins. One can definitely get a feeling of a civilization from visiting their ruins, be it Greek, Roman, Aztec, Inca, or Khmer. A ruin can be a direct link to the lives of the people who lived there. By closing one's eyes and absorbing the feeling of a place (and by somehow ignoring the busloads of tourists), one can be transported back to a previous era.

My grandparents and other relations are buried at the romantically named Sweetheart Abbey—the Abbey of Dulce Cor—in Dumfriesshire, Scotland. The Cistercian abbey was founded in 1275 by Dervorguilla of Galloway in memory of her husband, John Balliol, whose embalmed heart was buried with her when she died. I've been to many family burials there and have always felt that the red sandstone ruins keep something of the romance of Dervorguilla and John Balliol alive. For many years I paid an annual fee to reserve a plot there for myself. My grave would certainly have been hard to visit—a long journey for most people—but I thought that being buried in such a romantic and peaceful place among my ancestors would somehow justify the difficulty. However, I have let the reservation slip and think I will end up in London.

During a week spent in North Yorkshire during the summer of 2019, I managed to visit many ruined abbeys and monasteries, including Jervaulx Abbey, Fountains Abbey, and Mount Grace Priory. Fountains is always busy, but there was no one else at Jervaulx, and so it was easy to conjure up its past. In a cloister I find it easy to summon up the thought of the many silent devotions that would have been prayed there. At Jervaulx, my sister and I wandered through the ruined cloister into the adjacent ruin of the church—Chapter House, kitchen, and dormitories—all the time calling up images of the monks leading their mostly silent lives. When the English writer the Reverend Richard Coles visited the ruins at Rievaulx for a television program,[2] he commented that although we need silence to be at the center of what we do, in modern life we have mostly lost that core silence. At Rievaulx, though, he felt that the silence was still palpable.

But not all ruins have benign feelings attached to them. Ruins that are a result of war have a very different feel, as do those caused by natural disasters—not a silent connection and communion with the past but rather a feeling of haunting, horror, and violence. These are not silent ruins but ruins that seem to be screaming out to have their painful past recognized. Photographs of bombed cities have the feeling of a looming silent terror; each scene seems to be holding its breath, silently.

CATHEDRALS AND CHURCHES

Historic cathedrals are also on the tourist circuit, and with their pillars and columns they can be bastions of silence, their very solidity and substance generating a feeling of calm. If you are lucky enough to visit an empty cathedral or church, the silence can be intense. The silence of a Romanesque cathedral is tangible; it exists as a substance.

Churches can carry silence from previous ages. David Tas wrote "The Walnut Tree" about a visit he had made to the church in La Chataigneraie in the Vendée with his late wife. It was a hot day, and it felt as though the church invited them in:

To the cool darkness where silence
Absorbed our prayers into the candle's glow.[3]

The Swiss philosopher Max Picard describes cathedrals as growing around the silence that is locked inside, in the same way as ivy, by growing up a wall for centuries, imprisons the wall. He bemoans the fact that today (the 1950s), "the cathedrals are like silence inlaid with stone and are deserted just as silence is deserted"; they have become silent museums. "But they are still interrelated, cathedral with cathedral, silence with silence. They stand like ichthyosauri of silence, no longer understood by anyone."[4]

One of the most memorable descriptions of silence in cathedrals was written by J. K. Huysmans who in several of his novels addresses many different aspects of silence. He discusses the iconography of Christian architecture at length in *La Cathédrale*, the third volume of the trilogy featuring Durtal, his spiritual alter ego who converts to Catholicism and goes to Chartres in order to find silence. But the silence Durtal finds is not altogether positive. Reflecting Huysmans's own deep pessimism: "When we peer down in appalling silence into a black void."[5] In his novel *À Rebours* (*Against Nature*),[6] the antihero Jean des Esseintes surrounds himself with mute servants, old people who are bowed down by years of silence. He manages to create an environment where he does not have to endure hearing the footsteps of his servants. In *En Rade* (*Becalmed*), Huysmans, who detested the countryside, conveys the tactical importance of silence as shown by an elderly couple. Huysmans's poetry was strongly influenced by the French poet Charles Pierre Baudelaire, and Baudelaire, despite his dissolute life, liked to be alone and in silence. When he went into his bedroom, he would say that he had escaped "the great woe of not being able to be alone."[7]

Most churches have at least a chapel that is, or aims to be, silent. In Westminster Abbey, very much on the busy and noisy tourist circuit, a frequent announcement is made asking people to be quiet. This also happens regularly in the Sistine Chapel, and it is extremely distracting—possibly even more distracting than having people talking.

The artist Mark Cazalet often, but not exclusively, works in silence. Before drawing or painting, he does a reading or a meditation. For him, this is a way of letting go of the surrounding world. The drawing he then begins is a process, often with no thought-out plan. Cazalet sees the fact of being able to return to a designated and dependably silent place as a gift, and once back in that silent space being able to reengage with a work that's in progress is a satisfying, albeit somewhat scary process. What happens if that silent creative space can't be found again? It can be like getting to the edge of a cliff and having to take a step into the unknown. Between the seeing eye and the moving hand of the artist and the viewer there is "a cat's cradle of exchange, the tauter and better formed the richer the pattern becomes," and then the paradox—the letting go and allowing the "silence to expand and fill the anxious uncertainty of creativity."[8] Cazalet has described silence as a splint that allows the pieces to reconnect.

In 2016, Cazalet had an exhibition called *Silent Colour Meditation: A Great Cloud of Witnesses* in St. Edmundsbury Cathedral in Bury St. Edmunds in Suffolk, England. It was composed of a series of 153 paintings made when he was artist in residence. (One hundred fifty-three is the number of fish referred to in the Gospels of Luke and John and is often thought to be an inclusive number, representing all nations, all people.) In Bury St. Edmunds, anyone could volunteer to sit for him for thirty minutes; the stipulation was that they had to sit in silence while he painted their portraits. All the paintings were oil on wood, and all were the same size; each sitter chose two colors and a background hue of their choice. He began each session with a basic introduction to silent meditation, and at the end the sitters were able to talk about their experience of the sitting. Some felt euphoria, others desolation, and the deal was that while Mark would listen to what they wanted to say, he would stay silent. When completed, the paintings were hung around the cathedral at head height. It was a powerful experience to walk around looking at them. Some people gazed out at the viewer, while others had their eyes closed. What struck me was the feeling that I felt I knew more about those people who had their eyes closed than those with their eyes open—

something that belies the adage that eyes are the gateway to the soul. It was a deeply moving experience.

I think it only needs an exhibition like Cazalet's in Bury St. Edmunds to show that even today, cathedrals are holy places and are much more than museums. The fact that Cazalet's paintings were painted and shown in a cathedral was important, since being in a space that originated in the eleventh century and has had hundreds of years of worship meant that the silence of hundreds of years became an inherent part of the exhibition.

BUILT FOR THE PURPOSE OF SILENCE

When the UK department store Selfridges first opened in 1909 in Oxford Street, Gordon Selfridge created a Silence Room on the lower ground floor where shoppers could go for peace and quiet. Sadly there were no records of what the original Silence Room looked like, but in 2012 the architect Alex Cochrane reinvented the space as a refuge for shoppers. They described it as a room within a room, an inner chamber of silence. The outer room became a corridor connecting the shop floor to the Silence Room while serving as a buffer against noise and traffic. The singular light bulb in each corner guided visitors down the black corridors toward the narrow entrance of the chamber. It was built with oak and natural wool felt, both chosen for their acoustic and tactile qualities, and there was a bench running around the perimeter on which it was possible to lie down. The room was created for the No Noise campaign launched by Selfridges in 2013. Sadly it seems to have been a one-off, short-term event.

The noise in New York was described by the writer Malcolm Lowry as "like the unbandaging of great giants in agony."[9] Some people suddenly feel that they cannot bear this kind of constant urban noise anymore. This happened one day to the writer George Michelsen Foy as he was waiting for the subway in New York; the combined noise of the trains and the whining of his children set him on a mission to find the quietest place on earth.[10] In Foy's quest he visited a Cistercian monastery, an American Indian sweat lodge, and a nickel mine two kilometers underground. Finally, he went to the anechoic (having no echo) chamber at Orfield Laboratories in Minnesota, which *The Guinness Book of Records* claims is the quietest place on earth, being 99.9 percent sound absorbent. It is a small room insulated with layers of concrete and steel to block out any exterior noise; inside, it is lined with crosshatched buffers that absorb all sound. Most people who stay in the chamber for more than fifteen minutes get extreme symptoms of claustrophobia, nausea, panic attacks, and even aural hallucinations. Foy booked a forty-five-minute session and managed to stay the course. Initially he felt that his peace was being spoiled as he was very aware of the sounds of his breath, the blood in his veins, and his heartbeat. But when he stopped obsessing about these sounds, he began to enjoy the silence and only emerged because his time was up. Afterward, he said he felt wonderfully rested and calm. NASA even sends its astronauts to do part of their training in an anechoic chamber to prepare them for the silence of space. But, of course, outer space is not silent, and an astronaut told Foy that if you didn't hear constant noise in a space capsule, it indicated that there was a problem as it meant that the interior ventilators would have stopped circulating air.[11]

I couldn't imagine myself spending time in an anechoic chamber—it makes me anxious just to think about it. I once had a boyfriend who did an experiment in Germany, involving him spending time underground—it was for about a month, I think. There was no natural light, and he wasn't allowed a clock or a watch, and one of the things that was constantly monitored was how much time he spent asleep. I am hazy about the reason for or the results of the experiment—but I think it must have been something to do with investigating circadian rhythms; I think the twenty-four-hour day rapidly expanded into a forty-eight-hour day. Being deprived of sound and natural light quickly upsets your body clock.

SPIRITUALITY

6

Religious Perspectives

THERE HAVE ALWAYS been deities and idols dedicated to silence. Stone seals from the Indus valley civilization (3000 B.C.E.), long predating the Buddha, have been found depicting men sitting in the classic yoga meditation position. Most religions and spiritual traditions see silence as fundamental and have it at their core, and it is this silence that can link us to the past and to the essence of spirituality. Jesus went into the hills to pray, Jewish prophets went into the wilderness, and Hindu yogis and Tibetan sages traditionally went to meditate in remote caves.

ANCIENT CIVILIZATIONS

In ancient Greece, Harpocrates was the god of silence. Greeks adapted him from the Egyptian child-god Horus, the son of the Egyptian divinities Isis and Osiris. Horus represented the newborn sun rising each day at dawn and overcoming the darkness; he was often portrayed with his finger on his chin, showing the meaning of the hieroglyph "child." However, the later Greeks and Romans misunderstood this gesture and identified him with secrecy and silence, and in Ovid's *Metamorphosis*, he is described as "the child-god asking for silence with finger pressed to his lips."[1]

The silencing of women can be traced back to *The Iliad*, when Hera was silenced by her husband Zeus, who had threatened violence when she disagreed with him over a matter concerning the Trojan War.[2] In *The Odyssey*,[3] the spoiled adolescent Telemachus tells his mother, Penelope, that stories are only for men—that women should be doing "women's work." He also tells his mother to shut up when she complains about one of the performers in the communal male space in Odysseus's palace. In her novel *The Silence of the Girls*,[4] Pat Barker tells the story of *The Iliad* from the viewpoint of women, especially Briseis, the childless wife of King Mynes. But as the title suggests, most of the novel has Briseis being silent and only describes her internal thoughts.

When it comes to the Roman Empire, the goddesses Angerona, Tacita, and Muta seem to merge into one another and are difficult to tell apart. Ovid wrote that Angerona came to be called both Tacita and Muta, but actually all three were personifications of silence. The goddess Muta, the "mute one," was probably identical to Larunda, a naiad nymph. Angerona, like Harpocrates, is often shown with a finger on her lips encouraging us not to speak, while Tacita is often shown with her tongue ripped out, showing us the consequences of too much speech.[5]

In around 70 C.E., still lives were being painted on the walls of Pompeii. One of the qualities of a still life is an absolute quietness and silence, and this is a stillness beyond the stillness of something not moving: "Painting is silent poetry, and poetry is painting that speaks,"[6] the Greek philosopher Plutarch tells us. I had never really thought about the meaning of a still life beyond it being a collection of objects that didn't move, but still lives can and do evoke a feeling of calm and satisfaction. Still lives probably originated in Egyptian tomb decoration, as offerings for the dead to take into the next life.

Examples of these Egyptian wall paintings still exist in some of the discovered tombs. One of the first recorded Roman still lives is from Pompeii; it survived the volcanic eruption and is now in the National Archaeological Museum in Naples. It depicts vases and a glass bowl overflowing with fruit; and having survived silently for two thousand years, the apples and grapes that fill this glass bowl still look good enough to eat. As I wandered round the ruins of Pompeii a few years ago, the numerous instances of graffiti on the walls are a silent reminder of what a prosperous place it once was. I found it easy, in the silence, to reconstruct a thriving city in my mind.

SILENCE IN EASTERN TRADITIONS

The Buddha (fifth century B.C.E.) was liberated through silent meditation while sitting under the bodhi tree. After he became enlightened, when he was asked a question, he would often say nothing in reply, and it was this silence that was known as the practice of the "noble silence."

When Buddhism reached China, the Naga, or Serpent God, morphed into a dragon, which came to be the sign of an enlightened teacher—its presence being associated with the pursuit of silent illumination, a Zen meditation practice. Each of the Buddha's gestures has a symbolic meaning, and at around the same time that the Buddha was alive, Plato recorded the first use of sign language.[7] Although sign language is a silent way of communicating, I wonder whether those who practice it feel that it is, since silence is more than the absence of sound. True silence needs to be internal too.

The ancient Chinese writer and philosopher Lao Tzu, the reputed author of the Tao Te Ching, believed that wisdom was achieved through inaction (*wu wei*) rather than action and that solitude was healthy as an escape from the pressures of society. These Taoist sages appreciated the value of silence as a necessary precursor to creativity;

they went into their mountain hermitages where they would spend their days in silent contemplation. The Jungian analyst Anne Baring wrote of them: "If they were artists, they perfected their brushstrokes and observed every detail of the life surrounding them. If they were poets, they invited the words of a poem to enter the stillness, holding their breath so as not to disturb its emergence."[8] Those who practiced Taoism believed in living in harmony with the Tao (the Way) as the method of achieving perfection and becoming one with the rhythms of the universe. Tai chi chuan, the martial art now widely practiced in the West, embodies the principles of Taoism, its practice bringing one into harmony with the world.

THE MYSTERY RELIGIONS

Practitioners of Zoroastrianism have revered "towers of silence" (*dakhmas*)—circular raised structures on which their dead are exposed to vultures or other carrion birds. Bodies are divided into male, female, or children and put into different circles. Dead bodies were considered unclean and were meant to avoid earth and fire, both sacred to the Zoroastrians, hence their exposure to birds that would eat away the flesh and tissue. Then once the bones have been bleached by the sun, which can take up to a year, they are pushed into an opening in the center, where they disintegrate with the help of lime and are eventually washed away. In the mid-fifth century B.C.E., Herodotus knew about this and other mystery religions, the secret cults of the Greco-Roman world whose main characteristic was the secrecy and silence around the initiation and ritual practices. But he was such a loyal devotee that maddeningly he felt he needed to keep silent about them: "All the details of these performances are known to me, but I will say no more."[9] Although Herodotus was the first to mention Zoroastrians exposing their dead, the first mention of towers built specifically for this purpose does not occur until much later in the ninth century C.E., and the term "tower of silence" wasn't coined until the early nineteenth century by Robert Murphy, a translator for the British colonial government of India. Why he called them "towers of silence" is unclear, but the name stuck and that is how they are known today. I believe you can book a tour to see the tower of silence near Mumbai.

In the Roman mystery religion Mithraism, a Roman mystery religion centered on the god Mithras and inspired by Zoroastrianism, those being initiated held their fingers to their lips and whispered, "Silence! Silence! Silence." Long before the advent of Christianity, the Egyptian mystery religions that worshipped Isis and Osiris were "closed to him who speaks, but open to the silent."[10]

CHRISTIAN CONTEXTS OF SILENCE

Silence weaves its way through the different books of the Christian Bible with many differing attitudes—often paradoxical. In the beginning, the Word of God was born in silence, and because Christians believe in a God who speaks to them, it is necessary to be silent in order to hear him. While this is empowering to believers who are drawn into the silence, to many, God's silence feels like an absence or maybe even an indifference: "Then shall they call upon me, but I will not answer" (Proverbs 1:28).[11]

Often when we are suffering, all we want is for someone to be there. Human company can be soothing, and a silent presence can be a consolation. Despite being unwavering in his commitment to God, Job loses everything—his children, his wealth, even his health. When his three friends heard of what had befallen him, they went to mourn and comfort him: "So they sat down with him upon the ground seven days and seven nights, and none spake a word unto him; for they saw that his grief was very great" (Job 2:13). They knew it was best to allow him to grieve in silence. In contrast to the comfort of silence, the Bible also used silence as a means of control—a husband had the right to hit his wife to silence her, and St. Paul's first epistle to the Corinthians states, "And if they will learn anything, let them ask their husbands at home: for it is a shame for women to speak in the church" (1 Corinthians 14:35).

Jesus was silent for thirty years before he started preaching. In the gospels it was largely Martha, a disciple of Jesus, who spoke, while Mary her sister remained silent. Monastic Christians who built silence into their daily rituals were following the silent way of Mary, while the secular clergy followed Martha. Laurence Freeman OSB writes that through observing the death of Christ on the cross on Good Friday, we can learn the meaning of silence, since death is the ultimate silence. Of course, the void caused by death is painful, but if we are able to embrace silence, we can learn that the emptiness and poverty of spirit can also become a fullness. An ancient homily that is often read at Tenebrae on Holy Saturday draws one into a deep silence: "Something strange is happening—there is a great silence on earth today, a great silence and stillness."[12]

Early Christians themselves were noisy, often shouting their praises in the same way that many contemporary Christians do. There is no mention of monasteries in the Bible, but when early Christians journeyed from Syria to India, they discovered that both Hindus and Buddhists had traditions of monks and monasteries and that with those came some degree of silent practice. The monastic ideal and way of living was imported into Christianity in the second century C.E. and of course went on to become a very important part of Christianity, with monasteries becoming places in which to contemplate God in quietness.

Carthusians

St. Bruno of Cologne who founded the Carthusians, an order of the Catholic Church, was celebrated as a teacher and in 1075 was appointed chancellor to the Archdiocese of Reims. But since he was unwilling to accept the pomp and ceremony associated with the ecclesiastical hierarchy, he refused to become a bishop. In 1084 he went to Haute-Savoie where he built an oratory that later became the Grande Chartreuse, the head monastery of the Carthusians. The building had individual cells, and Bruno lived there in isolation and poverty, declaring that "only those who have experienced it can know what heavenly joy and benefit the silence and solitude of the desert can bring to those who love it."[13] The statutes of the Carthusians emphasize the importance of exterior silence, but even more emphasis is put on the practice of interior silence as a form of attentiveness and a positive receptivity. To some this might be alarming; for instance, Alberic, a Cistercian monk of the twelfth century, said, "Silence is a place for bumping into yourself,"[14] and silence does make you confront yourself and your inner demons.

The Carthusians still live by very strict rules, never smoking and never eating meat or poultry, and from September until Easter they keep a fast with only one meal a day. Once a year they are allowed to take a picnic on a long eight-hour walk, but the rest of the time is spent in mostly solitary silence. If anyone tries to relax the rules, the attempt is met with fierce resistance. In charterhouses, as Carthusian monasteries are known, novices initially try their vocations for a month to see whether they will be able to endure the tough life of being a Carthusian monk.

The Carthusians, hermits by instinct, have a motto: *Soli Deo* (God alone). They have always been fiercely independent, and their lifestyle has changed little since the Council of Trent in the sixteenth century. They were never reformed as they were never "deformed." They have a "walking about" on Mondays, and during this walk the monks are allowed to talk, although serious discussions are not encouraged; every thirty minutes they have to change their walking companion so as not to get too intimate. Novices and those monks who have taken vows—the solemns—are not allowed to walk together; in fact, their routes are kept strictly apart. "But even more important is interior silence. . . . The longer he lives in a cell, the more gladly he will do so."[15] It is unlikely that a Carthusian who fears silence will remain in the monastery, and it's not the silence that is frightening but what it reveals. A Carthusian wrote that "our silence is not something negative but a form of attentiveness, a positive receptivity."[16]

The film *Into the Great Silence*[17] about the Carthusian Grande Chartreuse monastery in the French Alps, was released in the UK in 2006. It had taken sixteen years for the director Philip Gröning to be granted permission to film in the monastery. He spent around six months immersed in monastic life; and his film, which is nearly three hours long, has few words. He did all the camerawork and sound recording himself and didn't use any extra lighting. No additional music or archival footage was added to the film, and there is no voiceover commentary, leaving the viewer in charge of interpretation. Since there is so little speech, other sounds tend to dominate, adding to the intensity of the film. The church bell summons the monks to prayer, and practical noises such as the chopping of wood and the sound of footsteps can occasionally be heard. But overall there is a feeling of deep silence. In this largely silent film there is a sequence in which snow falls silently onto the monastery roof; it is mesmerizing to watch, even though nothing happens other than just that—snow falling silently onto the monastery roof.

I went to see the film in a theater during lunchtime one day. I had taken a sandwich with me, but I found it almost impossible to eat, as with each bite I felt I was interrupting the silence, which indeed I was. As it was a daytime showing, there were mainly two groups of people—the retired and students. I could tell from their body posture that many of the retired were unenthusiastic—they were restless and whispering to their companions, many leaving before the end—whereas the young seemed rapt and found it hard to leave, even after the last credits had rolled. There is obviously a yearning and need for silence among younger generations. Timothy Radcliffe, OP, who saw it in St. Louis, reckoned it should have been called *Into the Great Popcorn Crunching*; he had been in the same kind of audience—young and old—with the St. Louis reaction being the same as in London.[18]

SHIFTING SILENCE

The eleventh century saw a dramatic shift away from the silence tradition, with far more emphasis being placed on external ritual. Although this appealed to many, it was in fact counter to the deep inner understanding that had been acquired over the ages and had been encouraged by the Wisdom Traditions, the idea that there is a perennial or mystic core to all religious or spiritual traditions and in which silence was important. The saints Thomas Aquinas and Bonaventure had kept the balance between silence and speech, but both died in 1274, and with their deaths this precarious balance disappeared and silence was sidelined. The increase in contemplatives at the end of the thirteenth and during the fourteenth centuries—such as Meister Eckhart, Julian of Norwich, and the anonymous author of *The Cloud of Unknowing*—was in part a protest against the general move away from silence. Julian of Norwich was one of many who recognized that prayer was a summons to silence, acknowledging the inherent poverty of speech. Meister Eckhart encourages us to let go of all of our preconceptions of God and to immerse ourselves in the silent wilderness of the Godhead—the purpose of human's existence being to love, know, and be united with the immanent and transcendent Godhead: "There is nothing so like God as Silence."[19] To enable the Word of God to filter through the bands of noise and clutter that we have erected, silence needs to be cultivated. Mysticism is a silent route to God, and a mystic's path ends in a craving for the cloud of unknowing, an unknowing that is beyond knowledge and comes with a silence that is beyond speech. Most people who claim to hear God speaking to them hear God in the silence of their hearts.

Away from monastic life, silence for the layperson in organized religion became increasingly rare but was promoted by some, including the fourteenth-century author William Langland. In his book *Piers the Ploughman*, a dreamer falls asleep on the Malvern Hills and begins his spiritual quest for "kynde knowing," a personal, silent, and transformative experience of God.[20] Nicholas of Cusa, a German philosopher, theologian, jurist, astronomer, and one of the first proponents of Renaissance humanism, was the last member within the hierarchy of an institution (he was made a cardinal and then vicar general of the Papal States) to teach kynde knowing, and after his death the tradition of silence was effectively lost to institutional Christianity for hundreds of years.[21]

In *The Divine Comedy*, Dante describes the sphere of Saturn as a transition point between the six lower spheres of heaven and those above. This is the heaven of the contemplatives, which Beatrice, Dante's muse and inspiration, called the "Seventh Light." Each sphere of heaven is governed by angels, but in this sphere the angelic choirs are silenced; here there is no singing or dancing. The Pilgrim sees a ladder of gold stretching out of sight, a symbol of the perfection of the contemplative life. When he reaches the Empyrean, or place of pure light, he suffers from temporary blindness; however, when his sight returns he is in ecstasy—a state that can only be achieved through silent contemplation.[22]

Isabella d'Este was a major cultural and political figure in the Italian Renaissance. The poet Ludovico Ariosto described her as the "liberal and magnanimous Isabella," and the diplomat Niccolo da Correggio called her "the First Lady of the World."[23] She had received a fine classical education and as a young girl in Ferrara had met many humanist scholars and artists. In Isabella's lifetime, women were praised for being silent, but she famously broke the mold by being vocal. As well as being a prolific letter writer, she served as regent when her husband, the Marquess of Mantua, was absent. In her *studiolo* in Mantua, there was a bronze figure of Pan playing his pipes, silently of course, and he seems to embody the interplay between music and silence. If he had looked up to the ceiling of the grotta, he would have seen one of Isabella's favorite devices, the *impresa della pause*—a line of musical notation in Isabella's own contralto clef. This had nine silent pauses with a repeat sign, portraying "infinite time and infinite silence."[24]

Martin Luther was an almost exact contemporary of Isabella. He was excommunicated by Pope Leo X for refusing to renounce his writings on, among other things, the efficacy of indulgences. When these were nailed to the door of All Saints' Church in Wittenberg in 1517, they came to be known as the "Ninety-Five Theses." One of Luther's main concerns was the increase of silence in church services, and from his time on, silence continued its general disappearance from the mainstream and was only kept alive by marginal organizations.

Although Isabella and Luther were against silence, St. Ignatius Loyola, another contemporary of theirs and the founder of the Jesuits in 1540, viewed silence differently. In order to create the right conditions for the Jesuitical spiritual exercises, the Jesuits made silence compulsory. St. Ignatius would spend up to seven hours a day in interior silent prayer: "God bestows, God trains, God accomplishes his work, and this can only be done in the silence that is established between the Creator and the creature."[25] A few other organizations and individuals—such as the Quakers, Shakers, some Mennonites, and a few Catholics including the mystics St. Teresa of Avila and St. John of the Cross, and during the twentieth century Dietrich Bonhoeffer and Simone Weil—did their best to keep silence alive as well, but these mystics were often viewed with suspicion by the conventional church.

So the reality was that for many hundreds of years, the Christian church, with a few exceptions, continued to ignore the silent meditative aspect of its heritage. From the Reformation onward, individual private prayer was viewed with suspicion, and this was one of the reasons that churches began to be locked outside of services. It is strange to think that churches were closed to prevent silent prayer. I had never considered that churches became out of bounds to prevent people praying or visiting in silence; I had always thought that they were locked to stop theft. Of course, silence can be seen as threatening—you cannot know what is going on in someone else's mind. It was therefore seen as safer to minimize public occasions for silence. Often when churches opened their doors, they were used for walking and talking, as can be seen in the Dutch genre of paintings by artists such as Pieter Saenredam, which show churches with groups of people strolling around and chatting.

The Eastern Orthodox Church

The Eastern Orthodox Church was far more effective in keeping the tradition of silence alive. Gregory Palamas, a monk on Mount Athos, promoted hesychasm, the Eastern Orthodox mystical tradition of contemplative prayer through the contemplation of icons. The tradition has continued up until today.[26] The idea is that icons exist to be a means of communion with those whom they depict—one person is looking at one other person with no need for words. This is why the only text on an icon tends to be the name of the saint. Hesychasm— from the Greek meaning "stillness, rest, quiet, silence"—was based on Jesus's teaching that "when thou prayest, enter into thy closet, and when thou hast shut thy door, pray to thy Father which is in secret" (Matthew 6:6). Presence rather than speech is at the heart of the Orthodox tradition: "Love to be silent rather than to speak. For silence heaps up treasure, while speaking always scatters,"[27] wrote the Christian ascetic Abba Isaiah. When the light of the Holy Spirit rises in the heart of the hesychast, the words of the seventh-century saint Isaac the Syrian become meaningful: "Love silence above all things, because it brings you near to fruit that the tongue cannot express."[28] St. Isaac wrote that one of the reasons he practiced silence was so that what he was reading should fill him with delight and understanding, and when his tongue was silenced, he could enter into a dreamlike state with "ceaseless waves of joy."[29]

St. John Climacus, a monk at the monastery on Mount Sinai, spoke about hesychia as "accurate knowledge and management of one's thoughts. Stillness of soul is science of thought and a pure mind."[30] Silence is linked to the heart (in Greek, *nous*), and the eye of the heart is arrived at through God's grace and inner stillness. One of the pitfalls and dangers for hesychasts is pride; having experienced their own light, they can sometimes wrongly think of themselves as enlightened. But the reality for this tradition is that the search for God's grace and divine light should never stop and should continue until death.

St. Teresa of Avila was a Spanish mystic who reformed the Carmelite order. Her life was based on contemplative prayer, and her seminal work *The Interior Castle* had an important place in Spanish Renaissance literature and Christian mysticism. In "Room 4" of this work, which describes the very inner part of ourselves, God produces delight with the greatest peace, quietness, and sweetness. Cardinal Basil Hume described this "place" as like being in a dark room with someone you love, while St. John Chrysostom in the fifth century said that it was a listening in silence, an expectancy. Many people today are not part of an organized religion, but they often do find solace and God in nature, a view understood by St. Teresa of Avila in *The Interior Castle*: "For those who walk the path of silent prayer, a book can be a useful device to prompt recollection. I have also found it helpful to gaze at meadows, flowers and water."[31]

Another Spanish mystic and Carmelite, St. John of the Cross, who authored "Dark Night of the Soul," wrote that "silence is God's first language."[32] He and his mentor, St. Teresa of Avila, both wanted to reform the Carmelite order by reimposing, among other things, long periods of silence. Those who followed the reforms became known as the Discalced Carmelites. But some Carmelite monks who opposed the reforms had John imprisoned and tortured, though after eight months he managed to escape and was nursed back to health by St. Teresa.

Mount Athos is a densely wooded and mountainous area of Greece. From the 1960s, this Eastern Orthodox community of monks, which bans all females, had a resurgence of monks to its twenty monasteries. From 1972 to 1976, 143 new monks arrived; but from 1987 to 1996, there were 609 new monks. [33]

Aidan Hart, one of the best-known Orthodox Church icon painters of today, explained his thoughts on silence and icon painting to me: "For me, silence is not absence of words or outward noise but a path for communion with Christ. It is the removal of inner rubble so that I can walk to Christ. It is ultimately positive, not negative. Words are conceived out of this contemplating silence, and these words born of communion have life and grace. They do not disturb the silence but give it meaning, fecundity."[34] While he was living as a hermit in Shropshire, Hart felt that the deeper he entered into his own depths of inner stillness, the more he became aware of the mystery of God and the more he was aware of where his words came from and the effect that they had on other people. Those words that came from his "still heart" (i.e., his deep internal silence) proved to be true, full of grace and just right for anyone who visited him— something he attributed to divine grace. When Hart is painting, he becomes aware of a strong sense of inner beauty, "like some paradisiacal music." He matches his painting against this feeling, observing whether his color combinations and rhythms correspond with this silent music. Is this the music of the spheres? When he feels he has reached this harmony, he continues. He also notices this in the students he teaches—the best are those who are inwardly still and can hear this silent music. The journey toward enlightenment lasts a lifetime. As St. Isaac the Syrian wrote, "Be at peace with your own soul; then heaven and earth will be at peace with you."[35]

Sister Teresa Keswick, a present-day Carmelite nun at Quidenham in Norfolk, told me that although nuns are encouraged to keep as quiet as possible, Carmelites do not actually take a vow of silence, an instruction that dates back to medieval times with the papal approval of the Rule of Saint Albert, which was drawn up to help the hermits on Mount Carmel. Although modern employers are not concerned with the holiness of their employees, Sister Teresa suggests that far more work would be accomplished if work were carried on in silence. Both office chatterboxes and those within earshot are affected by constant talk and gossip at work. Much sarcasm and criticism can be stopped in their tracks by silence: "What is certain is that under many circumstances, silence is a huge help to kindness." She explained that there are two kinds of silence in the convent. The "Great Silence" lasts from 8 p.m. until 6:30 a.m., and this silence should only be broken in the case of a real emergency. Silence at other times of day need not be adhered to so strictly, but the Rule of Saint Albert warns against too much talk, as the Gospel of Matthew (12:36) says: "Every rash word will have to be accounted for on Judgment Day." Another nun from Quidenham has said that living in silence has given her "a sense of the movement and meaning of time."[36]

In his comprehensive book *Silence: A Christian History*, Diarmaid MacCulloch states that both silence and contemplation were also constructed in the midst of ordinary society, and by the fifth century, the ideals of the Desert Fathers—"Go and sit in your cell—your cell will teach you all things"[37]—had spread widely and had been brought to Bardsey Island off the coast of Wales.[38] Bardsey became known as the Island of 20,000 Saints: "The island of hermits . . . the island of solitude where one is least alone."[39] This tiny island, less than a square mile, became a major center of pilgrimage in medieval times and remained so until 1537, when the monastery and its buildings were demolished by Henry VIII. It still attracts pilgrims today, although it is now better known for its spectacular bird life and its mass of gray seals. Sister Helen Mary moved to Bardsey in 1969 where she created an oratory. Initially she avoided conversation and kept a strict silence, but toward the end of her thirty years there, she started to speak to visitors.[40] Sister Mary's oratory has become a chapel, and Bardsey now has a retreat house where visitors can stay. There were also many Celtic solitaries and hermits on Lindisfarne, Iona, and on Skellig Michael, where the hermits lived in one of six beehive huts that are still standing today and that you can visit, provided the sea is calm enough. During the summer season, a boat trip from Kerry, Ireland, takes around forty-five minutes, but landings can only happen if the sea is calm. When I went, the summer season hadn't quite started, so we were unable to land, something I was glad about as the path up to the huts is treacherous. Apart from the gannets making this an extremely noisy place (Were they as vocal when the monks were there?), this is also one of the locations for the filming of *Star Wars*.

St. Benedict emphasized silence in his Rule—"A disciple should be silent and listen."[41] Although the three rules of Benedictine monastic life—poverty, chastity, and obedience—did not actually include silence, there were many times set aside for silence. At the Benedictine Abbey of Cluny, a regime of silence led to the invention of a monastic sign language.[42] Bread was signed by making a circle with the thumb and two fingers, while that for cheese was by bringing both hands together as if pressing cheese. The Trappists, a Christian order that initially branched off from the Cistercians in 1664 but only became a separate religious order in 1892, had a far stricter policy of silence. Their emphasis on strict austerity was in reaction to the perceived laxity that had crept into many Cistercian monasteries. To sustain their silence, the monks developed additions to the sign language that had originated in the original Rule of Saint Benedict—the sign for God was the thumb and first finger of both hands joined together to form a triangle, and the first two fingers of the right hand on the left wrist was the sign for coffee, whereas the thumb of the right hand on the left wrist indicated a fever.

Quietism and Quakerism

In the seventeenth century, the Spanish mystic Miguel de Molinos described three kinds of silence: silence of the mouth, silence of the mind, and silence of the will.[43] Molinos, described by the philosopher and historian William James as a "spiritual genius," was representative of a religious revival known as quietism. Pope Innocent XI in the seventeenth century declared it a heresy to elevate "contemplation" over "meditation," promote intellectual stillness over vocal prayer, and promote interior passivity over pious action. Once again, the authorities feared not having control over what someone was silently thinking, as in the silence subversive thoughts can rage. In 1687, Molinos was imprisoned in the Castel Sant'Angelo in Rome, where he died in 1696.

Quietism influenced the thought of St. Francis de Sales, who stressed pure love resulting from spiritual practices: "Nothing other than a loving, simple, and permanent attention of the mind to divine things."[44] We should think about the quality of our words, not the quantity—only speaking when we have something relevant to say. Quietism spread widely, as Madame de Maintenon was a convert and influenced many at the court of Louis XIV. When English writer and Anglican cleric John Donne was dean of St. Paul's Cathedral, his approach to silence was different. He gave many sermons, of which

160 have survived, and his powerful rhetoric was so persuasive that he was often able to reduce the usually noisy congregation to silence.

Quakers shared many of the same beliefs as the quietists. The Quakers were founded by George Fox, and the tradition does not follow any stated creed but believes that religion and life are all one and that there is something sacred in everybody—God is present in each and every one of us. They became known as Quakers because they trembled, or quaked, when they heard the name of the Lord; initially some even went naked in a symbolic return to Eden. The Quaker William Law wrote that "the Spiritual life is nothing else but the working of the spirit of God within us, and therefore our own silence must be a great part of our preparation for it";[45] and William Penn wrote that "Silence is wisdom; where speaking is folly and always safe."[46] Although silence can be shared by religions worldwide, it is the Quakers who are known for their silent meetings. Theirs is a silence of listening. They say that even within their meetings, there are different kinds of silence. Through their silent sitting and quiet stillness interesting words can emerge, and through the silence the self emerges. If someone speaks, even if that includes asking a question, there is no verbal answer; questions are answered with silence.

I went to my first Quaker meeting while writing this book. I had no idea what to expect other than that I would be sitting in silence. The meeting house I went to is in Wandsworth; dating from 1778, it is the oldest Quaker meeting house in greater London. It has its original paneling and ministers' gallery and is in the middle of a vast new development. Luckily it is a listed building and cannot be pulled down and has therefore been saved. The moment I arrived and left the busyness of Wandsworth High Street behind, I felt extremely welcome; and from the time I sat down, I felt at ease and at peace. Being a weekday afternoon, only about ten people were present, but there was a feeling of real harmony and calm in the room. I'm sure this has something to do with the fact that Quakers have met in this room for nearly 250 years. Reflecting on the amount of positive silence that has been in that room over that length of time is a powerful feeling. The half hour I sat there passed extremely quickly—something I have not often found with meditation. I'm not sure why, but the feeling of sitting with the Quakers and meditating felt very different. I didn't feel anxious, I didn't feel judged, I didn't fidget—I just felt accepted. So why have I never been back? I had always thought that if someone felt moved to speak in a Quaker meeting, although I certainly didn't, what was said would either be personal or spiritual. But on that rainy day in Wandsworth, the sole speaker's concern was wonderfully mundane and was about the carpets.

The Quaker George H. Gorman described a meeting as having "a greater depth of silence (which has) an eternal quality that diminishes the limitations of time and space," and he goes on to say that "without silence we cannot reach our inner self, and it is from this inner self that all creative energy radiates."[47] The silence adhered to by the Quakers continued to be important throughout the nineteenth century. Caroline Stephen, Virginia Woolf's aunt, was a Quaker theologian. She describes Quaker silence as "the silence we value is not the mere outward silence of the lips. It is a deep quietness of heart and mind, a laying aside of all preoccupation with passing things."[48] Quaker communities support the promotion of freedom, equality, justice, and peace and try to live simply. "Quakerism is premised on vulnerability, on stripping away all constructs and safety nets and laying ourselves bare to the real presence of the living God in our midst. And that's an excruciatingly beautiful vulnerability."[49]

PRAYER AND WORK

Writers have always bemoaned the lack of silence. Annoyance about the lack of silence is nothing new and has exercised people for thousands of years. In the first century, the Roman philosopher Seneca lived above a bathing establishment and described in an essay that silence was learned through the many sufferings of life and that the sounds emanating from below made him want to hate his very powers of hearing. He related how when men are exercising with weights and are either working hard or pretending to work hard, "I can hear him grunt; and whenever he releases his imprisoned breath, I can hear him panting in wheezy and high-pitched tones."[50] As Seneca sat trying to write about silence, with men grunting in what sounds like a modern gym underneath him, one can imagine his rage but also his powerlessness to shut them up.

It was always assumed in the ancient world that reading was something that was done out loud, but there are those who say that it is a myth that the ancients read out loud. Certainly there are many examples proving the opposite, showing that people did indeed read silently: Theseus read the letter he found on the dead Phaedra silently; and in a speech called "On the Fortune of Alexander,"[51] Plutarch informs us that Alexander silently read a letter from his mother. But maybe there's no such thing as true silent reading since when we read to ourselves, most of the time there is a voice in our heads saying the words.

Scholars continue to dispute when silent reading became widespread since it wasn't until the twelfth century that internal or silent reading began to be common and corresponded with the rise of the sense of self. Things began to be done privately, not needing to be communal. Much earlier, St. Augustine had written in his *Confessions* about the reading habits of St. Ambrose, bishop of Milan, who when he received unannounced visitors was always found to be reading silently: "When Ambrose read, his eyes ran over the columns of writing and his heart searched out the meaning, but his voice and his tongue were at rest."[52] St. Ambrose was described as a "clever-looking man with big ears and a neat black beard"[53] and as a very popular speaker. Legend has it that as a baby, a swarm of bees had settled on his face, leaving behind a drop of honey. His father took this as a sign of his future eloquence and honeyed tongue, and he was thus later associated with bees. As a result, bees became a symbol of eloquence.

The ancients were suspicious of silent prayer, wondering what those who did pray silently were trying to hide, and the trend that developed toward silent reading alarmed the Christian fathers. Silent reading meant that the reader had to be trusted, since it allowed them to communicate directly with the author, without any guidance from the person who was reading aloud. This change to silent and therefore mostly solitary reading was a massive step. Prior to this, reading had been oral, either aloud in groups or in a muffled voice to oneself. On a practical level, one of the things that made silent reading difficult was that Greek and Latin manuscripts were transcribed with the words running together, with no spaces left between words. And so, with silent reading, punctuation developed, and text was later divided into lines of sense, which made reading easier and also possibly easier to retain. The separation of letters into words and sentences developed slowly, something that didn't seem to be a problem for early Christian monks, as they mostly knew by heart the texts that they were transcribing. Although, of course, there was room for error since by leaving out one or two letters from a word, the whole sense can change. An apocryphal story is that over the years, "celebrate" became "celibate"—quite a difference for monks! In the seventh century, Isidore of Seville appreciated the fact that when he read silently, it was harder for what he was reading to "escape from memory."[54] Different parts of the brain and cognitive skills are required when reading to oneself versus when reading out loud, since when you read out loud you are automatically looking a few words ahead in the text. I am a reader in my local church, so I know the reality of my eyes scanning ahead in the text. St. Benedict thought that prayer should be more "pure," more internal, characterized by the silence of the heart and less taken up with the externals. He felt that the silent hours after Compline (the prayers at the end of the day), known as the Great Silence, was the holiest time. In monastic medieval life, the silence was only broken by church bells that rung out the Angelus daily. These bells were an important sound, as they were often the only way that people in the surrounding areas would know about the time of day or the start of a service. Medieval monks who spent much of their lives in silence were allowed to have music on their sick beds. This must have had a wonderful harmonizing effect on them and in great contrast to the silence they had been used to. If you live immersed in almost total silence, there must be times when you long to break out of it. While I am sure that some of the medieval monks met for clandestine chats, most of their days were spent in silence. Over time, Western monasticism began to forget about the importance of silence, which is one of the reasons why the Trappist monk and author Thomas Merton in the twentieth century had to fight so hard to become a hermit in his Abbey of Gethsemani in Kentucky.

Since all religions suggest that the best method of communicating with God and pondering the Divine is through silence, it seems counterintuitive that Christianity turned its back on it. Church services became very wordy with little attention paid to silence, and the silence and meditation practiced by the Desert Fathers disappeared from the mainstream for centuries. "Poor talkative Christianity," wrote the English novelist E. M. Forster in *A Passage to India*, comparing it unfavorably to the deep silence of the Malabar caves.[55] Imagining screaming children in a swimming pool elicited the following from the Anglican priest W. H. Vanstone: "The church is like a swimming pool in which all the noise comes from the shallow end."[56]

In Judaism, the absence of sound has an energy—a soft whisper; the silence in Judaism is therefore a listening silence—faith being the ability to hear the music beneath the noise—the silent music of the spheres referred to in Psalm 19. In Torah scrolls, the final letter of the first word of the biblical book Leviticus, *aleph*, is written in miniscule. This changes the meaning significantly—what would have meant "and God happened upon" is changed to "and God called." Aleph, the first letter of the Hebrew alphabet, is a silent letter, and Hasidic teaching holds that it contains the entire Torah compressed within it. In Jewish mysticism aleph represents the oneness of God. In the eighteenth century, the Baal Shem Tov, the founder of Hasidic Judaism, walked in the woods and sat in silence beside rivers in order to learn the art of listening. Central to his teaching was a direct connection with the Divine. This link pervaded every aspect of life and, as in other religions, taught that if we want God to speak to us, we have to learn to keep silent. If the belief is that life has a purpose and meaning, then it's necessary to hear what's in the internal silence. Silence can contain the possibility of every conceivable sound. In Jorge Luis Borges's short story "The Aleph," a strange sphere in the basement is called the Aleph; although only about an inch in diameter, it was all-encompassing: "All space was there, actual and undiminished."[57]

When the writer and Nobel laureate Elie Wiesel was asked about the lack of silence in Judaism, he replied, "Judaism is full of silences . . . but we don't talk about them."[58]

INTERRELIGIOUS DIALOGUE

Silence is revered in Hinduism, but it is the attitude of mind and how one approaches silence that really counts. As the spiritual leader Sri Ramana Maharshi said, "What is the use of a vow of silence if one is engrossed in activity."[59] Very often when a student asks a Hindu master a question, the teacher remains silent. This is similar to the Chinese *wu wei*, doing nothing or inaction, that emerged from Confucianism, described as the ideal form of government, and that became important in Taoism.

All this is very different from much that occurs in Christian monastic life, in which the monks can be in silence but at the same time busily working. But some monks do cross religious boundaries: Henri Le Saux, a French monk from Brittany who became known as Swami Abhishiktananda, was an exciting bridge between Hindu Advaita and Christianity. He went to live in India and showed the value of religions meeting at a spiritual level, describing his own experience of awakening as discovering "the cave of the heart." When Abhishiktananda, who loved talking, was on his walks along the Ganges and keeping a strict silence, he would often pass another sadhu, who was also in silence. They would gesticulate at each other about the beauty of the world and their love of God. It was said of Abhishiktananda, "Now there's someone who can talk about silence for 24 hours a day."[60] He often visited Sri Ramana Maharshi at his ashram in Arunachala in Tamil Nadu in southern India. The English writer W. Somerset Maugham also visited Ramana Maharshi's ashram in 1938. There are many different versions about what happened, but he fell ill and almost certainly met Ramana Maharshi, who seemingly visited him in his room, where they sat looking at each other for about half an hour without speaking. Maugham began to feel uncomfortable and wondered whether he should say something. Ramana Maharshi told him that "silence is best. Silence is also conversation."[61] In his novel *The Razor's Edge*, Maugham based the spiritual guru Sri Ganesha on Ramana Maharshi.[62]

Spiritual ties to silence are so powerful that some have died for the virtue. The French mystic Marguerite Porete,[63] the author of *The Mirror of Simple Souls*, a book of Christian mysticism about divine love, was burned for heresy in 1310 for refusing to recant her ideas about the merits of silence. She went to the stake in defiant silence, and it is for her silence that she is remembered. Silence runs through religious traditions, mostly in a positive way since silence is almost universally appreciated as the way to the center or to unity with the Supreme Being—but of course, it can also have negative consequences as in the case of Marguerite Porete.

7

Meditation

THE WORD *meditation* comes from the same Indo-European root as *medicine, measure,* and *meter,* meaning "to attend to" or to "reflect on." It is something that is shared by every great spiritual tradition and has been both practiced and written about for centuries. It has long been recognized as an important element of Eastern religions. It is also part of the Western spiritual tradition, though only relatively recently acknowledged, mainly through the works of John Main OSB, Thomas Merton OCSO, and Bede Griffiths OSB. These twentieth-century figures were all instrumental in bridging the gap between East and West, with meditation being one of the main links they found between the traditions. For many centuries, the fact that meditation was inherent in Christianity hadn't been appreciated, which was why, especially during the 1960s, so many people looked to the East and its traditions for the deep silent prayer of meditation. Many were astonished when they discovered that the meditative tradition already existed in the West.

Meditation is the way for God to become a conscious reality since God cannot be directly contemplated or known. This is as true for Christian meditators whose aim is to transcend themselves and enter the silence, stillness, and inward depth of their being as for Buddhist meditators who aim to free themselves from the delusion of self. Both Eastern and Western spiritual traditions stress the importance of not wanting anything from meditation, something that Westerners can find difficult since our society is very goal-orientated. As the English Benedictine monk Aelred Graham said, "The fine point of meditation is not to think about something, but rather that we should think about nothing (no-thing)."[1] We are so driven by the desire to achieve that I'm not sure how many people, even those practicing Buddhist meditation in the West, just "do" it without expecting anything to happen.

The silence of contemplation is a great unifier of the past, the present, and the future and can bring a "the peace of God, which passeth all understanding" (Philippians 4:7). When language ceases, silence begins, but this silence is not just a cessation of language, not just an absence of sound but, as the Swiss philosopher Max Picard describes, "a mark of divine love, that a mystery of the Faith always spreads around itself a kind of cloak of silence."[2] Meditation has been key to all the major religious traditions, and it is at its central point that Christianity makes contact with the religions of the East, as Aelred Graham wrote: "The Hindu-Buddhist tradition perhaps teaches more clearly than the Christian that the only place we can commune with God is here and the only time we can do so is now."[3] God is more present in silence than in words, and we have to be brave enough to accept this silence. Canon John Fenton said in a lecture in Oxford, "The most obvious characteristic of God is his silence. He does not cough or mutter or shuffle his feet to reassure us that he is there."[4] In *Finding Oneself 1*, Laurence Freeman gave the following description of silence: "Silence is a very powerful force, true silence."[5] Freeman emphasizes that he doesn't mean the negative silence of shunning somebody or hiding something in case it upsets people or any repression or deception. Rather, he means the true silence when our minds expand and our hearts open and we experience a new affinity with others. This silence brings us peace for ourselves and others, and it is a silence in which our true self can emerge.

In the West, psychology is concerned with the self, whereas in the East it is concerned with the transcendence of the self. Eastern spiritual traditions, especially meditation, have had a profound effect on Western psychology. The self has no real solidity or continuity, but (especially in the West) we try to cling on to our identity and sense of self. Meditation offers a way of learning to let go of self, and from it we can learn that while thoughts come and go, they prove to be ungraspable. Whatever the reason and whatever the motivation for meditating, and regardless of the context, there can be benefits. However, if meditation is reduced to purely psychological terminology, vast areas of spiritual experience are omitted. In the West, a polarization between active and contemplative life has caused some Christians, the majority of whom lead active lives, to feel alienated from the deep silent prayer that transcends complexity and restores unity.

What is it that leads someone to meditate? For many, it can be a dissatisfaction with the material world we live in or rather a feeling that there must be more to life than just being producers or consumers. The Benedictine monk John Main said that if we can't find any satisfaction in producing or consuming or any meaning in the outside world, then we should begin by looking at ourselves, which can begin through meditation. Perception changes in meditation, since what happens is not a conscious process but rather a breakthrough to another level of awareness. "You meditate not to experience the experience," Main explains. "You meditate to enter into the experience. Meditation is a coming to consciousness and a going beyond self-reflective consciousness."[6] The Trappist monk and author Thomas Merton saw great danger in neglecting the rich spiritual traditions of the East. "If the West continues to underestimate and to neglect the spiritual heritage of the East," he wrote, "it may hasten the tragedy that threatens man and his civilization."[7] However, since we do have a rich tradition of meditation in the West, I think it behooves us to stay with our roots: "We human beings cannot reject our past. The consciousness of the West was different from that of India and the East."[8] This is something on which the Dalai Lama, among many others, comments and the poet and peace activist Zen Master Thich Nhat Hanh wrote, "A tree that has no root cannot survive; you cannot grow well spiritually if you have no roots. You should not abandon your root religion."[9] Yes, we can learn much from other religions and traditions, but when it comes to our ultimate loyalty, it seems better to stick with our origins.

One's own tradition is a fact, and William Johnston, a Jesuit priest who lived most of his life in Japan where he was actively involved in interfaith dialogue, echoes Thich Nhat Hanh in saying how important our own traditions and roots, which include silent meditation, are: "It has always seemed to me that the psychologically realistic way of doing things is to stand in the stream of one's own tradition and humbly take what is good and valuable from another."[10] Since he knew Japan so well, Johnston wrote: "In Japan any clown can tell the difference between wise talk and foolish talk; but it takes a good master to distinguish between wise silence and foolish silence."[11]

Lama Yeshe Losal Rinpoche of Samye Ling Monastery, the Tibetan Buddhist monastery near Eskdalemuir in Dumfriesshire, one of the wettest places in the UK, said one of the reasons that Westerners find it so hard to endure solitude is that we carry so much anger and pain. The monastery, founded in 1967, has around sixty full-time residents and guest accommodations. Many years ago, I stopped and spent a night there on my way back from staying with friends further north in Scotland. I was made to feel very welcome and remember being told about people who were on three-year silent retreats—for men, these took place on Arran, and for women, Holy Isle—both islands off the coast of Scotland. I recall being told that when these people emerged, they wouldn't have heard about any world-changing events. I would think it must feel very strange to not know what is going on in the world, but perhaps we're too concerned with the news. It feels that we have a responsibility to know what's going on in the world, but I sometimes wonder why.

The Buddhist nun Tenzin Palmo lived in Britain as Diane Perry until she was ordained. She lived in India for twenty-four years. She spent twelve years meditating—three of those in a cave with no contact with any other human being—and at the end, she said that she had never been bored. For her, the purpose of life was to realize its spiritual nature, and she wanted to be the first to attain enlightenment in female form. Surprisingly after so long on her own and in silence, when she left her solitude and came back to England, she was able to slot straight back into society. She was very chatty but found herself particularly sensitive to the needs of others; she sensed that she had gained great compassion and become totally nonjudgmental. She felt an inner peace and clarity, saying that through an understanding of self, one can understand others, since all things are interrelated. After all those years in India, she believed she needed to get back to her Western roots and found that everything she had learned in the East was in fact deeply present in Christianity.[12]

Both Eastern and Western monastic traditions have silent meditation at their heart. As Thomas Merton says, "The religious contemplation of God . . . is a transcendent and religious gift."[13] At Tyburn Convent in Bayswater Road, in one of the busiest and noisiest parts of London, there is a silent order of nuns who have renounced the world and who only leave the convent for medical appointments or to vote. There are recreational periods when the nuns are allowed to talk, but there is always one nun wearing a white habit in silent prayer in the chapel. The order, founded on the Rule of St. Benedict, was established by Marie Adele Garnier, Mother Mary of St. Peter, in Paris in 1898. Because of the anti-religious laws in France, she had to flee to England in 1901. She died at Tyburn in 1924, and there are now convents in ten countries.

Until the Second Vatican Council in the 1960s, the Catholic Mass had had a silent contemplative core, but after the Council, Thomas Merton, among many others, felt that mysticism, silence, and contemplation had all been sidelined.[14] He felt that there was a grave danger of losing spiritual knowledge gained over generations by contemplatives and that since silence was being left out of church services, it was up to monks in their monasteries to keep it alive. Now it is as if there is a fear of silence during the Mass; Mass in the vernacular is very wordy and is often accompanied by guitars, leaving little space for silent reflection. I recently went to a church in north London where the priest started Mass with a few minutes of silence. It was something that I wasn't prepared for, but it felt welcome, albeit unusual. Priests tend to believe that their congregations cannot tolerate silence, but laypeople often say that they long for more silence in their services.

The day after my first Quaker experience in Wandsworth, I went to a memorial service in a packed Catholic Church. I arrived early while the choir was practicing. However, their singing was drowned out by the noise of the talking among the congregation, and I couldn't help contrasting my two experiences. Did I join in the chatter? Probably, yes. It's hard to keep silent when you are surrounded by people—many of whom you probably haven't seen for a while—since funerals, as much as weddings, are good places to catch up with friends.

After the Second Vatican Council, chanting was discontinued in some Benedictine monasteries. This turned out to be a disaster. Monks, if allowed to chant, had been able to survive on four hours sleep per night, but when they could no longer chant, they felt ill and exhausted. When this was realized and chanting was reinstated, the health of the monks improved.[15] Silence is not always what's needed. However, silence is actually a part of a monastic chant—the sound rises out of silence and then descends back into silence. In a monastery, monks face each other in the choir; the first part of the psalm is sung by one group and then the facing group finish it, with silent pauses in between. Most monasteries today still lack the shared experience of silence. Pre-Vatican II, there were times of communal silences, but no one knew quite what to do in them.

But like everything else, silence is not static. It changes, and we have to keep reassessing it. As Merton wrote, "Inner silence depends on a continual seeking, a continual crying in the night, a repeated bending over the abyss. If we cling to a silence we think we have found forever, we stop seeking God and the silence goes dead within us."[16] Through it, we get in touch with what is most basic in human existence. Merton believed that the purpose of meditation was to enable us to release ourselves from worldly affairs, the things that often only entail confusion and sorrow; and by letting these go, it is possible to enter into a loving contact with God. And by giving God praise, honor, thanksgiving, and love, we will also receive much needed help. The Benedictine monk and pioneer of interspiritual thought Bede Griffiths wrote that the wisdom of the great religions was necessary for the survival of the world in crisis—a marriage of East and West.[17]

Southeast Asian Buddhism has twenty-one different words for *silence*, which goes to show the importance there has always been for silence in Buddhism. Silence can unite those of diverse faiths; paying attention to this silence involves listening, a very different discipline from reading scripture, which involves using the sense of sight. India has many gurus, sannyassins, and monastics who have dedicated their lives to silence, so I shall only mention a few who have had particular relevance in the West. Meher Baba, who kept silence for forty years, advocated to "live more and more in the Present, which is ever beautiful and stretches away beyond the limits of the past and the future."[18] Sri Aurobindo, who was silent for the last twenty-four years of his life, believed that we could evolve the lives that we have in this world and make them into divine lives. Man would become superman. And an unnamed Hindu monk reinforcing the benefits of silence said, "If I could get one percent of the world to practice silence, the world would be transformed."[19]

Raimon Panikkar was a Catalan Roman Catholic priest whose father was Hindu. "I left Europe for [India] as a Christian, I discovered I was a Hindu and returned as a Buddhist without ever having ceased to be Christian."[20] He was a big proponent of interfaith dialogue, which ultimately led to him being expelled from Opus Dei[21] in 1962 for disobedience to the organization. On his relationship to silence, he wrote, "For silence to be a response, / a silent query must go before."[22] You need to think deeply about silence before using it as a reaction to what's going on.

It was John Main, a Benedictine monk, who reintroduced silent meditation to the West by means of a mantra. Having left the priesthood, Main was working in the Colonial Service in Kuala Lumpur, where he met Swami Satyananda Saraswati, who taught him about meditating with a mantra. Main returned to England, eventually becoming a monk at Ealing Abbey. He was sent as headmaster to St. Anselm's in Washington, DC, and while he was there, he studied the works of John Cassian, the fifth-century Desert Father who traveled as a monk in Egypt and Palestine and to southeastern Gaul. Main realized that the practice he had been taught in Malaya by Swami Satyananda was very similar to that which had been practiced by the

Desert Fathers. When he returned to England, he set up Christian meditation groups with another monk, Laurence Freeman. This group eventually became the World Community for Christian Meditation (WCCM), which today remains an international and truly vibrant organization still run by Laurence Freeman who travels all over the world giving talks and retreats; the headquarters are now at Bonnevaux in France. Aelred Graham, an English Benedictine monk who spent sixteen years in America as administrative head of Portsmouth Priory and who wrote, among other books, *Zen Catholicism*, commented that John Main was the most important spiritual guide in the contemporary church.

Main described meditation as the way to fully accept the gift of our being. He explained, "I think what all of us have to learn is that we do not have to create silence. The silence is there within us. What we have to do is to enter into it, to become silent, to become the silence"[23] And . . . that nothing happens in meditation and we must learn to ignore anything that does happen. It is certainly not a quick fix, but if we persist, "this space for expansion of spirit is to be found in silence, and meditation is both a way of silence and a commitment to silence which grows in every part of our lives."[24] And as Laurence Freeman says, nothing is more important in our era of fake news than to remember what this truth is. Thomas Merton didn't live to see the world of misleading information presented as news as we often have now on the internet. Nevertheless he wrote, "I make monastic silence a protest against the lies of politicians, propagandists and agitators."[25]

BENEFITS

Though both Eastern and Western traditions stress not trying to gain any particular results from meditation, since the twentieth century, psychologists have shown a great interest in meditation as a method of improving psychological health and as a way of relieving stress and anxiety.

Though religious or spiritual meditation does not aim to be therapeutic, it might have therapeutic consequences. The American Jesuit writer William Johnston said, "Christian contemplation is the experience of being loved and of loving at the most profound level of psychic life and of spirit,"[26] and being loved at a deep level is, of course, therapeutic. For Johnston, "If institutional religion has somehow failed those in search of meditation, this is partly because it has been unable to keep pace with the sudden evolutionary leap in consciousness that has characterized the last decade."[27] He believed that in a practice like Zen or for deep meditation, some kind of faith is necessary. He had reservations about Aldous Huxley's motives for meditation: "You can't go on detaching yourself indefinitely in the hope that something may or may not turn up inside,"[28] for although Huxley was a great believer in meditation, he had no spiritual beliefs.

Many people today are no longer aware if it is spiritual or psychological help that they need—although I believe the two are linked. All that they know is that their life seems empty and without meaning. Meditation is, of course, not religious if it is used to improve health or enhance business acumen, but does this matter if it can help someone develop psychologically or provide health benefits? And although meditation can start out having purely psychological benefits, it can—and often does—develop into a spiritual practice. Meditation can indeed be taught to people with little or no faith, and sometimes sitting and breathing can become the beginning of a spiritual search, with many eventually finding God or the Divine Being and *not* the anthropomorphic God they have rejected. Bede Griffiths commented that "we have first of all to enter into silence, to shut out the world of the senses."[29] For whatever reason meditation is begun, with practice it can become what it is at its true core—a way of connecting to the center and encountering the Divine Presence.

Buddhists say that enlightenment shouldn't be sought after; many people "sit" for years with nothing happening. This is not wasted time, as Johnston notes: "One leaves all that is familiar . . . to enter into the cloud of unknowing."[30] There should be no judgment involved in meditation. Therefore, whether one meditates badly or well is not the issue; it is enough just to do it. It is not a competition; there is no winning or losing. One of the advantages of seemingly nothing happening is that you do not get into the trap of believing that you are a special spiritual person.

There are many atheists and nonbelievers who meditate. Sam Harris, the author of *Waking Up: Searching for Spirituality Without Religion*,[31] is a committed meditator who teaches online meditation courses.[32] A wide variety of methods are used in the practice of meditation, but the aim of all methods is generally to calm and focus the mind while gently noticing when random thoughts and fantasies arise and letting them pass—all this with the intention of gaining experiential insight into the nature of reality. Modern mindfulness, which is much in vogue, involves focusing one's awareness on the present moment, but as a result some people can become preoccupied with their troubles, and for some, staying with a demanding experience can turn out to be counterproductive. In meditation we experience the whole spectrum of life, including pain and discomfort, and since we live in a comfort culture, the uncomfortable or seemingly negative aspect is often seen as a problem. But everyone experiences suffering, and the compassion that we learn to feel for others during meditation should include ourselves as well. If we stick with whatever comes up in the silence of meditation, we expand our window of consciousness.

The vagus nerve controls our immune system, and calmness and relaxation activate it. Consequently our immune system is boosted by meditation, hence the positivity attributed to it on a purely physical level. The results of experiments published in the journal *Neurosci-*

ence Letters while preliminary, suggest that silence could be therapeutic for conditions such as depression and Alzheimer's disease, both of which are associated with decreased rates of neuron regeneration in the hippocampus. In one experiment, two hours of daily silence led to the development of new cells in the hippocampus.[33]

Another indirect advantage of meditation is that it can help clarify one's thinking. By concentrating the mind and directing its flow, the process of thinking can operate more efficiently. Meditation provides an intense period of awareness that serves as a training for being aware for the rest of the day. The writer James Roose-Evans acknowledged the benefits: "At the centre and heart of true ritual is silence . . . deep, contented, grave awesome and joyous."[34]

However, as the American philosopher Ken Wilber observed, no matter the psychological benefits, meditation in any tradition is ultimately spiritual. From a spiritual perspective, it is a union with God, with the Divine, or an insight into the Ultimate Reality. This is something to which all religions aspire and that, if worked at, can be encountered in the depths of one's being. In the Theravada tradition of Buddhist *vipassana* meditation, which is penetrative seeing or mindful awareness, the mind is trained to perceive each thought as it passes without lingering on any one of them. In some forms of vipassana, the attention is deliberately moved over the body, part by part, with any perceptions or distractions that arise just being let go.

Meditation is free and doesn't need any props; it can be done anywhere and at any time. The scientist Rupert Sheldrake wrote that many people in the twentieth century believed that science would reign supreme and religion would simply wither away. This has certainly not happened. Sheldrake both meditates and prays and sees the difference between the two as like breathing in and breathing out. Prayer is about intention, whereas meditation has to do with letting go of thoughts and detaching from the everyday; it is about being in the present. The repetition of a mantra can help with finding stillness.

I heard of a scenario with a mediator who headed a meeting during which there was a long silence. She had looked from one party to the other during this silence without interrupting it, and when one of the parties spoke again, it was in a less hostile manner. The silence had enabled some of the anger to evaporate. In interviews, a fear of silence can often encourage people to speak, often with unnecessary and meaningless babble. But why should silence feel threatening? What is there to fear? The noted author and lecturer Sam Keen believes that words are a way of structuring, manipulating, and controlling our lives. Therefore, when they are absent, there is a fear of loss of control; if there's something we cannot name, there is a loss of power. Silence can mean impotence and the surrender of control. Control is power, and power is safety. But conversely, silence can also be very powerful.[35]

Although meditation is essentially an inward-looking practice—mostly done in silence with closed eyes—there is a special dynamic to the shared experience of meditation done in groups, and there are many meditation groups that anyone can join. During lockdown, I became part of a group called Benedict's Well, associated with the World Community for Christian Meditation (WCCM), that meets every Monday morning on Zoom for a silent meditation and a talk, often given by Laurence Freeman.

So, although through meditation we respond to the depths of our own particular nature, and by getting to the core of our being we can become our true selves, it is also a supremely unifying practice. In group prayer or meditation, a deep interior silence can emerge. It is at this level—where words are superfluous—that religious dialogue can be most effective. The ideal is to go beyond thought and images into a state of consciousness characterized by deep silence. The West had more or less lost the universal wisdom, or perennial philosophy, because of our tendency to lean toward science and philosophy, but recently with the transpersonal movements, this wisdom has started to reemerge. This is something that Eastern religions have always known—God is beyond the rational mind and is therefore not accessible by thought.

MY PERSONAL PRACTICE

How do I go about trying to find this silence within me? Since I live alone, I spend much of the day in silence without giving it much thought, although I am quite prone to listening to the radio. I do meditate every morning and have done so for years; my initial introduction to it was a course I did in Transcendental Meditation (TM) about thirty years ago. Maharishi Mahesh Yogi, the founder of the Transcendental Meditation technique, embarked on his first global tour in 1958 and over his lifetime claimed to have trained forty thousand TM teachers who taught the TM technique to over five million people. In the 1960s and '70s, he became famous as the guru of choice for celebrities such as the Beatles and the Beach Boys. Three weeks before he died in 2008, he retired from all activities and retreated into silence.

The TM course that I took was promoted, oddly, through my local gym in Notting Hill. As I remember it, the training lasted a weekend with a few evenings tagged on. We were each given a secret mantra and told never to divulge it. Somehow or other I worked out that my secret mantra was composed of letters from Maharishi Mahesh Yogi's name. I didn't like this fact, and I decided that since I had no belief in the Maharishi as a master, I didn't want to be endlessly reciting his name. It was then that I chanced upon the World Community for Christian Meditation (WCCM). They suggest the universal mantra *maranatha*, which is Aramaic for "Come, Lord," for one's daily practice.

I still find meditation extraordinarily difficult, but I persist; and I appreciate the discipline and the fact that so much that is positive has been written about it and that so many people I admire practice it. However, I am usually a once-a-day meditator, and Laurence Freeman of WCCM has told me that it becomes easier if it's done twice a day. The "not having any expectations" aspect is also challenging for me, especially when random thoughts bombard my longed-for internal silence. It is simple but not easy.

THE INFLUENCE OF THOMAS MERTON

Thomas Merton was a huge spiritual inspiration during the 1960s and '70s as well as being a social activist. He wrote more than seventy books, including his widely acclaimed autobiography *Seven Storey Mountain* (published in the UK as *Elected Silence*), which sold six hundred thousand copies when it first came out in 1948. I remember reading it when I was in my early twenties and being very excited to discover that there was a way of approaching Catholicism that was completely different from what I had been taught at my convent school.

Merton was born in France; his father was a New Zealand painter and his mother an American Quaker artist. He was baptized into the Church of England, and soon after the family left for America. He returned to England to be educated, and it was while he was on holiday in Rome that he first entertained the idea of becoming a Trappist monk. After leaving Cambridge, he went to Columbia University where he became very interested in Catholicism. Two books that intrigued him enormously were *The Spirit of Mediaeval Philosophy*[36] by Étienne Gilson and Aldous Huxley's *Ends and Means*,[37] which introduced him to mysticism. While he was at Columbia, he met Mahanambrata Brahmacharia, a Hindu monk who was visiting New York from the University of Chicago. Merton was impressed by him and his ideas but, Brahmacharia, like the Dalai Lama and Thich Nhat Hanh nowadays, recommended that rather than changing religion, people should reconnect with their own spiritual roots. "Blossom where you're planted."

Merton graduated from Columbia in 1938 with a bachelor's degree in English and later that year became a Catholic, deciding that he wanted to join the religious life, but he went on to gain his MA in English from Columbia in 1939. He met with the Franciscans hoping to join them, but when they heard about his rackety past, he was denied entry. He started teaching English at St. Bonaventure University in New York State, and while he was there, his spiritual life blossomed. He more or less gave up drinking, quit smoking, and stopped going to see films. One year during Holy Week, he went to the Trappist Abbey of Gethsemani in Kentucky for a retreat and found it spiritually satisfying. He went back to New York for a while, but fearing the draft, he returned to Gethsemani, and in 1941 he was accepted as a postulant. Throughout his time there, he kept journals, and in 1944 he took a profession of vows. In 1947, he took his final vows and in 1949 was ordained as a priest and became known as Father Louis.

At Gethsemani, he had a very hard time persuading his superiors to let him be solitary. Until he was allowed to be a hermit, he felt very restless and unfulfilled. However, in 1965, with Merton at the forefront of the change, other Trappist monks were allowed to be hermits.[38] By then he was living as a full-time hermit at Gethsemani. He loved being in the hut he had been given in the grounds of the monastery; the surrounding countryside reminded him of England, and he christened it St. Anne's. He felt that it was only when he was there that he was a true monk: "This solitude confirms my call to solitude. The more I am in it, the more I love it. One day it will possess me entirely and no man will ever see me again."[39] Silence and solitude should never be an escape from those people you don't like but rather a true and deep searching for God, he argued: "My heart consents to nothing but God and solitude."[40] Solitude wasn't a theory to Merton; it was his practice and he felt that it was his "place in the world."[41] He had found God in an interior solitude, and he felt that there was no true solitude other than this interior solitude.[42] He believed that the justification for deliberate solitude is that not only does it help in getting to know and love God but it also helps in relation to other human beings: "The further I advance into solitude the more clearly I see the goodness of all things."[43] When he had first arrived at Gethsemani, he was struck by the different and deeper feelings attached to silence when it was shared by many people. This is in some ways a contradiction to his love of solitude, but he found the silence that involved others more profound than the silence experienced on his own: "The Silence, the solemnity, the dignity of these Masses and of the church, and the overpowering atmosphere of the prayers so fervent that they were almost tangible choked me with love and reverence."[44] His teachings on solitude have a validity that connects with the wisdom of the ages, and he urged people in the "technological age" (the 1960s) to find interior solitude. He believed that there is a hidden wholeness at the heart of things that can only be discovered if we get to the deepest level, and the language that we need to get there is the language of silence—the language of God and the language of intimacy.[45]

He understood that not everyone is called to be a hermit but that nevertheless we could all do with more solitude and silence. However, speaking as a hermit, he wrote: "It is clear to us that our greatest and most unique service to the Church is precisely our life of contemplation itself. Our silence and solitude are not mere luxuries and privileges."[46] He goes on to say that it is not possible to find an inner peace unless one is in harmony with one's true self. Silence grants one an opportunity to understand oneself and others better: "And I felt the deep, deep silence of the night, and of peace, and of holiness enfold me like love."[47]

Along with Merton's fame came a mass of visitors to Gethsemani and an adoring fan club that he said made him feel "cheap" and part of a "liturgical vaudeville." But by the 1960s, toward the end of his life, in spite of his years of trying to become solitary, he used any excuse to leave the monastery for conferences and meetings. In 1966 he had an operation on his back in a Louisville hospital and it was there that he met M (Margie), a young student nurse with whom he fell in love. They went on to meet many times, despite promising his abbot he would stop seeing her, before she returned home to Cincinnati.

At the end of 1968, the new abbot at Gethsemani, Flavian Burns, allowed Merton to travel to Asia. Merton was a big proponent of interfaith understanding, a belief that dated back to his school days. In India he met the Dalai Lama three times, as well as the Tibetan Buddhist Dzogchen master Chatral Rinpoche. In Darjeeling, he befriended Tsewang Yishey Pemba, a prominent member of the Tibetan community.

Merton is inevitably controversial, as are many great figures, but some of his later behavior, as when he fell in love with the student nurse Margie Smith, can't detract from the immense significance of his writings. There's no doubt that his writings influenced generations of Catholics; in 2015, Pope Francis even singled him out as worthy of study and as someone who opened new horizons for the church. Merton is often quoted and has become extremely influential in spiritual circles worldwide.

Another influential Catholic teacher was the American Cistercian monk Thomas Keating, who was instrumental in the Christian contemplative prayer movement, which used Centering Prayer to facilitate the development of contemplative prayer. The movement presents ancient Christian wisdom teachings in an updated form. This was based on advice from Matthew 6:6—"But thou, when thou prayest, enter into thy closet, and when thou hast shut thy door, pray to thy Father which is in secret." Keating wrote that the silent prayer is "the human method for discovering what the interior presence, in us and around us, that penetrates us, actually is."[48] It is transformative as, in due course, we are rewarded with "a deeper, more intimate, more reliable, more appropriate, more delightful relationship with God."[49] In this "inner room" that silence helps us access, Keating says we can develop both the courage and the humility to face the dark side of our personality—our shadow.

CHALLENGES

The great traveler and writer Patrick Leigh Fermor visited several monasteries and wrote about his experiences in *A Time to Keep Silence*.[50] Leigh Fermor was a very sociable person who didn't easily adapt to the solitary life, and he took time to adjust to monastic seclusion, initially feeling very depressed: "The mood of dereliction persisted sometime, a feeling of loneliness and flatness that always accompanies the transition from urban excess to a life of rustic solitude."[51] He found the silences in the monasteries very taxing: "The desire for talk, movement and nervous expression that I had transported from Paris found, in this silent place, no response or foil, evoked no single echo."[52] However, in a relatively short time, he found that the abbey became the reverse of a tomb—"not, indeed, a Thelema or Nepenthe, but a silent university, a country house, a castle hanging in mid-air beyond the reach of ordinary troubles and vexations."[53] What had initially felt like a graveyard became very desirable, and it was the outer world that seemed unnatural—"an inferno of noise." He understood that it takes time to gain an understanding and appreciation of silence and that the beneficial effects of it are cumulative. He wrote, "For, in the seclusion of a cell—an existence whose quietness is only varied by the silent meals, the solemnity of ritual and long solitary walks in the woods—the troubled waters of the mind grow still and clear."[54] He had the feeling that Compline (end-of-day prayers) was most like what it would have been like in the medieval church and that the darkness present in the church reinforced the silence. Leigh Fermor described the silence that happens after music in one of the monasteries he visited—silence being at the very center of sound: "The anthem was followed by a long stillness which seemed to be scooped out of the very heart of sound."[55] The monks at the Trappist monastery he visited were only permitted to break their silence when they tended the abbey livestock; they were allowed to talk to the animals. Apart from that, the rule of silence was absolute, the only exceptions being that the abbot and the guest-master were occasionally allowed to speak. When Pico Iyer went on one of his many visits to a Benedictine hermitage in California, he wrote, "I was inside a silence that was not an absence of noise so much as the living presence of everything I habitually walked—or sleep-walked—past. . . . This was a solitude that clarified; a silence so enveloping and deep that it made me forget the word for silence."[56]

During the retreat that I went to in Spain, mentioned in chapter 1, I found that I was fairly comfortable with the silence. However, I found that the meditation made me feel anxious. I was encouraged to embrace the anxiety, and for very short periods of time I felt I could do that. But it wasn't long before I was composing endless lists in my mind and the anxiety came creeping back. My concentration or ability to meditate wasn't helped by sitting on an uncomfortable chair in an airless room; it was too noisy to have the windows open. And of course I couldn't resist looking at other people, and I would occasionally meet someone else's eyes looking at me. So perhaps I wasn't the only one finding this difficult! That was reassuring. It even seemed possible that the person in the very back had a hangover—perhaps they had snuck out for an illicit drink in secret, whereas my glass of red wine had been brazen. As I was metaphorically patting myself on the back for at least being honest, I wondered what on earth was I doing thinking of all of this? Most of my fellow meditators seemed to be in deep meditation. What was wrong with me?

Meditation is not right for everybody; many people have had bad experiences during meditation. This may in part have something to do with the fact that our society wants instant gratification from meditation or mindfulness, whereas in a religious context, meditation is about connecting with the Divine over the long term. Many Christian mystics experienced the "dark night of the soul," and some people today suffer the same symptoms of disconnection, terror, and suicide. Today's "dark nights" seem to occur with many people having no sense of self or how they fit into the world. When this is the case, meditating or practicing mindfulness can unloose negativity and can be dangerous. Many people are frightened of the silence that meditation requires because it means that they are left alone with themselves. This fear can be a real obstacle to the practice of meditation; people have even been known to run out of meditation halls in a panic. A minimum of mental health is necessary for the discipline of meditation, since negative emotional states, which have been suppressed rather than examined, might return and cause distress, and images released by the unconscious might be hard to integrate. However, for most psychologically healthy people, staying with the pain that can arise from meditation can be transforming and prove illuminating.

In a 2016 article in *The Economist* called "The Power and Meaning of Silence," the anonymous author starts the piece by describing the sound that the striking of two gongs made in Burma, breaking the total silence of the monastery. But he then goes on to bemoan the fact that even in the monastery, silence was an aspiration rather than a reality, since the monks at Mingaladon monastery now have Myanmar's busiest airport nearby. Presumably the monks have found ways to nurture an interior silence despite the noise from the planes, but the author found this plunge into a silent retreat from a noisy life very disconcerting. He missed outside stimulation and found that the imposed silence made him feel bored. He lasted fewer than seventy hours of the seven-day retreat he had booked, admitting that it was conceivable that had he stayed there, he might have had a breakthrough rather than a breakdown. Solitary retreats are part of the Buddhist tradition, but the silence in solitude can drive even experienced meditators over the brink.

A skeptical Tim Parks, a British novelist who lives in Italy, was encouraged to try paradoxical relaxation, focusing on sensation rather than thinking, to help relieve his chronic abdominal pain. The aim of this therapy, mostly used for chronic pelvic pain, is to take attention away from all thought. Parks was initially resistant to the process and was told to not try to relax consciously but "just" to try to empty his mind of verbal thought. It is almost impossible to be silent while words whirl around your head; "silence" is noisy if your head is full of words. Parks suggested that the noise in the world outside helps to drown out the noise in our heads and that in order to achieve any deep inner silence, it is interior noisiness that first needs to be tackled. The outer din can evaporate if deep inner silence is achieved. When Parks was told by a friend that what he was doing with his relaxation was a form of meditation, he vehemently resisted the label. Eventually he went on a silent retreat: "Silence is hard work. Because it's not just a question of the absence of sound. In the end, there is always a dog barking somewhere, a fellow meditator sighing. Silence is your ability not to react with irritation, but to soak up these sounds into an intense inner stillness."[57] He found that not only did he have a very real sense of who his companions were but also that the natural world felt nearer and clearer and brighter, things echoed by many people who spend time in silence. Parks had always carried earplugs with him, but on the train back home after his retreat, he realized that he didn't need them.

The panic and fear are not uncommon. The writer and theologian Belden Lane had considered himself something of a contemplative, but when he went on a desert retreat, he found the silence so devastating that he wasn't sure he could endure a whole week of it. In *The Solace of Fierce Landscapes* he wrote, "I need to be careful in describing the silence, the nothingness, to which I've been drawn in the writing of this book."[58] He realized the danger of romanticizing monastic silence, though he appreciated that in the shared silence of a retreat you can quickly learn to value others. After a few days of silence at retreats, buried emotions tend to bubble to the surface, and these can be distressing.

YOUNG PEOPLE

I spoke to Andrew Willson, the chaplain at Imperial College in London, and he told me that many of the students were "looking for" silence and stillness, seeing both as being unifying and having healing properties. They felt the need to slow down in a group context and came together for mindfulness sessions using guided prayer and both Muslim and Zen meditation techniques. He referred to both John Main and M. Basil Pennington, a Trappist monk, speaker, and spiritual writer, as important guides.

Central to trying to stamp out loneliness is teaching people how to value their solitude and silence, and teaching children how to meditate at a young age ensures that they can be better prepared to deal with possible loneliness in the present and when they are older. I have never meditated with children, but I'm told that even very young children love it; and there are many benefits, including improved attention, focus, relaxation, and calm. Schools are increasingly aware of this need for silence. The Dharma School, a primary school in Brighton that is guided by Buddhist principles, offers a meditation session in the morning for all the pupils; and mindfulness sessions are now well established in some primary schools in West Sussex. With society now being more secular, there is little time dedicated to self-reflection or spirituality, and the feeling of connection with others and something larger than oneself is often lacking.

At Quaker schools, each day begins with a silent assembly. After a while, the pupils really appreciate this and begin to feel a powerful sense of community while feeling a strong sense of individuality. Both of former US President Barack Obama's daughters went to a Quaker school in Washington, DC, which doubtless helped center and ground them from the inevitably rarefied atmosphere of the White House.

The American writer Kathleen Norris realized that elementary school children's imaginations could be liberated by silence; they became much more thoughtful when they wrote about silence rather than when they wrote about noise, perhaps because there are fewer clichés about silence than there are about noise. Some of the ideas that the children produced were poetical and original, such as, "As slow and silent as a tree" and "Silence is spiders spinning their webs," but perhaps the most profound of all: "Silence reminds me to take my soul with me wherever I go."[59]

Michaela Community School, the free school founded by Katharine Birbalsingh in 2014 in Wembley Park in London, has what Birbalsingh calls conservative values, and many of these involve silence. She is critical of many of today's methods of education and is therefore inevitably controversial, but the outstanding exam results from her school show the overall importance of education and so-called old-fashioned values.

Hornchurch High School, which was known as the Albany School and is now an academy in east London, introduced a policy of total silence between lessons. Pupils had to walk in an orderly line without speaking and queue in silence before their lessons, and four times a week year-ten students had to stay on at the end of the school day and work for an hour in silence. The head teacher, Val Masson, said that after the new rules were introduced, the number of pupils in isolation for poor behavior halved in a month. She said, "Silence creates a very mutually respectful relationship between students and staff."[60]

My cousin Kate Sapera wrote to me that "learning to sit with silence was an important part of my counselling training."[61] By remaining silent, the client is given the space to tap into deeper feelings—to enable this to happen, the therapist has to feel comfortable with the silence. A valuable service for children can be offering this kind of emotional listening support. Kate trains volunteers to work with primary-age children. Often her trainees feel uncomfortable with the silence and feel that they need to talk to and direct children in their activities. But the reality is that by sitting with the child in silence, the child can learn to feel that they are capable and can be trusted to make their own decisions—and that they are therefore okay. It can be liberating for a child—even if it's only for an hour a week—not to be told what to do, think, or say. This feeling of not being judged is important. And many children report loving the quiet time away from their noisy classrooms.

THE ARTS

8

Literature

IT IS NOT SURPRISING that many poets and writers have written about silence since it is present in so many parts of our lives, often as something longed for—and it bookends our lives. When we die, we go into an unknown silence.

POETRY

Profound silence can come through an appreciation of any of the arts—architecture, art, music, literature, and poetry. Poetry can give us deeper insights into what it means to be alive. At its best, it can be a fusion between what lies on the surface of our lives and what is in the depths within. In his collection of essays *Language and Silence*, the philosopher and writer George Steiner wrote that the poet's "song is the builder of cities; his words have that power which, above all others, the gods would deny to man, the power to bestow enduring life."[1] He investigated the role that language plays when it has been used to articulate falsehoods in totalitarian regimes and what part silence played in the thoughts and feelings of the poets Percy Bysshe Shelley and Paul Valéry.[2]

An early example of the motif of silence in poetry is *Beowulf*.[3] Set in Scandinavia, the world where the monster Grendel lives is described as dark, joyless, and silent—even as somewhere where the peoples are defined by their silence. Grendel seized his victims in silence, capturing thirty men. The silence here implies that the people of the north who live by silence have a resilience and a strength, but their world is one without pleasure since it is also frightening, monstrous, cold, and dark. The protagonists in *Beowulf* are an inherently silent people, but in much of literature, silence has to be learned, and it is often recommended or suggested as the best way to be.

In Norse mythology, Vidar, son of Odin, is mentioned in the *Poetic Edda*,[4] which was compiled in the thirteenth century. Vidar was known as the "silent god," and in times of immense difficulty was relied on by other gods. It is likely that Vidar's silence may have originated from a ritual silence that often accompanied acts of vengeance. He is usually depicted wearing a thick shoe consisting of all the leather that people have thrown away from their own shoes. Vidar is also immensely strong—almost as strong as Thor, the thunder god—but Thor was anything but silent, being associated with thunder, lightning, and storms.

Poets have described silent moments in very different ways. William Wordsworth "wandered lonely as a cloud," and his 1802 sonnet "Upon Westminster Bridge" reminds us how much silence has been lost in the London of today. Certainly London was always noisy (as discussed in chapter 2) but was not the twenty-four-hour city that it is now:

This City now doth, like a garment, wear
The beauty of the morning; silent, bare,
Ships, towers, domes, theatres, and temples lie
Open unto the fields, and to the sky;
All bright and glittering in the smokeless air

The sonnet finishes with:

> Dear God! the very houses seem asleep;
> And all that mighty heart is lying still![5]

Inanimate objects, innately silent, are useful devices for poetic descriptions of silence. John Keats uses porcelain to tell a silent story about looking at a Grecian urn. Since an urn is a three-dimensional object, it can be viewed from many angles, and Keats does this in the poem, examining each perspective. It is as if he would like to engage more fully and verbally with the urn and does this by picking out various scenes. A young man plays his pipe—of course silently, unheard—yet without cease:

> Heard melodies are sweet, but those unheard
> Are sweeter: therefore, ye soft pipes, play on;
> Not to the sensual ear, but, more endear'd
> Pipe to the ditties of no tone:[6]

Nothing needs to change; there is no suggestion that the vase will break—it will last silently into the future, its truth and beauty enduring:

> Beauty is truth, truth beauty,—that is all
> Ye know on earth, and all ye need to know.

In his search for God, Arthur Hugh Clough describes how when we reach the line that we had thought was our limit—our horizon—it becomes a shadow that we are unable to distinguish: "We approach, and behold leagues away, and receding and receding yet again beyond each new limit of the known, a new visible unknown. You have found God, have you? Ah, my friends! Let us be—silent."[7] By saying that God can only be found in silence, Clough is more or less dismissing organized religion. The Divine can be found in the "darkness deep," and only poetic language can take one to the essence of the divine as he writes in "Uranus":

> When on the primal peaceful blank profound,
> Which is its still unknowing silence holds
> All knowledge, ever by withholding holds.[8]

Alfred, Lord Tennyson, devastated by the death of his friend Arthur Henry Hallam, who had died suddenly in Vienna in 1833 of a cerebral hemorrhage, completed the long poem "In Memoriam A. H. H." in 1849, as a requiem. There are several mentions of silence throughout the poem:

> There twice a day the Severn fills;
> The salt sea-water passes by,
> And hushes half the babbling Wye,
> And makes a silence in the hills.

> The Wye is hush'd nor moved along,
> And hush'd my deepest grief of all,
> When fill'd with tears that cannot fall,
> I brim with sorrow drowning song.[9]

The hushing of the Wye evokes a hush or a silence; his grief is such that he cannot speak and cannot even let his tears fall.

The negativity of silence is referred to by D. H. Lawrence. In a poem called "Silence," he finds silence harmful and is haunted by it.[10] However in a later poem, also called "Silence," Lawrence has a far more positive attitude to silence, referring to it as "the great bride of all creation," appealing for it to come, seeing it as a creative energy.[11]

In "Snake," my favorite poem by Lawrence, the heat of the Sicilian summer permeates the verse. He does use the word "silently," and although it's an important word in the context of the poem, you can feel the heavy silence even without it, as he describes the heat of the day.[12]

"Ash Wednesday" is often called T. S. Eliot's conversion poem. While searching for the Word—meaning the words of Christ as well as Christ himself—he is concerned with the difficulties of religious belief and how hard it is to find it without silence. He enumerates all the places where there is not enough silence: the sea, the mainland, islands, and deserts and rain lands. One time when he was walking in Boston, he had had the experience of being "enfolded in a great silence." That feeling of being "enfolded in silence" is a feeling of being cocooned against the rest of the outside world within a cotton-wool cloud of silence.[13]

In *The Book of Hours*, Rainer Maria Rilke connected silence and the Divine, remarking that peace is important for finding silence. Rilke describes what is so familiar to many of us—the "noisy riot" of the senses. The challenge is how to get past these distractions and reach a deep interior silence where we can become aware of God. Rilke postulates that a way to do this is through meditation.[14]

The need for silence arouses great passions. As stated in the introduction Søren Kierkegaard wrote, "If I were a physician and I were allowed to prescribe one remedy for all the ills of the world, I would prescribe silence. For even if the word of God were proclaimed in the modern world, how could one hear it with so much noise? Therefore, create silence!" Kierkegaard took the idea of silence seriously, even taking the name Johannes de Silentio as a pseudonym for his 1843 book *Fear and Trembling,* a meditation on the sacrifice of Isaac.[15]

Ludwig Wittgenstein considered that the chatter he heard in the salons in Vienna was so shallow that it threatened the meaning of life. Much of his philosophical work *Tractatus Logico-Philosophicus* was conceived in the nature and silence of Norway. It aimed to identify the relationship between language and reality while defining the limits of science. "I cannot imagine that I could have worked in any other place as I have done here. It is the silence and, perhaps, the magnificent landscape; I mean its quiet gravity," he once said.[16]

The English poet Philip Gross reflected on the different silences needed by prose writers and poets. His collection of poems *A Bright Acoustic* has a sequence of thirty poems called "Specific Instances of Silence" in which he picks out thirty different kinds of silence.[17] He writes that poets work with words and silence and that the white space of the page controls the flow of words. He says that as a poet, "between the lines he plants seeds, hints, implications of the unsaid, the unspoken irony, the clue withheld."[18] Having a silent work environment is one thing, but what interests him is how to write silence on the page; that, to him, is the heart of poetry: "White space is a powerful tool. Few words, however well chosen, work as hard as it does . . . the break at the end of a verse line is more than a pause."[19]

Gross grew up with a bad stammer, and silences felt like the enemy to him. When he first attended a Quaker meeting, he felt extremely tense until he realized that the people there had not been silenced, nor were they sleepy or passive, but rather they were calmly, actively *listening*. And listening does become more acute within the context of silence.

The American poet Jorie Graham uses lots of gaps and spaces in her poems, and these areas of unspokenness create little islands of silence. If you're reading them to yourself, you're jolted into a pause. I'm not sure how they would work if they were read out loud; it might sound as if you were stuttering.

When thinking about his writing, the poet and gardener Sean Swallow thinks he might be pushing silence and faith away and wonders how he can get them back. But then he worries that he might have gotten this the wrong way around—maybe the words in his poems should flow out of silence rather than struggling to get in to it.[20] He considers that poets such as R. S. Thomas and W. S. Graham got things the right way around: *silence first, words second.*

In "The Untamed," R. S. Thomas refers to the special peace that can be found in wild places. He writes how this silence can still the mind, using the image of silence holding "the wild hawk of the mind," demonstrating the power that silence is able to have on our minds. Because that's what our minds so often feel like—untamable birds of prey—definitely in need of a "gloved hand" to help control them.[21]

The Swiss philosopher Max Picard wrote that "the floor of silence is inlaid with poetry. Great poetry is a mosaic inlaid into silence."[22] How wonderful to see silence as a mosaic and to have poetry as one of its inlaid tiles. There is a moment beyond words where even the words of a poet cease, and that moment is silence—somewhere where unfathomable deep feelings can happen. All art can move us and can be a way into harmony, peace, and silence; in literature it has always been so. And yet paradoxically, since I'm writing about silence, poetry can often be more appreciated if it is read out loud— and that even includes poems about silence.

PROSE

In Hans Christian Andersen's fairy tale *The Little Mermaid,* the mermaid trades her voice for a chance of life on dry land. On her first visit to the surface of the sea, she falls in love with a handsome prince and rescues him from drowning. Determined to somehow get back to her prince, the mermaid sacrifices her beautiful voice, condemning herself to silence. Although she is given legs, she is told very cruelly that when she walks it will feel as if she is walking on sharp knives. To compound the cruelty, in spite of losing her voice, she will only obtain a soul if she marries her handsome prince. She swims to the surface and meets her prince, who loves her in spite of her muteness.

But he says he can only marry the princess who rescued him, not knowing that it was she, his silent companion, who saved him. In her silence she can't enlighten him. Her sisters come to her with a knife and the assurance that if she kills the prince, she will once more become a mermaid. Thinking of all the sacrifices she has made, she despairs, but she cannot bring herself to kill him. So, she throws herself and the knife into the sea and her body dissolves into the foam.[23] So much of this tale involves sacrifice and silence that it's quite a jolt to discover that it has a relatively happy ending (although the poor mermaid never gets to marry her prince).

Ralph Waldo Emerson drew up a list of classics or sacred books of each nation and wrote a spirited defense of the importance of them being read silently, saying that they are all representative of the universal conscience and are of far more use to us than the barrage of daily news: "Let us be silent—so we may hear the whispers of the gods . . . and by lowly listening we shall hear the right word."[24] He picked out the Vedas, the Upanishads, the Bhagavad Gita, the works of Confucius and Mencius, Pascal's *Pensées*, and Thomas à Kempis's *The Imitation of Christ* as worthy of this kind of study. And he was strict as to how they should be read—on bended knee and on one's own. "Their communications are not to be given or taken with the lips and the end of the tongue, but out of the glow of the cheek, and with the throbbing heart."[25] Emerson's approach was exacting—the sacred works that he recommended had to be read with reverence and care and in silence.

There are also, of course, instances of religious silence in books that are not overtly "religious." For an example, there is a description in George Eliot's *Adam Bede* of Dinah, a Methodist preacher, sitting in silent prayer thinking about the community she is about to leave: "She closed her eyes, that she might feel more intensely the presence of a Love and Sympathy deeper and more tender than was breathed from the earth and sky. That was Dinah's mode of praying in solitude. Simply to close her eyes, and to feel herself enclosed by the Divine Presence; then gradually her fears, yearning anxieties for others, melted away like ice-crystals in a warm ocean."[26] By closing her eyes and sitting in silence, Dinah's fears about leaving her community diminished.

The Irish-born English clergyman Laurence Sterne's largely experimental novel *Tristram Shandy*,[27] considered by the philosopher Arthur Schopenhauer to be one of the greatest novels ever written, was originally published in nine volumes. It is full of double entendres and deviations; it claims to be a biography of the eponymous hero and focuses on the problems of language: asterisks are used when decorum dictates that things cannot be said, and death is symbolized by black pages. Words would be superfluous; only silence counts. I'm not sure how one would go about reading it out loud. I think you'd need to know the book well to work out how much time you would you need to give to the many pauses and silences.

The French writer Marcel Proust was a master of silence and needed a silent space within which to create: "Books are the creation of solitude and the children of silence." He had the walls of his bedroom covered with cork and would bribe the workmen above him not to work.[28] Lydia Davis, a translator of Proust, noted that he was meticulous in his requests about when his upstairs neighbors could use a hammer and nails. He described how this noise affected him: "Since a noise so discontinuous, so 'noticeable' as blows being struck, is heard even in the areas where it is slightly diminished." He also described the effect that an unexpected loud noise had on him: "What bothers me is never continuous noise, even loud noise, if it is not struck, on the floorboards. . . . And everything that is dragged over the floor, that falls on it, runs across it."[29] Proust portrayed the quality of silence in moonlight: "I dined with Legrandin on the terrace of his house by moonlight. 'There is a charming quality, is there not,' he said to me, 'in this silence; for hearts that are wounded, as mine is . . . there is no remedy but silence and shadow.'"[30]

When Michael O'Dwyer writes about François Mauriac's *Thérèse Desqueyroux*, he identifies ten forms of silence linked to speech, including a silence that takes the subject to the "shadows of their being."[31] In Joseph Conrad's short story "An Outpost of Progress" in the 1898 collection *Tales of Unrest*, the silence between the two Europeans who were working together in a trading post in the African jungle is hostile. This is an acrimonious silence: "When the two men spoke, they snarled; and their silences were bitter, as if tinged by the bitterness of their thoughts."[32] In *The Shadow-Line*,[33] Conrad describes the calamitous nature of the dead calm of the tropical high seas and its terrible silence.

Virginia Woolf said that she wanted to write a novel about silence—the things people don't say—and in *The Voyage Out*, she has the character Mr. Hewet pursue that aim.[34] In Woolf's *To the Lighthouse*, the character Mrs. Ramsay sits alone and muses that now what she so often needed was time: "Not even to think. To be silent; to be alone."[35] A different approach is in Robert Walser's novel *Jakob von Gunten*, where Jakob is sent to school to learn to think of nothing, since "who can ever feel at ease when he cares about the world's praise."[36] Work that is silent and unacknowledged can be just as valid as work that is out there in the public domain, as Jiddu Krishnamurti explains: "And you need to have a mind that is absolutely silent, absolutely, not relatively—there is the silence when you go of an evening in the woods, there is great silence, all the birds have gone to bed, the wind, the whisper of the leaves has ended, there is great stillness, there is the outward stillness."[37]

The novelist Colm Tóibín finds that "the amount of silence around things"[38] is a frequent starting point for his work, but for the American-British writer Tracy Chevalier it was the reverse. She was trying to make a phone call on a street in New York when she was suddenly overcome by the noise around her—cars, people, planes. When did it get so loud? she asked herself. She puts that moment down to her interest in the value of silence and her attendance at Quaker meetings—something she hadn't done since childhood. She remembered that Quakers had been active in the abolitionist movement and had worked on the Underground Railroad, a network of secret routes and safe houses established in the early nineteenth century and used by African American slaves to escape into free states.[39] All this led to her writing the novel *The Last Runaway* in which her heroine Honor Bright is, as Chevalier put it, as quiet as possible,[40] something that is difficult to accomplish in a novel. Chevalier found it hard to describe silence but hoped that her attempts would pique readers' curiosity, since "it is worth quieting the mind for."[41] When Honor stops talking, it upsets her community. Some take her silence for guilt; and others, even though they are Quakers, take it as a judgment on them. Eventually they stopped asking her questions, and when her husband introduced her to newcomers, he said, "My wife has extended the silence of Meeting into her whole life."[42] When she attended meetings, Honor found that her attitude toward them had changed; rather than feeling she might have to speak aloud, "now she simply watched the sun cross the quiet room, catching dust motes kicked up by shifting Friends. She listened to the insects outside and learned to distinguish between the chirping of the cricket, the sawing of the grasshopper, the ticking of the beetle, the buzzing of the cicada."[43] By deciding not to speak, her powers of observation had increased.

Novels that are set in unfamiliar and different landscapes can have silences that one wouldn't necessarily have thought about otherwise. In Halldór Laxness's Icelandic novel *Under the Glacier*, the priest gives a silent glacier as his reason for stopping preaching, comparing its silence to the silent lilies of the field saying that words are misleading.[44]

There is much to be written about silence and love—or rather, lovers. When two people first meet, there is often much chatter, but this can turn into a companionable silence. As the philosopher Blaise Pascal explains, "In love, silence is of more avail than speech . . . there is an eloquence in silence that penetrates more deeply than language can."[45] Indeed, silence can grow more comfortable between couples over the years. The American novelist Nicholas Sparks observed his wife's grandparents who had been married for more than sixty years, sitting quietly and watching the world around them. This kind of silence takes a lifetime to learn, and it is only the old and those who are comfortable with each other who can experience it; in fact, this holy silence between the couple was the inspiration behind Sparks's *The Notebook*, which was found on an agent's slush pile: "The young, brash, and impatient must always break the silence. It is a waste, for silence is pure. Silence is holy."[46] It went on to get a $1 million advance, immediately hit the *New York Times* bestseller list, and was made into a film.

Silence as a topic ranges over many disciplines. In 2016, the British Society for Eighteenth-Century Studies had a conference in Paris called "Modes of Silence in the Seventeenth- and Eighteenth-Century Anglo-American World." In its call for papers, delegates were asked to consider the following topics: silence and speech in scientific books; silence and speech in rhetorical treatises; silence and speech in commonplace books, educational treatises, conduct books, and the place given to women; silence and speech in religious writings and spiritual practices; expression and function of silence in literature; representation and expression of silence in art (painting, emblem books and music); institutional repression of speech, its effect and censorship; and speech in political and social rituals. All kinds of prose find the themes of silence intriguing enough to explore it in various ways.

Governments and those in authority also can and do use silence as a form of censorship by banning certain books. This can take place on many levels. The Catholic Church had an index of books listing forbidden reading for Catholics. It was started in 1559, was updated annually, and was in existence until 1966 when it was finally terminated by Pope Paul VI. Twentieth-century authors whose books were forbidden included Sartre, Gide, Anatole France, and Simone de Beauvoir. Although the index was abolished, there are still guidelines for Catholics concerning forbidden books, and of course there must have been many that slipped through the net.[47]

Sadly censorship of books is no longer a thing of the past—this is now happening today on an ever-increasing scale in the US and to a lesser extent in the UK. Shockingly in the US during the last school year, thirty-two states banned 1,648 individual titles from libraries and classrooms,[48] including titles by Toni Morrison, Margaret Atwood, Harper Lee's *To Kill a Mockingbird*, André Aciman's *Call Me by Your Name*, Sylvia Plath's *The Bell Jar*, Sally Rooney's *Normal People*, Alice Sebold's *The Lovely Bones*, and John Steinbeck's *Of Mice and Men*.[49] Where will this end? In some places, Shakespeare plays already have "trigger warnings." Surely the point of literature is that it can be unsettling and take you to places you had never imagined. I fear our retreat to a Puritan age bodes ill for the children of today. Censorship imposed by a government or any other authority is a prime example of negative silence.

Another unwelcome silence in the written world is writer's block, a silence experienced by many writers, including Thomas Hardy, Herman Melville, Arthur Rimbaud, and Gerard Manley Hopkins.[50] One of Hopkins's early poems, "The Habit of Perfection," was written in January 1866 while he was at Oxford, a few months before his conversion to Catholicism. The word *habit* here refers both to the religious dress and the behavior of doing something regularly:

> Elected Silence, sing to me
> And beat upon my whorlèd ear,
> Pipe me to pastures still and be
> The music that I care to hear.
>
> Shape nothing, lips; be lovely-dumb:
> It is the shut, the curfew sent
> From there where all surrenders come
> Which only makes you eloquent.[51]

In the first two verses, he refers to silence as the kind of music that he wants to hear and how he wants lips to be dumb and therefore not to speak. He could be referring to his own lips, as just before he became a Catholic, Hopkins "gave up" poetry for Lent. Shortly afterward, when he had started his novitiate with the Jesuits, he burned what he had written and gave up writing poetry completely. He vowed never to write again, something he adhered to for seven years. Fortuitously in 1872, he read the work of the philosopher and theologian John Duns Scotus and realized that writing poetry need not conflict with a religious life, and in 1875 he was asked by his religious superior to write a poem commemorating the wrecking of a German ship. The result was "The Wreck of the Deutschland,"[52] which, like much of his poetry, was not published until after his death. In an earlier poem, "Nondum," he prays that God hasn't deserted him:

> And Thou art silent, while Thy world
> Contends about its many creeds[53]

THE ACT OF READING

Reading, silent or otherwise, is a great link to other people and other times. A daring innovation in eighteenth-century Europe was the "new" practice of reading alone in bed. This was considered hazardous and depraved. The danger was twofold: one was understandable—the fire risk from candles; but the other—allowing women to read in bed—was deemed to be particularly dangerous and immoral. The private fantasy world conjured up by books might contravene moral boundaries, since once people had started reading silently and in their own beds, there could be little control over their reading habits and what they were reading. I remember the thrill of reading the series of salacious books about Angelique by Sergeanne Golon[54] under the bedclothes at my convent school. Ever since, a flashlight has been part of my essential travel kit.

If a book is read out loud, everyone in the vicinity can hear it, regardless of whether they want to, but when a book is read silently, there is more of a direct link between the author and the reader. Reading to oneself can be an immersion into a silent world, but it is only superficially silent since by being absorbed in a book one is often entering another—nonsilent—world. As I live on my own, most of my reading is done in silence, but having grown up in a large family, I find it relatively easy to ignore the sounds around me if I am immersed in a good book. Since I read on the bus and the subway, I always have a Kindle in my bag—something I find invaluable for travel but something I hardly ever use at home, and of course as an ex-bookseller I buy as many actual books as I ever did.

Hours of silent reading are hours salvaged from the cacophony of sound that there would have been with everyone reading out loud. The Chinese graphic tradition allows Chinese children to develop silent reading at an earlier age than we do in the West. As a result, adult Chinese readers are able to read exceptionally fast.

There has been a recent surge in Silent Book Clubs, the idea behind them being that to read surrounded by a group of friends is "awesome." These started in 2012 in San Francisco, and there are now three hundred chapters around the world. Pre- (and presumably post-) COVID-19, these meetings took place in physical spaces; people would come and read their own books over a glass of wine and trade book recommendations. The London Silent Book Club, founded in 2017, currently has 1,450 members. During pandemic-related lockdown, they took place online; the one I attended had about twelve people. We began by being asked what we were reading. There was quite a large range of books. One person even confessed that she wasn't reading anything but just wanted to meet people. Someone else said that he was now halfway through the book he'd started six months ago; it seemed more like a meeting place than a book group. We were instructed to read silently for an hour and then rejoin the group to chat about our books. I felt a great desire to chicken out, since as well as being about fifty years older than everyone else, surely no one would be interested in the Sylvia Plath biography I was reading. It seems to me Mark Twain should be left to have the last word, having recommended that it was better to keep one's mouth shut and be thought a fool than to open it and remove all doubt!

In 2018, audiobook sales rocketed by 43 percent in the UK, but during the first half of 2022, they slowed dramatically.[55] So it seemed that in our noisy world even reading silently was declining; it was also feared that the e-book was going to become responsible for the death of the print book, but e-book sales peaked a few years ago and although at the time it seemed that audiobooks might bear responsibility for this, the reality is that in 2022 the number of independent bookshops in the UK and Ireland rose to a ten-year high, and there are now 1072 independent bookshops.[56] One statistic that I read is that busy people tend to listen to an audiobook at twice the normal speed, although they say that this makes it sound more normal and matches typical reading speed.[57]

THEATER

At the beginning of Shakespeare's *King Lear*, when Lear's three daughters are declaring how much they love him, Cordelia says, as an aside, "What shall Cordelia speak? Love, and be silent."[58] Her contention is that as a good and loving daughter, she has no need to profess to the world how much she loves her father—he should understand that her silence is proof enough. Of course Lear misinterprets her silence, saying, "Nothing will come of nothing."[59] He says that she is untender, while she says that she is true. In other plays, Shakespeare uses the dramatic pause, the silence, to both increase and release tension. Act 5 of *Hamlet* has a stage full of dying or dead bodies. Gertrude is poisoned as is Laertes, the king is killed, and Hamlet—who has long thought about death, is also poisoned, and is taking a while to die—has his last words before death, "The rest is silence."[60]

Although the assumption is that literature needs language, there are a significant number of playwrights who use silence as a tool to help navigate today's complex world—for example, Harold Pinter, Samuel Beckett, and Eugène Ionesco. Ionesco said that "Not everything is beyond the reach of words, but the living truth is."[61] Beckett found speech futile, declaring in his first novel, "I shall state silence more competently than ever a better man spangled the butterflies of vertigo."[62] These playwrights use the silences in their plays to express what is unspeakable and find a freedom in it. Beckett referred to the abysses of silence; and in his mimed plays *Act Without Words I* and *Act Without Words II*, silence is used to emphasize the frustration of life.[63] He believed that "every word is like an unnecessary stain on silence and nothingness."[64] In Beckett's very short play *Breath*, there are no characters and no action—just two cries and the raising and dimming of stage lights.[65] But Beckett could also be very wordy; in his play *Not I*, most memorably performed by the English actress Billie Whitelaw and then the Irish actress Lisa Dwan, Beckett's instructions were to speak at "the speed of thought."[66] The intensity of the play and the fact that they were strapped to chairs unable to move sent both actresses temporarily mad.

By including silence as key in their work, Beckett, Pinter, and Ionesco are able to communicate the unsayable, and it is endlessly fascinating to get glimpses of the unsaid. They do this through one of the many different silences referred to by the writer Leslie Kane as the

> dumb silence of apathy, the sober silence of solemnity, the fertile silence of awareness, the active silence of perception, the baffled silence of confusion, the uneasy silence of impasse, the muzzled silence of outrage, the expectant silence of waiting, the reproachful silence of censure, the tacit silence of approval, the vituperative silence of accusation, the eloquent silence of awe, the unnerving silence of menace, the peaceful silence of communion, and the irrevocable silence of death illustrated by their unspoken response to speech that experiences exist for which we lack the word.[67]

This is such a wide-ranging, rich, and diverse list of silences, and as you think about each one, you can begin to appreciate how the many ways that the silences used by playwrights can be interpreted. Pinter said that "speech is a constant stratagem to cover nakedness."[68] He, like Beckett, has many silent or inarticulate characters—for example, Aston in the *Caretaker*.[69] To Pinter, silence is communication: "We communicate only too well, in our silence, in what is unsaid, and . . . what takes place is continual evasion, desperate rearguard attempts to keep ourselves to ourselves."[70] In the introduction to the first volume of his *Complete Plays*, Pinter wrote that speech is often about a language beneath it: "The speech we hear is an indication of that which we don't hear. It is a necessary avoidance, a sly, anguished or mocking smokescreen which keeps the other in its place."[71]

Pinter often uses silences to show both isolation and separateness. In his plays, we can tell much from the pauses and the silences about the relationships between people. There is also something unfinished and incomplete, and the end of a Pinter play is often an accumulation of what has been left unsaid. An early play of his *Silence* looks at the language of desire and the terrible gulf that exists between what we say and what we want.[72] I recently did a course at the City Lit in London that included studying Pinter's *The Caretaker*;[73] I learned to appreciate Pinter's language and pauses from the teacher, Hugh Epstein, himself a brilliant communicator.

In his plays, Ionesco ridiculed banal situations and portrayed the human condition as insignificant. At the Théâtre de la Huchette on Paris's Left Bank, Ionesco's *The Bald Soprano* and *The Lesson* had been performed to packed houses six days a week since 1957, surely the longest running double bill anywhere. The pandemic inevitably stopped this theatrical run; however, it has now reopened. The opening stage directions state, "There is a long moment of English silence. The English clock strikes 17 English chimes." What is an English silence? And why an English clock and English chimes? The silence created after a clock has struck or bells have rung does have a special resonance.

In the plays of the Belgian playwright, poet, and essayist Maurice Maeterlinck, what is suggested by the characters is more important than what they actually say. He found the use of silence in his early plays to be the ideal vehicle for exploring death and the meaning of life. The dialogue is lean and spare, and his characters have no foresight and very little understanding of themselves or their worlds. He considered humankind powerless against fate, and since he thought actors inadequate in portraying his symbolic figures, he often resorted to using puppets in his plays; puppets could represent fate's control over humankind.

Silence as a theatrical device was used by the French playwright Jean-Jacques Bernard, who was involved in a company that became known as *L'école du silence* (The School of Silence). It was known for its compact dramas about conflicting desires and the "unexpressed." In his plays, emotions are implied through gestures and facial expressions—and silence.[74] Another company the Théâtre du Silence, based in La Rochelle, France, was a dance company created in 1972 by Jacques Garnier and Brigitte Lefèvre, two Paris Opera Ballet dancers. It created many contemporary dance ballets and employed many well-known choreographers. Some contemporary dance is performed in silence, and the silence can make the audience feel awkward. Often a dancer can lie motionless on the stage. Music could make this feel acceptable and comfortable, but the silence can make it feel challenging, and it certainly makes you think.

The actor William Chubb told me that he feels that silence in acting is something you have to earn. He played the Tory chief whip in James Graham's frantically busy and noisy *This House*.[75] During a late-night scene when the chief whips bump into each other, there is a "glorious moment of silence" and then a pause when you don't know what's going to happen. This pause is an *earned* silence rather than one that is just dead air and boring.

In 1988, Anthony Minghella wrote a radio play called *Cigarettes and Chocolate*,[76] starring Juliet Stevenson and Bill Nighy, in which the heroine, Gemma, refuses to answer her phone. Eventually one discovers that she'd given up talking for Lent, having given up cigarettes and chocolate in previous years. Her silence provokes her friends into verbal diarrhea. Silence often has this effect of making people feel awkward, goading them into excessive chatter.

In the beginning, films, too, were silent. They had no dialogue in them, only subtitles, but there was often live music at a performance. Robert Bresson says in shouty capitals in his book *Notes on the Cinematograph*, "THE SOUNDTRACK INVENTED SILENCE."[77] In Ingmar Bergman's film *The Seventh Seal*, Death is largely silent, failing to respond to the pleas of the hero, Antonius Block. When Block cries out to God and gets no answer other than silence, Death tells him that "perhaps no one is there." Silence is present in many of Bergman's other films, including *The Silence* in which three travelers arrive in a country where they do not speak the language, making it impossible for them to communicate with the locals.

In *A Quiet Place*, a film directed by John Krasinski and starring Emily Blunt, the monsters portrayed are blind, and by keeping silent, the family can stay safe from them. Before the arrival of the monsters, as the daughter is deaf, the family had learned to communicate by sign language; they were therefore prepared for a silent world. But the mother is pregnant, and a major issue in the film is how is she going to give birth in complete silence. Could you mentally train yourself to do without sound? By suppressing all noise, the family start to yearn for it. They become increasingly uncomfortable with the silence.

9

Paintings

THE VISUAL ARTS are another interesting source of silence—paintings that both depict silence and those that instill a silent reaction. All paintings and images are silent in that they make no noise, but they do use a silent language to speak to us. While some paintings emanate the feeling of silence, others are noisy—for example, you can almost hear the clamor and noise in any painting by Pieter Bruegel the Elder, the sixteenth-century painter known for his landscapes and peasant scenes often portraying raucous village festivals. He was one of the first generation of artists not to paint religious scenes. Most paintings are good examples of how we can learn and absorb from a silent object by just looking. And I mean *really* looking.

I often go and draw in London's National Gallery, and I am always astonished by the hordes of tourists—many of them traipsing through with iPhones at the ready, snapping away, only glimpsing paintings through their lenses and never stopping to look and to allow themselves to feel the awe they might get by standing in front of a painting that the artist who painted it also stood in front of. You can be almost as close to a painting as were Leonardo da Vinci, Vincent van Gogh, or Michelangelo; it's like standing in their shoes and it's definitely worth taking the time, silently, to absorb this extraordinary privilege. We are transported to the world of the artist, where there is nothing except time between them and us and their world. And time can evaporate—what was in their mind comes straight to us, and we become part of the chain of every person who has ever looked at that specific painting. This silent connection stretching back through the ages to the time of the painter is a particularly gratifying thought. I find that by sitting in front of the same painting for several hours, there is a gradual osmosis with something of the artist transmitting itself to me.

For me, drawing the painting in front of me adds to this connection, but I know that there are people who just sit and look at the same painting for hours and on many visits. Having a particular theme in mind as one walks around a museum or art gallery is extremely helpful. To visit a gallery while thinking about silence can be very rewarding. I went several times to the wonderful *Spanish Still Lives* exhibition at the National Gallery in London in 1995. Looking at still-life painting can induce a real feeling of calm and peace, even though some of the objects in the paintings—for example, saucepans—are noisy when used. I couldn't see enough of the paintings, and soon after I flew to Dublin for the day to see a Spanish still-life exhibition there.

When I interviewed the writer Hisham Matar, he talked about his book *A Month in Siena*,[1] a wonderful example of a way of looking at and silently absorbing Duccio paintings. He told me that when he'd been a student in London, he would spend most of his lunch hour in the National Gallery in front of a different painting each week. For him, paintings require time, and they change in unexpected ways as you look at them hour after hour—and all of this is silent looking. Now he says it can take several months, even up to a year, before he moves on to a different painting.

Leonardo da Vinci said that "painting moves the senses more rapidly than poetry."[2] In Leonardo's day, most poetry would have been said out loud, but paintings would have been looked at silently. The Swiss writer Max Picard described the feeling he got when looking at old master paintings, explaining that it was as if the characters had stepped out from behind a wall of silence and were waiting for another opening to appear in front of them so that they could disappear into the silence again.

ALLEGORICAL AND RELIGIOUS PAINTINGS

The National Gallery in London has a set of Sienese paintings (c. 1490) telling the story of Griselda, or Grizzel as she's sometimes known, whose children were taken away from her by her husband and who was sent away, uncomplaining, to live in silence. Years later, her husband summonsed her back and reinstated her as his wife. And back she came—still uncomplaining. This silent ideal of womanhood was all pervasive, and many people wrote about her, including the Italian writer Giovanni Boccaccio and Petrarch; she also appears in Geoffrey Chaucer's *The Clerk's Tale*[3] in the late 1300s.

Max Picard wrote that in Piero della Francesca's paintings, "His human beings seem to wander in a dream of the gods, before the gods created man."[4] Piero della Francesca's painting the *Madonna and Child with Saints, Angels and Federico da Montefeltro* in the Pinacoteca di Brera in Milan radiates silence. A recent innovation in the Brera is that many of the paintings in the gallery have descriptions attached to them, written by contemporary artists or writers. The Piero della Francesca painting is described by the Japanese writer Yoko Ogawa as a picture of silence. In the painting, no one is looking at anyone else, the lips of everyone seem to be sealed, and silence fills the space. Each character is immersed in their own personal world and may be, according to Ogawa, listening to something we cannot hear.

The silence is certainly true of many of Piero della Francesca's paintings, but not for *The Nativity* in the National Gallery in London. Not only does it have two angels playing lutes but other angels are singing and a donkey is braying. It does have a dreamlike quality (it may be unfinished?), but to me it is not a silent painting—there is too much music and activity for that.

In paintings of the annunciation when the Angel Gabriel appears to the Virgin Mary to tell her that she will have a child who will be called Jesus, Mary always seems to be alone, often reading, and in silence—that is, until the Angel Gabriel comes to speak to her. In many paintings, the dove, or Holy Spirit, enters through the Virgin's ear—with sound or not, one doesn't know. We know she understood what was said, but had she heard it out loud—or in silence?

GENRE PAINTINGS

In complete contrast to the calm and quiet paintings of Johannes Vermeer, Pieter Bruegel the Elder was one of the first painters to paint scenes that were not religious. His paintings reflect ordinary life, and ordinary life was noisy—at least the ordinary life depicted by Bruegel was noisy. Small groups of people gather to perform their activities, almost all independently of other small groups. By studying them, one can get a good idea of what medieval life was like. Often known as Peasant Bruegel, he shows the work and rituals of daily peasant life—dancing, fighting, cooking, and hunting, as well as various other ceremonies and festivities. By looking at paintings for their sound, or for their silence, one is struck by the different noise levels. Medieval society thought hell was infernally noisy, and this is well represented by both Bruegel and Hieronymus Bosch who portrayed hell as full of hideous noises—with engines exploding, hideously loud farts (amplified with trumpets stuck up bottoms), and the wails of the tormented.[5] So even in medieval times, noise, in contrast to silence, was considered hellish.

A few years ago I met Clare Hornsby, the art historian and poet, at an afternoon gathering in Shoreditch in the east end of London. She told me that she had written about Arcadia (the poetic term for natural and harmonious nature) in eighteenth-century art from the perspective of silence and sound and very generously sent me her as-yet-unpublished manuscript, originally written for the Royal Academy of Music. Many of her examples contain musical imagery, and yet some of those paintings that are full of music and dance seem to me to be silent paintings. In many of Jean-Antoine Watteau's paintings—*The Music Lesson*, *The Music Party*, and *The Serenader*—instruments are being tuned, not played. There is a silence in them—the silence of anticipation before a piece of music starts. In *Les Plaisirs du Bal*, the performers depicted actually seem to be playing their musical instruments, unusual in a painting by Watteau. But the Goncourt brothers, Edmond and Jules who wrote all of their books together and didn't spend more than a day apart during the whole of their adult lives, pointed out that the dogs in the painting are not barking. So does this make it a silent or a nonsilent painting? I feel that it's a combination—silent dogs but a full *fête champêtre* with dancers and musicians.

Carle van Loo's painting *The Grand Turk Giving a Concert for His Mistress* has a convivial atmosphere, and the music and singing can almost be heard. Everyone is engaged; there is no silence. In *The Concert*, a painting attributed to Vittore Belliniano, four figures appear to be singing from a score held by the woman of the group. The men are possibly meant to represent the three ages of man, a subject painted by, among others, Giorgione and Titian. None of the group is actually singing, and it is likely that they have come to the end of their concert and are pausing in the silence that is often palpable at the end of a piece of music—that brief time at the end of a great performance before the applause starts. For a moment you can almost hear the silence. But, of course, silence never ceases to imply its opposite—you have to acknowledge a surrounding environment of noise or language in order to recognize silence.

PORTRAITS

Nicolaes Maes did a series of six paintings called *The Eavesdropper*, in which someone is observing a forbidden scene that's taking place in a room on a different level of the house. The subject, usually a servant, has her finger in front of her mouth, indicating *shhh*. In these paintings, the viewer is being asked to join the eavesdropper, and it is very effective—you can't escape being drawn into the conspiracy. By asking us to be silent, we become coconspirators.

There is a Salvator Rosa self-portrait in the National Gallery in London in which the artist wears a broad-brimmed black hat and holds up the motto *Aut tace aut loquere meliora silentio* (Be silent unless what you have to say is better than silence). In this painting it seems as if Rosa is setting himself up as the personification of silence. This wasn't immediately obvious to those who knew him, but it was a side of him that he wanted others to know about. Although his name was often associated with banditry, Rosa was also an intellectual and a poet.

STILL LIVES, LANDSCAPES, AND MORE

The genre of still life—*nature morte* in French, and *stilleven* in Dutch—first appeared in the Netherlands in the mid-sixteenth century. The Dutch artist Johannes Vermeer's interiors are full of silence. The philosopher Emil Cioran called him "the master of intimacy and confidential silences."[6] The French poet Paul Claudel wrote that a Vermeer painting is "full of the silence of the here and now"[7] and that many Dutch paintings have this "active silent space" and are "sources of silence." Although Vermeer is better known for his interiors, his landscape painting *View of Delft* has a particular calmness and silence. Marcel Proust, a great understander of silence, wrote about the novelist Bergotte's death and how just after Bergotte had gone to see Vermeer's *View of Delft* in an exhibition, he noticed "the little patch of yellow wall" for the first time. When Bergotte saw the painting, he regretted not writing more colorfully himself and died, repeating, "Little patch of yellow wall, with a sloping roof, little patch of yellow wall."[8]

One of the paintings I have particularly enjoyed sitting in front of and drawing in the National Gallery is Francisco de Zurbarán's *A Cup of Water and a Rose*. This deceptively simple still life with just three objects—a cup of water, a rose, and a silver plate—has immense depths and stillness. While sitting in front of it for hours attempting to draw it, I found that I could cut out the surrounding clatter and become completely absorbed in the stillness of the still life.

Chinese paintings can draw you into the world of silence that they portray. Many paintings have the moon as a focal point—and the landscape lit by the moon is a silent land. The people in these landscapes are described by the Swiss writer Max Picard as "like figures in a moonlit mist over the world of silence, woven from moon threads over the silence."[9] The people and objects in the paintings seem to exude silence—a fallen leaf attracts silence around it and the surrounding area seems hushed and peaceful.

Vanitas paintings are still lives that include symbolic objects—skulls, rotten fruit, hourglasses, extinguished candles—designed to remind the viewer of mortality and the shortness, fragility, and transience of life. The term comes from the opening lines from the book of Ecclesiastes: "Vanity of vanities, saith the Preacher, vanity of vanities; all is vanity" (1:2). One of the aims of vanitas paintings was to shock and preach through silence. These paintings, mostly of the sixteenth and seventeenth centuries, should ideally be looked at in silence since they invite us to contemplate death. The observer is also reminded of the worthlessness of worldly goods and pleasures, which are portrayed by musical instruments, wine, and books.

The Anatomy of Riches, the art historian Spike Bucklow's book about the painting known as *The Paston Treasure*, conjectures that still lives became so popular because fundamentally they were not "preachy"; their spiritual dimension was quiet and unassuming. They reward our attention without pushing themselves on us; they celebrate the riches of life while being aware of life's transience. *The Paston Treasure* is a large anonymous seventeenth-century painting commissioned by Sir Robert Paston that is crammed with exotic objects and curiosities from all over the world, each one obviously having had a special significance for their owner. Both Robert Paston and his father, Sir William, had traveled widely, and the painting, as well as being an insight into the mind and world of the Pastons, also tells us much about the life and interests of people at the time.

Chardin was an early master of still life in the eighteenth century. He painted very slowly, only completing about four paintings a year—two hundred in his lifetime: "Who said one paints with colours? One *employs* colours, but one paints with feeling."[10] He was called the "grand magician" by the French philosopher Denis Diderot and was the first artist to submit a still-life painting to the Royal Academy of Painting and have it accepted. Many of his paintings were painted under the heading of *la vie silencieuse* (the silent life); they are full of quietness, well-thought-out structure, and light, in marked contrast to many of his contemporaries such as Francisco Goya, Eugène Delacroix, and Francois Boucher, whose paintings are filled with activity and color. (Although Delacroix wrote, "Silence is always impressive."[11]) Diderot loathed Boucher, whom he referred to as "a deadly enemy of silence."[12]

As well as still lives, landscape painting, which rose to prominence between the sixteenth and eighteenth centuries, can invite silent contemplation, and this feeling of silence continued into the nineteenth century. Jean-François Millet's *The Angelus* conveys a tangible stillness and silence. It portrays two peasants who have stopped work to pray the Angelus after hearing the bells from the church on the horizon. In contrast, there is no companionable silence in Edgar Degas's painting *L'Absinthe*, also in the Musée D'Orsay, which is of a man and woman sitting in a café; that silence is one of despair. You can actually feel the agony of the woman sitting there.

Many of the paintings of the German Romantic painter Caspar David Friedrich emanate silence and presence, but perhaps especially *Wanderer above the Sea of Fog* in which we see the back view of a young man as he looks out over a vast landscape. The foreground of Friedrich's *Winter Landscape* shows a man who has thrown away his crutches and is leaning against a boulder and three trees—one with a crucifix—probably representing the Trinity. In the background, a ghostly cathedral looms out of the fog. In his journal of 1803, Friedrich wrote, "Close your physical eye, so that you see your picture first with your spiritual eye. Then bring what you see in the dark into the light, so that it may have an effect on others, shining inwards from outwards."[13]

The painting *Isle of the Dead*, by the Swiss symbolist Arnold Böcklin, shows an isolated island across a stretch of dark water; a small rowing boat is arriving at the shore with a figure all in white standing in the bow accompanying what is probably a coffin. The islet is dominated by a dense clump of cypress trees, hinting that it might well be a cemetery island. Could the boatman be Charon ferrying souls to the underworld? Although Böcklin never revealed the location the painting was depicting—and there are many versions of it—it might have been partly evoked by the English Cemetery in Florence where Böcklin's baby daughter was buried. She was one of the eight of his fourteen children who died. He described *Isle of the Dead* as "a dream picture: it must produce such a stillness that one would be awed by a knock on the door."[14] It is an enigmatic painting, but it has an extraordinary feeling of stillness and silence. It was very influential, inspiring paintings such as Salvador Dali's *The True Painting of the "Isle of the Dead" by Arnold Böcklin at the Hour of the Angelus*[15] and paintings by Michael Sowa, H. R. Giger, James Gleeson, and Fabrizio Clerici. It was also used by the Swedish playwright August Strindberg for his play *The Ghost Sonata*, appeared in television series such as *Pretty Little Liars* and *Neo Yokio*, and was used in films including *I Walked with a Zombie*, *The Tales of Hoffmann*, J. G. Ballard's science-fiction novel *The Crystal World*, and Bernard Cornwell's *The Warlord Chronicles*. Even pieces of music—by Sergei Rachmaninoff and Max Reger—were inspired by the painting. There can't be many other paintings that have inspired such a wide variety of art forms, but there is something very powerful in the silent quality of Böcklin's painting that makes it both compelling and inspirational.

Emblem books—books pairing allegorical illustrations with morals or poems—were popular in Europe in the sixteenth and seventeenth centuries. They were collections of three sets of elements: an icon or image, a motto, and a text explaining the connection between the two. These books were descended from medieval bestiaries, and many of the illustrations depict somebody—sometimes a putti, sometimes a monk—with their finger in front of their mouth, indicating silence. These are followed by a text explaining that particular silence. In Andrea Alciato's *Book of Emblems*, which has 212 Latin emblem poems, emblem 11 has the following text on silence: "When he is silent, a foolish man differs not a bit from the wise. Both tongue and voice are the index of his foolishness—therefore let him press his lips, and with his finger mark his silences, and let him turn himself into a Pharian Harpocrates."[16] Harpocrates was the god of silence in ancient Greece.

Ironically, I've always thought of Edvard Munch's *The Scream*, of which there are many versions including in the National Gallery in Oslo, as a silent painting. It's a scream of anguish and of not being heard, or as Munch put it: "One evening I was walking along a path, the city was on one side and the fjord below. I felt tired and ill. I stopped and looked out over the fjord—the sun was setting, and the clouds turning blood red. I sensed a scream passing through nature; it seemed to me that I heard the scream. I painted this picture, painted the clouds as actual blood. The color shrieked. This became *The Scream*."[17] It's as if through Munch we are experiencing the silent scream of nature, as we pollute her seas and rivers and poison her air—even more relevant today than it was in the late nineteenth century.

One of the many spin-offs from *The Scream* was created by Steven Moffat for the 2011 BBC television series *Doctor Who*, in which the main antagonists are called "The Silence." They were a scary religious order, represented by humanoids with alien-like physical characteristics with their looks loosely based on Munch's *The Scream*. Created to be the scariest-ever monster in *Doctor Who*, The Silence are only seen when they are looked at and are immediately forgotten when someone looks away. However, the terrifying suggestions made by the monsters are retained and are impossible to forget.

Artists don't need to be as dramatic as Henri Matisse, who once said, "Listen: do you want to paint? Well start by having your tongue cut out."[18] Nevertheless, creativity does flourish in silence. There are many painters who "paint silence." There's Millet's *The Angelus*, Berthe Morisot's *The Cradle*,[19] Pierre Bonnard's *L'Homme et la Femme*, and probably most of the paintings by Edward Hopper, many of which show utter desolation and the gulf that can exist between a man and a woman. His houses seem to breathe silence, and his painting *Gas* in the Museum of Modern Art in New York of three gasoline pumps exudes silence; it is dusk and a single figure stands by three solitary gasoline pumps alongside a deserted road. The single figure of a woman in *Automat* exudes desolation. Hopper's silences don't feel peaceful; they feel anguished. Earlier American artists had painted the frontier and were therefore outward looking, but Hopper saw that in the twentieth century, "The old frontier had moved inward and now lay within the self, so that the man of action was replaced by the solitary watcher."[20] I find it almost impossible to say anything in front of a Hopper painting; I am reduced to silence, but it is a silence filled with feelings of anguish and despair. Is life really that bleak? The answer for the people he was portraying was probably yes.

Many of the late nineteenth-century French symbolists were mystics; they were signaling a retreat from the word into silence using painting, poetry, and drama.[21] *The Silence*, a lithograph by the symbolist Henri Martin shows a girl whose long hair covers her mouth, and it is this covering of her mouth that evokes silence. With hair in her mouth, she can no longer speak.

The still life genre, which showed domestic scenes and people involved in silent activities such as reading and writing, was sidelined in the nineteenth century by historical, religious, and mythological paintings. However, it reemerged as a genre with painters such as Giorgio Morandi. There is absolutely no sound in a Morandi painting. He painted seemingly simple subjects, but his bottles, vases, bowls, and flowers have a huge depth of meaning and complexity. In the late 1960s, I lived with my American cousin in New York. She had been given a Morandi still life by her father—my uncle, Johnny Walker—who had won it in a raffle in Italy when he had been studying with Bernard Berenson at I Tatti. Walker later went on to become director of the National Gallery of Art in Washington, DC. I remember its position on the wall, but because it was surrounded by a mass of other interesting paintings, objects, and clutter, its silence did not break through. It was only later that I learned to appreciate Morandi.

In 1908, Piet Mondrian, a contemporary of the Italian Futurists, became interested in theosophy, the occult movement started by Madame Helena Blavatsky in the late nineteenth century. The roots of theosophy can be traced back to ancient Gnosticism and Neo-platonism, and one of its core beliefs is an emphasis on mystical experience, the idea that there is a deeper spiritual reality that can transcend normal human consciousness. In 1911, Mondrian moved to Paris where he lived as more or less of a recluse in a small one-room apartment near the Gare Montparnasse. Unlike other cubists, his art had a spiritual element, and in 1913 he began to fuse his paintings with his theosophical ideas. In 1914, Mondrian wrote, "Art is higher than reality and has no direct relation to reality."[22] When the English painter Ben Nicholson went to visit him once, the pauses and silences in Mondrian's conversation reminded Nicholson of "those hermit's caves where lions went to have thorns taken out of their paws."[23]

The German-French sculptor, painter, poet, and abstract artist Jean Arp wrote that "soon silence will have passed into legend. Man has turned his back on silence. Day after day he invents machines and devices that increase noise and distract humanity from the essence of life, contemplation, meditation."[24] Even at the beginning of the twentieth century, Arp was conscious that the world was becoming noisier and noisier—he was aware that machines were distracting people from silence.

However, if it's beginning to seem that the majority of artists were in search of silence, of course that is not the case. In fact, there were whole movements against it. The Italian Futurists, founded in Milan in 1909 by the Italian poet Filippo Tommaso Marinetti, loathed silence. Marinetti declared, "We want no part of it, the past . . . we the young and strong Futurists."[25] They loved speed, technology, youth, violence, the noise of accelerating cars and airplanes, and the industrial city. The Futurist Luigi Russolo, author of the manifesto *The Art of Noises*, written as a letter to his friend Francesco Balilla Pratella, was also a painter, composer, and builder of experimental musical instruments, which used acoustic noise generators and sculptures by Giacomo Balla. They glorified modernity wanting to liberate themselves from the past.

The movement known as monochrome painting, in which artists such as Kazimir Malevich, Alexander Rodchenko, Robert Rauschenberg, Robert Ryman, and Ad Reinhardt belonged, used just one color in their work. Their aim was to move away from composition and "vulgar subject matter," paring down their paintings to single colors and no objects. Reinhardt, who was a friend of Thomas Merton, wanted to make art purer and emptier. This purity raised the subject of silence and resonated with the mystical tradition in Christianity.

"Silence is so accurate,"[26] the American painter Mark Rothko remarked, echoing Kierkegaard, and his paintings certainly do resonate with a deep silence. The power of a Rothko painting can override most noise, even when a gallery is full of people. Rothko wanted to address modern human's spiritual emptiness, which he thought was largely due to the lack of mythology in modern life. He found it hard to describe his paintings in words, and indeed, why should he need to? But he felt that his paintings could release an unconscious energy. Dominique de Menil, the philanthropist and French-American art collector, and her husband commissioned the Rothko Chapel in Houston. The Italian architect Renzo Piano designed the building in Houston, Texas, that houses the Menil Collection; he described it as being serene, calm, and discreet. It is a small, windowless octagonal building that was built as a meditative space. Although it is now nondenominational, while he was doing the paintings for it in New York, Rothko believed that it was going to be a Roman Catholic chapel, and he took his inspiration from the Byzantine church of Santa Maria Assunta in Torcello,

Venice. Rothko took six years to complete the paintings; he wanted it to be a pilgrimage site, far away from New York and the center of art. "Perhaps only silence and love do justice to a great work of art," wrote de Menil.[27] Some people find the dark paintings, panels of pure color, claustrophobic. Others feel that when they look at them, they have a spiritual experience; they do force one to turn inward and to confront one's own existence, and this can be unsettling. The chapel is now used for colloquiums that foster mutual understanding on justice and freedom.

The Irish-born artist Sean Scully's abstract paintings seem to capture a tranquility amid a chaotic world. They have been described by the poet, historian, and art critic Kelly Grovier as "sounding boards for the soul" and "mute eye music." Scully named his series of Doric paintings after the least ornate order of Greek architecture. He liked the simplicity and power of Doric architecture, as evidenced by his "preference for the least adorned classical order, comparable to the simplified forms of the composition."[28] His abstract Doric paintings, with their bands of blacks and grays, combine a sobriety with a radiance and a movement and pay tribute to the Greek influence on Western civilization.

There have even been several exhibitions devoted to silence. The Rath Museum in Geneva had an exhibition from June to October 2019 called *Silences* that showed a variety of works of art all pertaining to and revealing silence. The exhibition started with a silent video by the French artist Camille Llobet called *Voir ce qui est dit* [See what is written], which used sign language to interpret an orchestra conductor's gestures. There were still lives, a selection of Christian art that had been used for meditative purposes to inspire devotion and as a means of getting closer to God. These included paintings of the mystic St. John of the Cross, St. Jerome depicted as a hermit, and St. Ignatius doing his spiritual exercises. And there were paintings by artists as diverse as Vilhelm Hammershøi, Henri Martin, Giorgio

Morandi, and Felix Vallotton. All had very different approaches, but all had silence as the theme.

The former Archbishop of Canterbury Rowan Williams wrote that every search for truth involves some kind of fleeing, some kind of asceticism—and indeed all imaginative creation needs silence.[29] Silence can play an important role in the actual process of creating. The journalist Andrew Marr agrees with Winston Churchill that painting is one of the most important things you can do in utter silence.[30] In that silence there can be a wonderful losing of oneself and an immersion, a place where time stands still. When I paint, I find I can be completely absorbed and drawn into silence.

OTHER ARTS

Paintings are far from the only visual art that can be inspired by silence. Other exhibitions on the theme of silence have featured sculpture, video, and even performance art. In 2017, the Catalan artist Jaume Plensa had an exhibition in New York called *Silence*, which took place in two rooms and featured sculpted heads. It was billed as a meditative two-room altar to one of the planet's most precious and rare commodities: silence. Plensa wanted us to become more conscious and proactive by producing silence for ourselves: "Our words are not always the best way to express feelings."[31] He urges us to *think* more. There is a sculpture by Plensa called *Anna* in the monastery in Montserrat where I went on my Buddhist retreat. Like many of his other sculptures, Anna has her eyes closed, indicating a withdrawal from the world and a silent looking inward.

In 2012, another exhibition called *Silence* opened in the Rothko Chapel in Houston and moved to Berkeley in 2013. It asked the following questions: What is silence? Why does it have a grip on the imagination? Why do we connect it to mystery? The exhibition considered the absence of sound in modern contemporary art and film and included works by Marcel Duchamp, Nam June Paik, Theresa Hak Kyung Cha, and Doris Salcedo. Silence is present in the important things in life such as memory, contemplation, and mourning. As the writer and philosopher Susan Sontag put it, "The art of our time is noisy with appeals for silence."[32]

One of Marina Abramovic's works, *The Artist Is Present*, featured Abramovic sitting in silence for over 736 hours while members of the public queued to sit opposite her, also in silence. It took place at MOMA in New York, March 14–May 31, 2010. She was meant to do something similar at the Royal Academy in London, but it was canceled due to COVID-19.

The empty spaces in sculpture evoke a silence that encourage us to pause and think about the spaces. For example, the gaps and holes in the large stone sculptures by Henry Moore are silent spaces. There is a sculpture, *Single Form (Memorial)*, by Barbara Hepworth that I often pass when I'm walking in Battersea Park. The broadly oval abstract sculpture has a circular hole near the top—a possible silent space. It was made by Hepworth after her good friend Dag Hammarskjöld, the secretary general of the United Nations, was killed in a plane crash in 1961. A larger version is outside the UN in New York.

There are films with silence as a theme such as Joseph Beuys's 1973 film *The Silence,* which is five original 35mm reels of Ingmar Bergman's 1962 film *The Silence,* lacquered and plated in copper and zinc baths. Earlier, in 1964, Beuys had done a piece as a reproach to Duchamp: *The Silence of Marcel Duchamp Is Overrated*—the implication was that Duchamp didn't have the nerve to answer his own manifestos. The conceptual artist Gillian Wearing won the Turner Prize in 1996 with her video called *Sixty Minute Silence,* in which a collection of people dressed in police uniform were meant to be as still and silent as possible for the hour—difficult for both watcher and watched.

Cities and Memory is a global field recording and sound artwork project that provides both the present reality of a place but also its imagined, alternative counterpart; it remixes the world of sound. Initial recorded sounds are reimagined by an artist who uses the original piece as inspiration. Human activity endangers the sounds of nature, and this project aims to reflect on the sounds—and silences—of the natural environment as well as urban noise. In March 2020 they launched a campaign to build a global crowdsourced sound map showing how the sounds around us changed during the pandemic. One of their projects is called Sacred Spaces, where by clicking on a map of the world you can listen to the sacred sounds from that place. These could be church bells from an English country church, drums from an evening Pooja in Sri Lanka, or the breathlessness and footsteps from someone climbing up the Duomo in Milan (something I did recently but would never have thought of recording—and anyway I think I took the lift!). Many of these sounds are used as preludes to a silence.[33]

Several years ago the contemporary English master potter Edmund de Waal gave a talk at Kings Place in London, in which he described the thoughts he has when he is creating his pots. He actively thinks about how to make silence—when he is making a bowl, he is making "a silence" and the whiteness of the clay is an additional kind of silencing. His pots have an echo of ancient Greek statues, which we look back on today as vessels of mysterious silence and as silent beacons from the past. Much poetry goes into de Waal's silent pots: "My life is full of silences," he says, and he refers to both poets and painters who help him achieve this silence, including Paul Celan (whose poetry focuses on the silence of annihilation); Wallace Stevens's *The House Was Quiet and the World Was Calm*; Osip Mandelstam's "When on the squares and in solitary silence, We slowly go out of our minds"; Sappho, "For when I gaze at you fleetingly, I can no longer utter a sound," and Proust.[34]

In his talk, De Waal encouraged people to look at the paintings of Chardin, Morandi, Cy Twombly, Sol LeWitt, Agnes Martin, and

Barnett Newman. He said that Newman used color to produce silence—spatial silence—and by looking silently at a painting, one can absorb it. One of de Waal's pieces entitled *The Origins of Silent Reading* consists of two black cabinets with white pots, a reference to the roots of silent reading.

Silence is important in the art of Japanese gardens. The water in the gardens is a purifying force for both ritual washing and punctuating the silence. The white gravel represents the void, or *ma* (emptiness), also representative of silence. Outside the Connaught Hotel in Mount Street, near London's Berkeley Square, is a fountain called *Silence*, designed by the Japanese architect philosopher Tadao Ando. The fountain is largely silent, with water trickling down the outside of the large round basin; every fifteen minutes there is a soft hiss and a cloud of water vapor starts up.

Although some say that the lack of silence in buildings is a failure of architecture, some architects, especially the American architect Louis Kahn would disagree. He spent his whole working life trying to answer the need for architecture to reflect life; he believed buildings could foster empathy and that they could have spaces that enfolded silence within them. Near the end of his career, *silence* and *light* were the words he chose for collecting together all his poetic ideas concerning the process of architectural creation; silence being a wish of expression present in the collective unconscious.

10

Music

"AFTER SILENCE, that which comes closest to expressing the inexpressible is music,"[1] wrote Aldous Huxley. And indeed, silence gives a vital shaping quality to all music. Musicians have always appreciated the qualities of silence—the pauses and the gaps. "Silence is the basis of music. We find it before, after, in, underneath and behind the sound,"[2] said the Austrian pianist Alfred Brendel. Another Austrian pianist Artur Schnabel is quoted saying, "The notes I handle no better than many pianists. But the pauses between the notes, ah, that is where the art resides."[3] And Schnabel was echoing Claude Debussy who said that "music is the space between the notes," which was repeated by the pianist Clifford Curzon, who said that "a performer's whole art could be detected in the 'space between the notes.'"[4]

Silence is at its most "audible" when the last note of music has died away. There can be a wonderful pause in a live performance before the audience starts clapping. This post-performance silence, quite rare, is very different from the silence that is built into the music and is also different from a pre-concert silence that signals expectancy, heavy with anticipation. And there's one hand clapping, which is of course totally silent and which derives from a Buddhist koan known as "the sound of one hand."

Neuroscientists have observed that it is the silent intervals in music that most excite positive brain activity. It is during these silent interludes when the body is the most relaxed, with blood pressure dropping and heart rate slowing down. That this silence comes within a piece of music, rather than on its own, is important. And it is the quality of the silence contrasting with the music that is most beneficial—silence after sound, the yin and the yang. Both are needed.

COMPOSERS

The best-known "silent" music is probably John Cage's *4'33"*. When he first wrote about what it meant, he said that the listeners had missed the point:

> What they thought was silence, because they didn't know how to listen, was full of accidental sounds. You could hear the wind stirring outside during the first movement. During the second, raindrops began pattering on the roof, and during the third the people themselves made all kinds of interesting sounds as they talked and walked out.[5]

Cage's silences are connected with his belief in Zen Buddhism, and the piece is effectively about the nature of sound. The pianist William Howard told me that attending a live performance of Cage's work can be very uncomfortable, as silence so often can be. But, as Cage had said, you do become very aware of the sounds around you; in fact, your senses are heightened.[6]

Cage's *4'33"* has become a point of departure for many different works that have stillness and contemplation at their core. He first got the idea for it after visiting the anechoic chamber at Harvard University in 1951, a space designed to totally absorb sound and electromagnetic waves: "Get thee to an anechoic chamber and hear there thy nervous system in operation and hear there thy blood in circulation."[7] The chamber was originally built to carry out secret military research.

Many other composers have based work on silence, often getting their inspiration from music makers of the past. The Catalan composer Frederic Mompou mostly wrote short "intimate" music, influenced by both Erik Satie and Gabriel Fauré. Mompou's work often had a meditative sound, and his 1967 masterpiece *Musica Callada* (*Voice of Silence*) was based on the poetry of St. John of the Cross. As well as writing music about and containing silence, some composers need absolute quiet in order to compose in the first place. The Austro-Bohemian Romantic composer Gustav Mahler needed total silence when he was composing and even demanded that the cow bells in the area surrounding him should be muffled.

The Italian Futurist Luigi Russolo believed that the Industrial Revolution had given people the capacity to go beyond traditional melodic music and to appreciate more complex sound. His 1913 manifesto *The Art of Noises* states: "At first the art of music sought purity, limpidity and sweetness of sound. Then different sounds were amalgamated, care being taken, however, to caress the ear with gentle harmonies. Today music, as it becomes continually more complicated, strives to amalgamate the most dissonant, strange and harsh sounds. In this way we come ever closer to noise-sound . . . Today, noise is triumphant and reigns supreme over the sensibility of men."[8] According to Russolo, music should no longer be sweet or melodic, but with an appreciation of more complex sound, music should be something that reflects the dissonance of the age.

The composer Walter Marchetti wrote "Song for John Cage" in 1984. This was electronic music consisting of offensively loud whistling with a few words dropped in every few seconds. He also wrote bodies of work incorporating silence, among which his *Composition for Eight Orchestras*[9] includes notes held for impossibly long times and lasting several hours. However, this is nothing compared to the composer Clarence Barlow's *Stochroma*, written in computer coding and calling for a pause of 109 billion years![10]

Another contemporary composer, John Tavener, said that there were two kinds of silence in his work: one literal (the pauses) and one metaphysical. He linked this to the feeling that can be obtained from icons (he was a member of the Russian Orthodox Church) in which angels are transfixed as they gaze on God "a frozen or uncreated Eros, because it comes in the form of longing. It is the longing for God."[11] He felt that silence was crucial to his art and that even when it was being played, if it was listened to correctly, there should be an inherent silence. He felt that if there was no implicit silence, the music wasn't doing what he wanted it to do. He achieved this in his 1982 piece called "The Lamb." John Rutter commented that Tavener had the "very rare gift" of being able to "bring an audience to a deep silence."[12] Tavener felt that silence was everywhere because God was everywhere. He found a spiritual aspect in Anton Webern's music, being able to sense what was beyond the notes: "His silence seems to acknowledge another dimension so that there is a wonderful transparency in his music which somehow allows God to enter."[13]

When the composer George Benjamin was a pupil of Olivier Messiaen's in Paris, Messiaen would talk about the different kinds of musical silences. First, there was the simple silence that he compared to punctuation, which separated sections and was like turning a page or taking a breath; movements would also be framed by silence. Another kind of silence was that of musical notes dying away. But the deepest silence was left for the end of a work—a silence that Benjamin calls "precious." In 1990, he composed the piece "Upon Silence," based on the William Butler Yeats poem "Long-Legged

Fly."[14] In an interview, one of the orchestra players said that it was in the silences of this piece that the impact of the music was felt.

EXPRESSION AND EXPERIMENTATION

In a BBC radio program commemorating Holocaust Memorial Day, after Anne Sofie von Otter had sung a lullaby composed in Terezin concentration camp, Petroc Trelawny, the presenter, allowed a pause for contemplation, saying that silence is important and that there must be time for music to sink in.

During the 1960s and 1970s, an international, interdisciplinary community of artists, composers, designers, architects, economists, mathematicians, and poets called Fluxus engaged in experimental art performances. They were very influential in broadening the definition of what is considered art. Loosely founded by George Maciunas, a Lithuanian American artist, their philosophy was to emphasize the artistic process over and above the finished result. John Cage was a big influence on Fluxus, whose artists included Joseph Beuys, John Cale, Yoko Ono, and Nam June Paik. George Brecht was a Fluxus artist and composer, and among his compositions is "Drip Music 1962" in which water is poured from a watering can on top of a ladder into a bucket below. He described his art as a way of "ensuring that the details of everyday life, the random constellations of objects that surround us, stop going unnoticed."[15] This is minimalist rather than silent, but it gives time for ample opportunity for one's own silent interpretation.

Yoko Ono and John Lennon included two silent pieces, "Baby's Heartbeat" and "Two Minutes of Silence," on an album in honor of their stillborn child.[16] The American composer Tom Johnson said that silence is often the only response to great sadness; he is a committed adherent of the sparseness minimalist/silent music movement. In 2000, he used the organ in the American Church in Paris, where he now lives, to compose his piece called "Organ and Silence." He says that silence resonates in big spaces, and half to three-quarters of this piece is silent. The sparser the music, the more space for listeners to interpret in their own way—something that requires a great deal of mental work.[17] The composer of experimental music Michael Pisaro wrote that "music traces the border between sound and silence."[18] Boundaries are redrawn and obstructions are put in place to be demolished; we measure distance by its limits and expand by pushing the limit as far as we can.

The jazz musician Miles Davis was known as the Prince of Silence and was famous for the dramatic silences in his performances, the spaces between the notes. In 1969, he released a studio album called *In a Silent Way*. It was recorded in one session, and although it was greeted with suspicion when it first came out, it was later acknowledged as one of his greatest and most influential works.

Where silence comes from is important. Silence originating in peace is beneficial, but silence that comes from anger can be very damaging.

The English author and biologist Rupert Sheldrake stresses the importance of singing and says that he goes to church most Sundays in order to sing hymns and psalms. His wife, Jill Purce, who teaches chanting, emphasizes that we can only chant in the present and that by listening to the sound that we make, we create a "circuit of attention." All traditions have their own sacred sounds that are repeated and that can lead to silence. "The gift of sound is silence,"[19] Sheldrake says. The ban on choirs and singing imposed by the coronavirus pandemic had devastating consequences for many who sing to help their mental health. Singing via Zoom was not the same.

When the pianist William Howard teaches piano, he encourages his students to listen to the silence between the notes—maybe not quite like in Siberia, where people listening to pianos tend to do so with a "suspicious silence." The term comes from *The Lost Pianos of Siberia*, a riveting book by Sophy Roberts in which she travels throughout Siberia in search of lost pianos and the people who play them. Nonetheless, listening to these silences is the key to performing well, and it is vital that the performers themselves are aware of the silence so that it can be transmitted to the audience. Howard tells his pupils that the silence is as important as the notes, and the discipline of this often surprises them. But while the left hand is playing the silence between the notes, the right hand can be on top of this silence. The tiny silences are the key to articulation, the parameter that determines how a note is sounded. Music can get into deeper places within us and can be more comprehensive than language, but the loudness of the music is pertinent.[20] As Thomas Merton once explained, "Music is pleasing not only because of the sound but because of the silence that is in it: without the alternation of sound and silence there would be no rhythm."[21]

One of my favorite pieces of piano music is Franz Schubert's Piano Sonata no. 21 (D960). Listening to it helps me calm down and, played so lyrically by Artur Schnabel, I find the silent pauses heartbreaking in their intensity. Music played like this makes me understand what silence in music means.

OTHERWORLDLY SILENCE

If there's silence in music, what might the "other world" sound like? The realm that we enter after our earthly death? If and when we reach this other world, do we imagine it as silent? The journalist and author Paul Johnson speculated that there was no reason to think that it would be noiseless, but surely if we do think of it as having sound, we hope it would be positive sound. A tradition preserved in the Talmud shares that in the fifth heaven, angels sing praises by night and are silent by day so that Israel's praises could certainly be heard. Higher-up angels fill the eighth realm of heaven with their silent singing (but can singing be silent?)—they were there in the eighth realm as a countering force to demons.[22] The Songs of the Sabbath Sacrifice, a group of thirteen liturgical songs that were found in fragments among the Dead Sea Scrolls and that are suggestive of silence, were also known as the "Angelic Liturgy." In them "the sound of glad rejoicing falls silent."[23] When a room becomes silent at twenty minutes past an hour, folklorically it is thought to be because an angel is passing through. More scientifically, this lapse into silence may actually be programmed into humans, as a moment that gave our hunter-gatherer ancestors time to listen for danger. Nowadays, maybe we can view this as a product of Carl Jung's collective unconscious.

The ancient Greek philosopher Pythagoras considered that since objects in motion vibrate and produce sound, the planets, which are large bodies in motion, must also produce a sound—hence he named it the "music of the spheres." We now know that everything in space emits sound waves, and we can already hear echoes of events from near the beginning of the universe. One day we may even be able to hear the big bang. Did the ancients have knowledge of this when they alluded to the music of the spheres? A hundred or so years after Pythagoras, Plato held that rather than being silent, the whole universe was united by musical concord.

In book 7 of John Milton's *Paradise Lost*, when Raphael tells of the creation of the world, silence and deep peace are linked. This is a recurring theme: silence brings peace with it.

"Silence, ye troubled Waves, and, thou Deep, peace!"
Said then the Omnific Word; "your discord end!"[24]

When Dante described heaven, he associated it with music,[25] and many composers have acknowledged this, including Franz Liszt in the *Dante* Symphony, a choral symphony based on Dante's journey through hell.

The world begins with silence, but when Milton attempts to describe heaven, in a similar vein to Dante, it is always associated with music; angels learn to sing before they can fly. The search for celestial music, which had begun with Pythagoras, continued as the German astronomer, astrologer, and mathematician Johannes Kepler published his work *Harmonices Mundi* in 1619. This was his attempt to discover celestial music. He explained the harmony of the whole world through the harmonies in planetary motion, and on a smaller, more manageable scale, he wrote about the harmony between math and a lute string.

In her memoir *A Silent Melody*, Shirley du Boulay remembers watching Jacob Bronowski's 1973 BBC television series *The Ascent of Man* in which the music of the spheres was recreated at the beginning of the program as a "curious, whispering, mysterious, complex sound." She felt that it was exactly what the music of the spheres would sound like if we could hear it and knew what it sounded like: "The OM that time and history utter on their way, the OM uttered by Space when entering into time."[26]

In 1997, the British Antarctic Survey asked the composer Peter Maxwell Davies to go on a voyage to the Antarctic—a journey that resulted in his Eighth Symphony, the *Antarctic Symphony*, which premiered in 2001. During his time in the Antarctic, he kept a diary in which he described what he heard: "Disconcerting, in the infinite silence, to hear ice crack and split before the ship's bow, then roar along the keel to the stern in a tumultuous clatter of slabs and shards."[27]

RADIO

In 1946, in *The Perennial Philosophy* Aldous Huxley wrote that the twentieth century . . . is the age of noise: "Physical noise, mental noise and noise of desire. . . . That most popular and influential of all recent inventions, the radio, is nothing but a conduit through which pre-fabricated din can flow into our homes."[28] He elaborated further by saying that of course this din penetrates the mind, filling it with a "babel of distractions." He felt that idle words got in the way of the perennial philosophy, the perception that all the world's religions share a single metaphysical truth from which all spiritual knowledge developed. This knowledge could be nourished and sustained by silence. The Swiss philosopher Max Picard, who died in 1965, was contemptuous of the radio—it was "a machine for producing absolute verbal noise. The content hardly matters any longer; the production of noise is the main concern."[29] He felt that the noise continued even when the radio was turned off and that "wireless sets are like constantly firing automatic pistols shooting at silence."[30] He felt that nothing had changed the nature of humankind so much as the loss of silence—something that had been taken for granted and was as natural as breathing: "There is more help and healing in silence than in all the useful things. . . . It makes things whole again."[31]

But radio doesn't need to be "prefabricated din"; there is always an off switch (which some people seem to forget), and some programs even actively encourage silence. In 2017, to celebrate the seventieth birthday of Radio 3, the BBC played a program called *Sacred River*, which was a continuous stream of music throughout the day with no verbal interruption but instead with pauses between the pieces. Of course in this digital age, it was possible to go online and read what was being played, but it was certainly not necessary. The music was played live and the decision about how long to leave between each piece was decided in the moment. As Kate Chisholm wrote in *The Spectator*, "It's in those pauses that the magic happened. The impact of carefully curated silence."[32] Another part of Radio 3's slow radio series had a five-part program called *Meditations from a Monastery*, an imaginative leap on the part of radio as many of the thirteen minutes of each program were silent. The Benedictine monasteries of Downside, Belmont, and Pluscarden Abbeys were featured, and there was little sound apart from birdsong, plainsong, and the occasional words of a monk. Kate Chisholm wrote in *The Spectator* that it was "remarkably cleansing; how to declutter on air."[33] She felt that time appeared to slow down and time and space seemed to lengthen before her.

Unplanned silence on the radio can also be very powerful. After the Beslan school siege in 2004,[34] the broadcaster John Humphrys interviewed the then archbishop of Canterbury, Rowan Williams, on BBC's Radio 4. Williams asked to take time before saying anything. He was silent for about ten seconds (which can seem an age on the radio) before he realized that there was no real answer as to the why of the horror; his silence was the answer.[35] This exchange shows, I think, that silence is far more than a lack of something; it can be a positive. It's unsurprising that Humphrys understands silence—he detests extraneous noise and won't even eat in restaurants with background music. Rowan Williams has said, "I believe these moments of silence are so very important not only for our humanity generally but for our Christian humanity in particular."[36]

The world-class percussionist Evelyn Glennie, who is profoundly deaf, has said, "There is no such thing as silence." She tunes in so acutely to the vibrations of her instruments that she can easily play in an orchestra, describing how she feels that "the whole body is like a huge ear," which constantly beats, breathes, and resonates with sound.[37] We could all learn something from Glennie. If we train ourselves to hear more of what our bodies are telling us, this would give us a chance to discover a connection to something bigger than ourselves.

DARKER SIDES
OF SILENCE

11

War

THERE WAS ALMOST constant noise during the First World War, with gunfire in the background at all times. During the Battle of the Somme, Private Fred Ball described the noise as "like a wall of roaring sound before us,"[1] and the poet Robert Graves said in an interview that the noise never ever stopped. Ironically, this contrasts the way we can experience the Great War now—through silent films. Some filmmakers have added music for effect, but the most powerful ones are those that are silent.

THE NOISE OF BATTLE AND FOREBODING SILENCE

The following lines from the English poet and soldier Wilfred Owen's "Anthem for Doomed Youth" emphasize the din of war:

> What passing-bells for these who die as cattle?
> — Only the monstrous anger of the guns.
> Only the stuttering rifles rapid rattle
> Can patter out their hasty orisons.

No mockeries now for them; no prayers nor bells;
Nor any voice of mourning save the choirs, -
The shrill, demented choirs of wailing shells;
And bugles calling for them from sad shires.[2]

Lines from David Jones's *In Parenthesis* also illustrate the persistent noise. He wrote, "Out of the vortex, rifling the air it came—bright, brass-shod, Pandoran; with all-filling screaming, the howling crescendo's up-piling snapt. The universal world, breath held, one half second, a bludgeoned stillness."[3] Even after leaving the trenches there was no escape from the noise. The English war poet and soldier Siegfried Sassoon knew that having once been in the noisy trenches, the noise continued, even when in a supposedly "quiet and peaceful" place. He conveyed the persistent or imagined noise in his poem "Repression of War Experience," written in 1917 when he was at Craiglockhart Hospital in Scotland being treated for shellshock. He was aware of the fact that he was never able to get the noise of the guns out of his head and that their noise continued to drive him crazy.[4]

The trenches were so noisy that when people tried to speak to each other, they could not be heard. They could neither hear words of encouragement nor talk to each other; voices were silenced, and some of the soldiers were made deaf by the constant barrage of noise. The noise might have been particularly negative for injured soldiers, as Florence Nightingale insisted that the sick and wounded needed quiet in order to heal.[5]

But there were also ominous silences in the trenches, and knowing how to decode the noise and the silence was a vital skill in war. It is appalling to imagine that the continuation of relentless noise was better than the threatening silence that sometimes followed it, but "the silence remained tense, more awful than ever,"[6] wrote B. Neyland, who as a sapper in the Royal Engineers served in France near Arras from January to June 1917, before being invalided home. On another occasion, he had written: "10.30 p.m. An eerie silence on the ether, pierced only by atmospherics crackling in my ears. As the time went on the strange quietude became ghastly."[7] He knew he was lying next to a dead soldier, and it was this memory of being next to the Tyneside Scottish corpse that stayed with him most vividly, especially as it contrasted with the "miraculous dawn of the following day."[8]

In Shakespeare's *Henry V*, the noise from both armies becomes so quiet that the soldiers imagine they can hear the whispers from the other camp. This is a silence in which anything could happen.

> The hum of either army stilly sounds,
> That the fix'd sentinels almost receive
> The secret whispers of each other's watch.
> Fire answers fire.[9]

The silence in the trenches was both positive and negative, but to many soldiers it came as a great relief. In his poem "That Centre of Old," Ivor Gurney was "grateful for silence" after the "thud, smack, belch of war" and "hell's hammering and clamouring."[10] There was a final silence, but also a safety, that came with death, although as Siegfried Sassoon wrote in "The Death Bed," the relentless noise of war continues.[11] Even after the "silence and safety" of death, the noise of the guns can suddenly reappear.

Frank Gardner appreciated the silence after he had been shot six times by terrorists in Saudi Arabia in 2004. When his attackers had left him, thinking he was dead, the BBC correspondent, described how he felt: "For me, lying punctured and bleeding on the ground, there suddenly came the sweetest sound in the world: the noise of my attackers revving up the engine and driving off. They were leaving me for dead. There followed total silence. No wail of sirens, no crying of children, no clatter of approaching feet."[12]

In his poem "Exposure," written in September 1918 a few weeks before he was killed, Wilfred Owen wrote about the freezing winter of 1916–17. The cold of that winter made men want to cry, something they had not even considered under shell fire. A mug of tea that started off boiling hot at one end of a three-quarters-of-a-mile-long trench had ice on it by the end of its short journey.

> Our brains ache, in the merciless iced east winds that knive us . . .
> Wearied we keep awake because the night is silent . . .
> Low drooping flares confuse our memory of the salient . . .
> Worried by silence, sentries whisper, curious, nervous,
> But nothing happens[13]

The soldiers have to stay awake because the night is silent and the unexpected might happen. The apprehension in that silent waiting is palpable. Soldiers in the trenches were often given orders not to move until they had received telephonic orders; however, it transpired that the lines of communication had often been cut and so the men waited in vain for orders that could never come.

And there is an implied silence at the end of Wilfred Owen's "Strange Meeting":

> "I am the enemy you killed, my friend. I knew you in this dark:
>   for so you frowned
> Yesterday through me as you jabbed and killed.
> I parried; but my hands were loath and cold.
> Let us sleep now . . ."[14]

Censorship, another kind of silence, is often prevalent in wartimes. During the First World War, negativity was silenced by the Allied Troops. Not wanting to cause unnecessary worry in their letters home, soldiers didn't tell the truth of what was happening. But, as Paul Fussell wrote, "If they ever did write the truth, it was excised by company officers, who censored all outgoing mail."[15] No one knows how much literature and poetry succumbed to the censor.

Far from the trenches during the Second World War in the Cabinet War Rooms in Whitehall, there were signs saying "No Whistling." Winston Churchill was fanatical about noise and had specially adapted Remington "noiseless" typewriters imported from the United States and installed in each of his offices.

THE QUIETING AFTERMATH

The end of the First World War, November 11, 1918, was known as the Great Silence. Six months later, Edward George Honey, an Australian journalist, wrote a letter to the *London Evening News* proposing a respectful silence to commemorate the dead. This was brought to the attention of King George V, who on November 7, 1919, issued a proclamation calling for a two-minute silence. He declared, "All locomotion should cease, so that, in perfect stillness, the thoughts of everyone may be concentrated on reverent remembrance of the glorious dead."

On Armistice Day, now Remembrance Sunday in the UK (the nearest Sunday to November 11), the dead of that war and every subsequent war are commemorated by having the two-minute silence at 11 a.m. In the US this is known as Veterans Day and takes place at 2:11 p.m. EST. In Britain, the Cenotaph in London is the focus of proceedings. The Royal Family and leading politicians attend the ceremony along with the military and the other services; they lay wreaths and events take place at war memorials throughout Britain. This silence demonstrates more than any other a direct link to those killed in war, and it is the silence that creates this link in a way that nothing else could. The BBC, quoting Ralph Waldo Emerson, said that the two-minute silence is a "solvent which destroys personality and gives us leave to be great and universal."[16]

Although from time immemorial people have used the arts to represent war, there was a fear that the horrors of the two world wars would also end up silencing much creation. "No poetry after Auschwitz,"[17] wrote Theodor Adorno. It was to do with the horrors of the First World War that Franz Kafka wrote, "Now the Sirens have a still more fatal weapon than their song, namely their silence. And though admittedly such a thing has never happened, still it is conceivable that someone might possibly have escaped from their singing; but from their silence certainly never."[18] Mutism became a common symptom of war neurosis and was something from which many soldiers suffered. Isaac Rosenberg was one of many who fought against this kind of silence; he wrote to the English poet Laurence Binyon in 1916, "I am determined that this war, with all its powers for devastation, shall not master my poeting."[19] It did, however, effect many. The English poet Wilfred Owen often used the words "muted" or "dumbed," and poets wondered how they could give adequate voice to "the speechless." How could they best honor the memory of fallen comrades with words?

The Franco-American literary critic George Steiner thought that the inhumane events of the twentieth century—the horrors of the First World War and the Nazi Holocaust—exceeded the boundaries of language. He stated that the inhumanity of the twentieth century has "done injury to language and Nothing speaks louder than the unwritten poem."[20] He quoted a message received from the Warsaw ghetto: "The world is silent, the world *knows* (it is inconceivable that it should not) and stays silent. God's vicar in the Vatican is silent; there is silence in Washington and London: the American Jews are silent. The silence is astonishing and horrifying."[21] Steiner questioned how educated Germans who read Johann Wolfgang von Goethe and Heinrich Heine could use the same language to send people to their deaths. What happens to a language that is so misused? The fear that the horrific events of the world wars would silence creation or do "injury to language," as Steiner had predicted they might, did not occur. In fact, the world wars produced a mass of literature.[22]

There are historic sites from wars that command silence, where it seems almost an insult to talk. When Rowan Williams as Archbishop of Canterbury met the then Chief Rabbi Jonathan Sacks at Auschwitz, the two spoke in whispers, humbled by the occasion. Williams said, "The quiet weighs very heavily here—[it's a silence] that swallows words and robs them of their meaning."[23] Sacks went on to say, "Walking through certain parts of Europe, I hear ghosts . . . a whole murdered generation in a quite small space of time."[24]

Memories of war attach themselves to a place and linger long after the event is over. What I remember of the Tuol Sleng Genocide Museum in Phnom Penh, Cambodia—the site of the interrogation, detention, torture, and extermination center used by the Khmer Rouge where an estimated twenty thousand people were detained with only twelve surviving—are the photographs that line the walls of several rooms of the museum. These are the black-and-white photographs of the faces of many of the victims who were incarcerated there. It sounds like a cliché to say that you feel as if they are staring at you reproachfully, but that is the feeling. When I saw those thousands of staring eyes, I was silenced. On an earlier trip, I had visited Hiroshima where there is a Peace Memorial Museum. Among its exhibits is a watch that stopped at the exact time that the bomb was dropped. Fifty years after my visit, it is that silenced watch that I remember.

According to the poet Chris Agee, the dreadfulness of war, the Holocaust, and the bomb compose "the literally unspeakable realities of the century's history."[25] The horrors of the First World War, a "sound hell," changed the meaning and significance of silence. The battles of the Somme and Passchendaele were, of course, worse than any description of them could possibly be and led the then Prime Minister David Lloyd George to say, "The thing is horrible, and beyond human nature to bear and I can't go on any longer with the bloody business."[26]

Today's warfare, with solitary silent snipers, is often more silent and more dangerous than the noise that occurred in previous wars. But modern warfare can be noisy in other ways. Suzanne Steele was the Official Canadian War Artist embedded with the First Battalion Princess Patricia's Canadian Light Infantry in Afghanistan from 2008 to 2010. The poetry and blogs that she wrote from Afghanistan refer to a constant noise—the thudding and the pounding were relentless. Now even louder weapons have been invented; the Israeli army uses sonic booms to "break civilian support for armed Palestinian groups responsible for . . . suicide bombing."[27] The United States military are also experimenting with noise-creating devices; these sonic bullets are narrow beams of noise that exceed the human threshold of pain and can be totally disabling.[28]

Janine di Giovanni has spent much of her working life as a journalist in war zones and has written that as she grows older, quiet and silence have become more and more important to her. In her twenties, thirties, and forties, she was surrounded by bombs, gun explosions, and shouting soldiers, all of which led to her to experience the kind of hearing loss unique to the military. When she arrived in New York in 2017 as a Fellow at the Council on Foreign Relations, she wrote to me saying that she felt the nature of people's manners had changed since she'd last lived in the States. She had asked a woman who was shouting into her phone on a train to Washington, DC, if she could conduct her business call outside the carriage, but the woman "turned on me like a demon," she said. "You are sick!" the woman shouted. "Is there something wrong with you?" To compensate for this and other New York noises such as garbage trucks and loud partying, di Giovanni would escape at weekends to her mother's home in rural New Jersey: "I walk on the beach, I walk in the dense forest. I see enormous deer, startled, and on my beach walks, empty spaces. I need this to think. Without it, I would go mad. This much I know." But she was also aware of how frightening silence can be and has always appreciated having people around: "The other day I climbed the stairs to my fourth-floor walk-up and my neighbor was playing *Fiddler on the Roof*. It is a sound track my son and I love, and I began to sing along. Sometimes silence can be terrifying, and so, I welcome the sound of something warm and embracing and alive."[29]

12

Prison and Solitary Confinement

SILENCE HAS OFTEN been used as a form of punishment. Keeping people in solitary confinement has been and continues to be a cruel form of abuse, although in the eighteenth century, the silence and solitude endured by those in prison was thought to be beneficial. In the eighteenth century, it was John Howard—after whom the Howard League for Penal Reform is named—who recommended silence and solitude as a benefit to prisoners: "Solitude and silence are favourable to reflection and may possibly lead them to repentance."[1] Howard traveled widely, visiting hundreds of prisons to investigate how other countries dealt with their criminals. He was very struck by the Hospice of San Michele, a house of correction for young boys in Trastevere, Rome, established by Pope Clement XI in 1703. In the middle of the house was a notice on which the word *Silentium* was written. It was this silence that most impressed John Howard—the silence was interspersed with prayers and Mass, and the silence also helped the guards with their observations. Idleness was often deemed responsible for the misdemeanors of the youths.

At least here they all learned a trade, such as bookbinding, designing, smithing, carpentry, tailoring, shoemaking, spinning, knitting, or barbering. But during the day, the boys were chained to tables as they worked, and while at one end of the room was an altar, at the other, in disturbing contrast, was a punishment stand where they were lashed. Jonas Hanway, the Evangelical social reformer, philanthropist, and opponent of tea-drinking, declared that his plan for prisons was "solitude in imprisonment." He believed that by being alone in a cell, a prisoner would reflect on their past and would *have* to start contemplation and would, as a result, be driven to God. In 1842, fifty years after his death, Pentonville in London was opened as a model prison and Hanway's ideas were implemented. Prisoners had their names replaced by numbers and had to wear masks in the chapel and schoolroom to prevent conversation.

The nineteenth century brought about other experiments with silence in prisons. In 1822, the Eastern State Penitentiary in Fairmount, Philadelphia, the vision of the Founding Father Benjamin Rush, opened. The idea behind it was to imprison thieves, forgers, highway robbers, and murderers in isolation and silence. Each prisoner was to remain alone in their cell for the duration of the sentence; on occasion, this punishment was made even worse when a prisoner was put into a dark cell or dungeon for a time. This led to great suffering and was especially hard to endure for someone who was probably already fragile. As the neurologist Oliver Sacks stated, "The brain needs not only perceptual input but perceptual change."[2] Charles Dickens visited the Eastern State Penitentiary once on his American tour and wrote, "The system here is rigid, strict, and hopeless solitary confinement. I believe it, in its effects, to be cruel and wrong."[3] He observed that the faces of the convicts showed "a depth of terrible endurance in it which none but the sufferers themselves can fathom, and which no man has a right to inflict upon his fellow creature."[4] Dickens also visited many prisons in the UK, writing about them in both fact and fiction. In *David Copperfield*, the lightly disguised Pentonville Prison is visited by the hero;[5] and Amy Dorrit, in *Little Dorrit*, was born and raised in the Marshalsea debtor's prison where Dickens's own father had been imprisoned.[6] In the nineteenth century, Auburn State Prison in New York State also experimented with silence. When the inmates were at work they had to work in total silence, they ate in a communal dining room also in silence, and at night they were housed in individual cells—echoes of the correction house in Rome visited by John Howard.

SOLITARY CONFINEMENT

An enforced silence of a different kind is imposed on those in solitary confinement. Many prisoners in solitary are driven to insanity. Those who fare best are those who are educated, often political prisoners who have a sense of purpose. What seems vitally important for people in this situation is to keep some decision—however small—that is their own. It could be deciding to eat the meager food rations at a particular time of day rather than when the food arrives, or it might be deciding to walk a certain number of steps in the cell each day.

Eugenia Ginzburg was imprisoned in 1937 during Stalin's Great Purge and was often in solitary confinement. For much of the time she was in Yaroslavl, east of Moscow, where she found the nights particularly hard. She found the silence oppressive, but she also made the link between mind and body, although in a negative way: "The silence thickened, became tangible and stifling. Depression attacked not only the mind but the whole body . . . I would have given anything to have heard just one sound."[7]

During the Spanish Civil War, the journalist Arthur Koestler went to Spain as a correspondent for the *News Chronicle*, and in February 1937 he was arrested in Malaga by Francisco Franco's troops.

His fellow journalists had fled, but because of his loyalty, courage, obsessiveness, or ambition, he had stayed. He was taken to Seville and put in solitary confinement where he remained for ninety-four days. After his arrest, there was an international outcry, and following interventions from the British Parliament, the League of Nations, the Red Cross, and the Vatican, a prisoner exchange was arranged. He wrote later in *Dialogue with Death* that in jail he had felt free and able to face the ultimate reality: "Not afraid of death, only of the act of dying; and there were times when we overcame this fear. At such moments we were free—men without shadows, dismissed from the ranks of the mortal; it was the most complete experience of freedom that can be granted a man."[8] Three years after this episode he published *Darkness at Noon*, his novel about a man confined, interrogated, and executed in a Communist prison.[9]

Christopher Burney was captured during the Second World War while working for the Special Air Service. He was held in solitary confinement for fifteen months in Fresnes, France, before being transferred to Buchenwald concentration camp. However hungry he felt, he used to keep his bread ration to eat at a time that suited him, rather than consuming it instantly, which gave him some kind of control. In his book *Solitary Confinement*, he confesses that when his neighbor in the cell next door tried to make contact by tapping, having become so used to silence and his own thoughts, Burney resisted the approach as he found the thought of conversation an embarrassment. He had also realized that his months of solitude had been an exercise in liberty: "I had been left free to drop the spectacles of the near-sighted and to scan the horizon of existence ... and I believed I had seen something there. But it was only a glimpse, a remote and tenuous apprehension of what lay behind the variety and activity of life."[10]

Although Burney resisted making contact by tapping, many in Russian and Soviet prisons had used tapping as a way of communicating with their neighbors. In her memoir *Memoirs of a Revolutionist*,

Vera Figner, a Russian revolutionary political activist who spent much time in solitary confinement, described the "prisoners' alphabet." Envisaged as a grid with horizontal rows, it was used to tap out messages to adjoining cells. So much knocking went on between the prisoner's cells that the guards often had to work hard to drown out the constant tappings.[11]

When the Hungarian-born Edith Bone was working as a freelance correspondent in Budapest in 1949, she was accused of spying for the British government and got detained by the State Protection Authority. She was kept in solitary confinement for seven years without a trial, without even being given a prisoner identification number. After her release, she wrote *Seven Years Solitary*, in which she wrote, "Fortunately for myself I am not at all noise-sensitive; I used to live in a place where a tube-train roared past every few minutes, and if one can stick that, one is immune to noise."[12] And so it seems that for Bone, either too much noise or no noise was not the issue. To deal with the isolation, she concocted many strategies that involved mentally recreating the plots of the books she'd read, imagining geometry problems, practicing her languages, and composing poetry with letters she'd made from the coarse black bread she was fed. She made all these into goal-orientated projects, which gave her the control so vital to survival.

In 1967 during the Cultural Revolution, the British journalist Anthony Grey arrived as the Reuters Correspondent in Peking at a time when there were many ongoing anti-British protests. A few months after his arrival, Red Guards smashed into his house and his "crimes" were read out. His whole house was daubed with black paint, including his toothbrush, and his beloved cat was killed. He was put under house arrest, ostensibly for spying, and was initially confined to a small room at the bottom of his house. Before his incarceration, Grey had been allowed to choose three books from his bedroom to take into the room where he was confined. One of the books he chose was about yoga, something he practiced compulsively. Since yoga involves both body and mind, he felt that it was this that kept him sane. He believed that it was his guardian angel who, on his way to Peking, had led him to buy the book on yoga in Hong Kong, and that it was also his guardian angel who had ensured that the book had been in his bedroom at the time of his arrest. He often got depressed but gradually adjusted to the horror. Even though he was on meager rations, food and drink became less and less important, although the first time he was allowed an apple, he was ecstatic. Of course priorities change when you're leading such a pared-down existence. He spent a lot of time watching ants, an occupation that allowed him not to think about himself. At one point he killed an ant, but he was immediately full of remorse, realizing that this sadistic behavior was comparable to that of his Chinese captors. After three months of house arrest, he was moved to a slightly larger room in his house, and having managed to secure a pen, he started writing a diary, mostly in shorthand. He was under house arrest for a total of 806 days. During that time, he was allowed very few visitors and only had two twenty-minute consular visits. On his release, he said that he felt neither joy nor elation, just a great feeling of relief, but he was aware that he had become obsessed with himself. Afterward, when he was asked by friends how he had been able to bear it, he said that in their own way, anyone would. In his book *Hostage in Peking*, he does not refer much to the silence he endured, or whether he had appreciated it or abhorred it; however, he did say that when he was released, one of his biggest pleasures was being able to talk freely.[13] During his confinement he was never accused of anything; and one of the worse things must have been, as it must be for many in captivity, that while he was under house arrest he never knew how long it would last.

In 1968, at the height of the Cultural Revolution, Gladys Yang, a British translator of Chinese literature and the first person to graduate in Chinese literature from Oxford, "disappeared" with her husband, Yang Xianyi. They were released in 1972, after she had spent four years in solitary confinement. In her first letter home after her release, she wrote that until you had been in solitary, you wouldn't know how to appreciate the world.[14]

In 1985, the British businessman Roger Cooper was imprisoned for five years in the notorious Evin Prison in Tehran after a farcical trial. The book he wrote on his release, *Death Plus Ten Years*, refers to the sentence he was given. While he was in prison, he invented math games, thought about bridge, and devised anagrams. Because he spoke fluent Persian, he was able to engage with his guards. While he was in jail, he too preferred being on his own rather than with other prisoners. On his release, after the initial elation, he suffered from post-traumatic stress syndrome, finding it hard to engage with people.[15] While he was in prison, his friends, of whom I was one, had formed a Friends of Roger Cooper Society, something that he said subsequently was comforting but probably did nothing to hasten his release. I had my bookshop at the time, and I remember choosing books to send to him. Some got through to him, but many didn't.

In 1987, Terry Waite was negotiating the release of four hostages in Lebanon when he himself was captured. He was held prisoner until 1991, much of that time in solitary confinement. While imprisoned, he realized the importance of creating a routine, something that would give him some kind of control. On his release, he became increasingly attracted to the silence of the Quakers and repelled by the verbosity of many church services. In 2008 he joined the Religious Society of Friends.[16]

The Black Panther Albert Woodfox spent forty-four years in solitary in a cell that measured nine by six feet in the notorious Angola Prison in Louisiana for a crime he didn't commit. He finally had his conviction overturned by the US Court of Appeals in 2014, and he was eventually released in February 2016. Remarkably, when he talked about his incarceration, he said that "mind, heart, soul, and spirit I always felt free." His experience is related in his book *Solitary: Unbroken by Four Decades in Solitary Confinement—My Story of Transformation and Hope.*[17] He later said that he had "prospered" and "wouldn't change a thing" and that he wouldn't be the man he became had it not been for his time in prison.

We all recently had to learn how to live "under lockdown." At times this compulsory isolation wasn't easy, but I found that a good way of dealing with it was to have a routine. Of course, most of us are immensely privileged, having access to the internet and as many books as we want, so there really is little comparison to spending time in solitary confinement. Nevertheless, there is an occasional flash of recognition.

THE GULAG

No opposition is allowed by one-party states—both the media and anyone who disagrees with the authorities are silenced. On a large scale, this kind of silencing can lead to genocide. In "Mystical Experience of Loss of Freedom," an article published over thirty years ago in the *Network Newsletter* (the magazine of the Scientific and Medical Network), an anonymous political prisoner wrote that many imprisoned in the Soviet Union say that the arrest, imprisonment, the camps—indeed, the loss of freedom—became the most important experiences of their lives. Despite the psychic and physical suffering these people endured, many had moments of intense happiness and a feeling of being one with the universe, in ways that they had never experienced before.[18] Aleksandr Solzhenitsyn said repeatedly that it is only the spirit that can save and only the spirit that can preserve the body.[19] In the Gulag labor camps, the most important thing became to preserve the soul. When the soul was given priority over physical needs, the physical body survived; but with the loss of the spiritual, the physical body disintegrated. The anonymous political prisoner mentioned above stated that those who gave priority to their physical selves lost both inner and outer strength. Conversely, if an individual chose to save his or her soul, the choice between saving either the body or the soul did not have to be made—the body would follow the soul, and both body and soul would be preserved. The physical body was able to survive by listening to the inner voice, the mystical power or "God"; it was up to the individual to access this internal force, the force that could lead to freedom.[20] This seems to be an indication that within each individual's soul there is an unexplained psychic force that cannot be separated from the physical world. Stronger than anything external, this force has the ability to combat all outward forms of oppression and can lead to a feeling of freedom. Since there is no objective proof of any of this, there has to be faith that it is a possibility.

In the Gulag, all feelings, both negative and positive, were experienced more acutely, but in spite of all the suffering, there were very few suicides. Maybe this was attributable to that positive feeling that some prisoners had, of feeling free and completely at one with the universe. "Some savage force within the spirit suddenly asserts its control," Dimitri Panin, the author of *The Notebooks of Sologdin* who spent thirteen years in jails and forced labor camps, asserted.[21] He went on to say that the whole universe is in some mysterious way linked to the depth of our soul. In very different circumstances, these are the same feelings that Rear Admiral Richard E. Byrd had in the Antarctic. Each person has the freedom to decide whether to follow this inner voice, and if this voice is followed, the terrible experience of suffering and isolation in prison can bring a sense of inner freedom. Both thought and silent prayer can bring about tangible results. Solzhenitsyn asserts, "You only have power over people so long as you don't take everything away from them. But when you've robbed a man of everything, he's no longer in your power—he's free again."[22]

Panin wrote that the world resembles a white tablecloth with black spots rather than a black tablecloth with white spots. No totalitarian system has a chance of winning against this internal faith and conviction. Soviet Russia realized this when religion, however much it was persecuted and forbidden, continued to exist. Panin went on: "He who lets go of all outward trappings and decides from then on to obey his inner voice—which is only another name for faith—and then discovers to his amazement this mysterious yet real force at work not only inside himself but in the outer world, realizes at the same time that he is not master of this force and cannot use it as he wishes. On the contrary, he begins to understand that everything in his life, indeed life itself, is entirely dependent on the mysterious inner power, which, in the language of religion, is called God."[23]

This was echoed by Solzhenitsyn, who said, "Above all, don't cling to life. . . . Possess nothing, free yourself from everything, even those nearest to you, because they too are your enemies."[24] In the *Gulag Archipelago*, Solzhenitsyn tells a story about an astrophysicist in solitary confinement whose method of coping was to think of specific astrophysical laws and problems. However, at one point he could go no further, since he did not have the information he needed in order to complete the problem he was wrestling with. He began to pray, and "by mistake," a book on astrophysics was brought into his cell by a guard. It had exactly the material he needed, and he managed to learn the data before the error was realized and the book was swiftly taken away.[25]

Though Solzhenitsyn and many other prisoners in the Gulag understood that by nurturing the soul, the body would survive, there were, of course, many dark moments. Of course, not everyone found freedom in solitary. Many suffered from the oppressive silence.

People released from solitary find it hard to adjust on their release. It is also difficult to know how those waiting for someone to be released will react. I was in the bookshop one day in 1987 when a familiar figure walked in. I say familiar, but this was someone I hadn't seen for months. It was Charlie Glass, who had recently escaped from captivity in Beirut after being held hostage for sixty-two days. I remember rushing toward him and him giving me the most enormous hug—words seemed unnecessary. I didn't know Charlie that well and hugging had not been part of our relationship—but that silent greeting was exactly right.

OTHER PUNITIVE SILENCES

Imprisonment isn't the only way silence can be forcibly imposed. Historically there have been various forms of punishment created specifically to silence offenders. Forcibly imposing silence can be a terrible punishment and is something that can be done by one individual to another as social punishment, as well as by those in authority as a punitive action.

When I was growing up in the 1950s, it was taken for granted that one didn't interrupt adults. I was a shy child, and I felt that I had nothing to say anyway, so keeping silent came naturally. But I do remember being told that "children should be seen and not heard." The old English proverb, which dates from the fifteenth century, was especially directed to girls and young women, who were expected to keep quiet. It was first recorded in a collection of homilies written by the Augustinian clergyman John Mirk in *Mirk's Festial*, circa 1450: "Hyt ys old Englysch sawe: A mayde schuld be seen, but not herd."[26] Even Queen Elizabeth I, an extremely cultured and far from silent woman, had to contend with the ignominy of being silenced because she was a woman. Thomas Wilson, an English diplomat and judge, was her secretary of state, and it does seem odd that the Queen should have allowed him to have written the following about women in *The Arte of Rhetorique*: "What becometh a woman best, and first of all? Silence. What second? Silence. What third? Silence.

What fourth? Silence. Yea, if a man should aske me till Domes daie, I would still crie silence, silence."[27]

One particularly barbaric abuse that was reserved almost exclusively for women was the "scold's bridle," also known as a witch's bridle or brank's bridle. It was first recorded in Scotland in 1567 and resembled a muzzle or cage for the head. It was made of iron with a padlock at the back and a projecting spike that would go in the mouth when the bridle was closed. A husband could request that his wife wear one for being a nag or a scold. As part of the humiliation, the offender would be led round the town. The wearer couldn't speak, as any movement of the tongue meant that the tongue would be pierced. Beyond its silencing and ostracizing effect, other side effects included excessive saliva in the mouth.

Many of us likely experienced being socially ostracized, at least to some extent, as a child. In England, we have a phrase for this: being "sent to Coventry." It's an ostracization that can be very painful; it is as if you no longer exist, since no one talks to you or acknowledges your presence. Why it is called "Coventry" is unclear, but it is probably something to do with the Civil War when Oliver Cromwell sent some captured troops to Coventry, where they were not well received.

Some parents use silence as a weapon to punish children, and from a child's point of view, the pain can feel like being cut by a knife. Children often don't understand the reason behind the silence, and the fact that silence is the weapon of punishment means they won't get an explanation. When silence is used as a punishment, the anterior cingulate cortex, the part of the brain found near the front, is activated in the same way as it would be with physical pain, meaning that relegating someone to silence can count as emotional abuse.[28] Few people realize that this part of the brain that is triggered to recognize physical pain, such as a broken arm, is the exact same part that reacts to emotional pain. So when you hear of someone suffering the anguish of a broken heart, the pain is as real as any physical pain. By subjecting someone to silent punishment, you are therefore inflicting real pain. Likewise, when couples give each other the "silent treatment," it can be extremely damaging and painful in a relationship and can become a dangerous pattern that is very difficult to break.

The recent "no-platforming" of people whose ideas some might find upsetting—a British term for a form of activism on university campuses of not allowing those whose ideas are disagreed with to appear on stage—is another form of censorship. Freedom means having the ability to hear repugnant ideas and being able to disagree with them; silence in this instance is the enemy. I remember watching Nick Griffin of the far-right British National Party (BNP) on television during a *Question Time* debate; the consensus was that he lost badly. The argument is that by allowing such people to speak, it legitimizes their views, but it was so much better to see him exposed in this way, allowing him to make a fool of himself with his ultraright-wing opinions, rather than no-platforming him. In February 2005, Griffin was asked to speak at St. Andrews University by the president of the students' debating society, who said—correctly, in my opinion—"We believe that the only way to get the truth of what the BNP are saying and to combat them is to do it in public in a debate." But the debate was canceled. Griffin was also asked to the Cambridge Forum, but this was canceled as well. Chris Paley, the president of the Cambridge Forum, called the decision an "own goal" for the values of free speech, but the Liberal Democrat politician Lembit Öpik said that it was his belief that in a democracy, people had a right to make their own decisions. In October 2017, David Thomas wrote a letter to *The Spectator* that said that the silencing of speakers in colleges was a "frightening sign of our fear of ideas." He had gone to college in 1970 not only to study and develop his life experience but also to meet and argue with people with diametrically opposed ideas: "It was an all-round education . . . I never felt the need to be protected from the ideas and words of other people, the enemy of freedom is not fascism and communism: the enemy is silence."[29] The students currently at college who are denying free speech may feel that they are in control, but when they leave and maybe find that it is they themselves who are being controlled, they might not be able to complain about it; they might well be silenced for their views.

Recently there has been a trend by the police of shutting down public protests as a way of silencing protestors, and minorities get silenced by racial profiling. All worrying developments.

Nowadays, prisons tend to be very noisy, but some prisoners long for silence. In the Massachusetts Correctional Institution—Shirley (a medium-security state prison in Shirley, Massachusetts), a prisoner discovered Thomas Merton's *Seeds of Contemplation*[30] under a mattress. He found it so helpful that he helped form the forty-first chapter of the International Thomas Merton Society[31] at Shirley and a large library of Merton's books was donated, with the prisoners meeting regularly to discuss his books.

Indeed, the unexpected discovery of the "right" book at the right time is fascinating—Anthony Grey in Peking had his book on yoga, a prisoner in Shirley, Massachusetts, found Thomas Merton's *Seeds of Contemplation* under a mattress, and the astrophysicist in Siberia had exactly the right book on astrophysics brought to him when he needed it.

Many prisoners, including both Arthur Koestler and Anthony Grey who were discussed earlier, experience moments of feeling that there was some kind of "higher order" of reality with which solitude and silence had put them in touch—a feeling of "inner freedom" and an ability to confront the ultimate realities of life.[32] Some prefer being on their own rather than having to share a cell. There is a description of solitary confinement being like a lotus flower growing from the mud, and the new awareness gained from it can give a more intense enjoyment of existence. But after time spent in solitary and after returning to an ordinary existence, the genuineness of the experience seems to rapidly diminish.

GOING FORWARD

13

Conscious Listening

THE BOOK HAS EXAMINED silence by looking at individuals' experiences—including my own—as well as looking at its relationship to places in nature, existing structures, and spiritual and religious traditions. Its timeless intrigue is well represented in literature, visual arts, and music (ironically enough!). And we have also explored the darker sides of silence—such as during wartimes and as punishment. After this exploration we have taken together, how might you approach silence moving forward in life? The main thing is to be mindful of both noise and silence, and to continue to learn and grow from a place of curiosity rather than fear.

LEARNING FROM CULTURE

"Talk is talk; silence is wisdom," according to an Algonquin saying. We can learn much from other cultures about the benefits of silence, as there certainly is a cultural element to talking and not talking. Indigenous people and other cultures understand silence better than most. According to Washakie, chief of the Shoshones in the nineteenth century, "The Indian finds words hard to utter because of his full heart. The white man speaks with his tongue but the Indian with his heart and the heart has no tongue."[1]

The British tend to try to fill awkward silences, often with inane chatter; it seems hard to remain silent. In *The Hitchhiker's Guide to the Galaxy*,[2] Ford Prefect cannot understand why humans have to fill their silences with inanities like "What a nice day." Karen Armstrong, the writer on comparative religion, was made aware of this when she was making her six-part television series about St. Paul.[3] In Jerusalem, on her first morning of filming, when she was trying to fill an awkward silence, the director Joel growled at her: "If you have something to say, say it! If not, *sheket*."[4] And very often he would say to her, "You are not in England now!" Later during that same journey, Armstrong was taken to Jericho to watch the sun rise over the desert. The car radio was playing the Mendelssohn violin concerto, so it wasn't actually a silent occasion, but she remarked that fortuitously there was no polite conversation to interrupt the mood.

It is not easy to break from the norms of the culture one has been brought up in. What is polite in one society could be considered rude in another, and silence is a prime example. For instance, Finland seems to have a different approach to silence than many other places. Horatio Clare traveled to the Arctic on a Finnish icebreaker and by talking to the crew learned to deconstruct "the different grades" of Finnish silence, eventually coming to conclude that Finnish reserve "out-reserves even the British version. . . . There are relaxed silences, companionable, puzzled, contented, unhappy, charged and thoughtful silences, even lyrical silences." He then attempted to join one of the crew in a thoughtful silence but realized that "I am doing this wrong. I am eating his silence—we can both feel it. No, worse, I am listening to his silence. Of course! How can you hope to share a silence if one of you is eavesdropping on the other? Quickly, I must listen to my own silence."[5] This is interesting and I suppose could be the reason that can make certain silences awkward—eavesdropping on another's silence feels like a huge invasion of privacy. Clare's book *Icebreaker: A Voyage Far North* has some first-rate descriptions: "In sheened black water ice floats in shattered fragments. The only motion outside is three hooded crows, heading in a straggle for an island through huge stillness. You can see silence here."[6] I have not come across many descriptions of visual silence, but this reminds me of my own experience of floating among the icebergs in Antarctica.

In order to experience and try to understand silence, the Norwegian explorer Erling Kagge wanted to be entirely alone in Antarctica for fifty days. In his recent book *Silence: In the Age of Noise*, which includes his solo trek to Antarctica, he admitted that on his journey there, he discarded the batteries from the phone that the aviation company insisted he take with him. Kagge thinks that the mind needs to be trained to "hear" silence and that it should be possible for everyone to discover silence within themselves. He addresses three questions: What is silence? Where is it? Why is it more important now than ever? For our sanity, I believe that we need to start thinking seriously about what we stand to lose if we ignore the need for silence. Looking back into the past we can tell that it has *always* been important, but never more so than now in this increasingly frantic noise-driven world in which we live. We are now permanently connected to one another through social media; this has never happened before. Our gadgets can, of course, be switched off, and this is a choice that anyone can make. But it's hard. It is difficult to put a value on silence because, of course, silence is free. And we tend to think of value in monetary terms. You don't have to go anywhere special to find it, and you can even be silent in a noisy environment. But once you have discovered your silence within, it is always there—hard as that might be to remember in a rowdy place. Kagge reminds us to "keep in mind that the silence you experience is different from that which others experience. Everyone possesses their own."[7]

People have different ways of getting to that place of silence. The psychotherapist Nicholas Pearson has realized that for him to get to a place of peace, there has to be a pursuit of No-Thing: "The pursuit of Silence is indeed a most fascinating subject and one I think, in our heavily overloaded and determinedly materialistically one-sided age, one of the most important pursuits of all."[8] Pearson says that it took him a long time to understand the true value of silence, despite many years of searching. He had tried meditating, but he had found all forms of meditation too busily in search of something. But his quest eventually changed: "Firstly I began to see that the thing I really sought was No-Thing . . . literally nothing." Many of us tend to search for what we think we need, when actually whatever this thing is, is often right in front of us. Pearson found "seeking No-Thing" in sources as diverse as Meister Eckhart, Taoism, and Sufism, and it led him to change his perspective into the quiet of his own "simple awareness." Through the work of Douglas Harding's *On Having No Head*,[9] Pearson found the place just behind his own head that was "nowhere" and "nothing," and it was here that he found both silence and peace. He quotes Carl Jung, who said that "the tricks we use in the first half of life don't seem to work quite so well in the second half." As we get older, it becomes more and more important to find a safe place for ourselves where we can just be. Having discovered this place of safety, we know that it can always be there, even though that is sometimes hard to remember, and this place—which for Pearson is just behind his head—is a place of "profound creative silence." There is a stillness that comes with seeking NOTHING: "It is as if the created world of our everyday experience arises from out of this place of Nothing. . . that the God, or the Awareness or the pure Consciousness we seek is most profoundly, to our limited human faculties, quite simply . . . NO THING." Out of this space, the whole plenitude of creation can emerge with all its manifestations . . . "and yet, the thing that is perhaps most real . . . is the No Thing."[10] Simple, but not easy.

Many cultures use drugs as an aid to spiritual awakening, and of course many Westerners have experimented with peyote and ayahuasca among others. In 1953, Aldous Huxley took mescaline, a psychedelic alkaloid that comes from the peyote cactus, for the first time and wrote about his experiences in *The Doors of Perception*.[11] When Stephen Batchelor took it, he wrote that all that mattered was the "undiluted intensity of the moment, the keen lucidity of the senses, the ecstatic silence."[12] He was so wrapped up in his own silence that even when he had been urged to participate more fully, he didn't. This led to one of the participants writing to him later to tell him that he hadn't realized how "beautiful silence is."[13]

The Southern Italian code of silence, *omertà*, is widely used by the Mafia and other criminal organizations to make certain that silence is maintained during questionings by the authorities and outsiders. Omertà also ensures that if one has been witness to a crime—or indeed, a victim of a crime—there is no informing to the powers that be. This imposed silence is regarded as an extreme form of loyalty, to the extent that one wouldn't betray even one's deadliest enemy. The breaking of omertà is often punishable by death. In 1963, the Italian-American mafioso Joe Valachi was the first to break this code of silence when, from prison, he testified to a US Senate committee about the existence of the Mafia, telling them about its structure, operations, rituals, and membership.

AUDITORY CONDITIONS

Of course, it's always important to remember that both silence and sound are experienced in different ways by everyone. The author Bella Bathurst started to lose her hearing when she was twenty-eight. It was a gradual process that she fought against, not admitting to her friends that it was happening. In her book *Sound*, she describes the process and reveals a particularly fraught occasion when she was working as crew on a sailing boat and could not hear the instructions addressed to her properly; she was reluctant to disclose this, even though she knew it could be putting everyone on the boat in danger. Eventually she became profoundly deaf, losing around 80 percent of her hearing. After twelve years, she heard about a French surgeon who she was told might be able to restore her hearing by doing a delicate operation on the inner ear. She had the operation and did indeed regain most of her hearing, rediscovering the marvels of sound. She wrote that she became a better listener, realizing that while sight gives you the world, hearing gives you a specific access to other people. At the book launch of *Sound* at the Wellcome Foundation in 2017, I asked her whether silence had different qualities for those who are deaf. She said that that indeed was the case and that silence for her as a deaf person had been a muffling, a double-glazing or solid thing between her and the world. When she had almost recovered from her operation, she went to hear the Berlin Philharmonic with Sir Simon Rattle and was so overcome by the beauty of the music—Beethoven, I think—that she ends her book with: "I think the whole thing was almost worth it just for that single experience. Almost."[14]

The incidence of depression is four times higher among those with hearing loss than for the population as a whole. But there is, of course, a distinction between those born deaf—around sixty thousand people in the UK and about two to three out of every thousand babies in the US are born with some kind of hearing loss. Those born deaf have their own community and culture, often using sign language and those who have become deaf later in life and who do not share this culture inherited at birth. There were many deaf people at the launch of Bathurst's book in 2017, obvious from the way people at opposite sides of the auditorium were signing with each other. Certain schools now teach sign language to all their pupils. At my great-nephew's primary school in Manchester, the whole class is learning sign language, as one of the children is deaf.

Sign languages are not universal and are not mutually intelligible with each other, though there are striking similarities. Deaf people have used sign languages throughout history. In Plato's *Cratylus*, Socrates says, "If we hadn't voice or a tongue, and wanted to express things to one another, wouldn't we try to make signs by moving our hands, head, and the rest of our body, just as dumb people do at present?"[15]

There is a theory that people with locked-in syndrome, a rare neurological disorder in which there is complete paralysis of all muscles except the ones that control the movement of the eyes and in which cognitive function is usually unaffected, are happy; the longer they are "locked-in," the happier they become. Seemingly the brain protects itself by not processing negative feelings. I'd like to believe this, but I'm not sure that I do! The French journalist Jean-Dominique Bauby had a massive stroke and suffered from locked-in syndrome. Bauby's book *The Diving-Bell and the Butterfly*, painstakingly written by blinking his left eye, charts his life in the hospital: "Far from such din, when blessed silence returns, I can listen to the butterflies that flutter inside my head. To hear them, one must be calm and pay close attention, for their wingbeats are barely audible."[16] The book was published to great acclaim, but Bauby died just two days after its publication. This enforced silence must have been extremely frustrating for him, but the people around him knew that he had the ability to speak and write. How much worse for those who are assumed not to have the ability to communicate with words. This was so for Jonathan Bryan, a boy born with severe cerebral palsy among other life-threatening illnesses. From an early age, Jonathan's mother read to him widely; although he was unable to communicate verbally, she could sense that he understood. His hidden abilities were recognized due to the dedication and belief of his parents, his caregivers, and a teacher named Sarah. A method was devised that allowed him to spell out words by looking at letters with his eyes.

The end result of this was an astonishing book called *Eye Can Write* in which Chantal, Jonathan's mother, writes about his life from her perspective—but the bulk of the book is written by Jonathan and is about his feelings, his belief in God, and the "garden" that he goes to during his many acute hospital stays and illnesses. He always finds it a wrench to come back from that garden where he feels free and able to move his limbs at will, and to have to reinhabit his extremely disabled body again. But one of the reasons that he does haul himself back is that he feels so passionately that other people in his situation should have the opportunity that he had to learn to read and write.[17] With this in mind, he set up a charity called Teach Us Too which promotes an education system in which all children are taught literacy regardless of their label (www.teachustoo.org.uk). The label attached to Jonathan was PMLD (profound and multiple learning difficulties). With this label, his lessons in his special school would be repeated every year and never advanced beyond the basics. At age seven, he was taken out of his special school for an hour a day to be taught by his mother and caregivers. He also started going to his local primary school where he excelled and where his fellow pupils helped him with his writing device. I'm sure that this was beneficial for them as well as for him. Imagine how many other people, both adults and children, have had to live with the label PMLD, thereby living a life condemned to silence. This is not a silence anyone would welcome. Of course, one of the main issues preventing dedicated help in such cases is funding, but just as importantly we should all be made aware that labels attached to people are often misleading and should be looked on with suspicion.

Misophonia is a condition in which certain sounds can be deeply disturbing to the sufferer. Sufferers experience changes in brain activity when they hear a particular sound, like paper rustling or someone eating popcorn in the cinema. This oversensitivity to noise can make much of modern life almost unbearable. Noisy restaurants, for instance, can reduce someone with misophonia almost to tears; it's not just the volume but some sounds or frequencies can trigger an adverse reaction that can also cause physical pain and headaches. A friend described her condition: "Apparently I used to scream as a small child when anyone rustled brown paper; these days it's more likely to be the sound of someone rustling a crisps packet (made from a kind of metallized plastic film) or unwrapping a sweet slowly: it's a harsh sound that seems to go straight through the head and set the teeth on edge."

The Musicians Union says that hearing damage is a major problem for orchestra players, and hearing problems among musicians are massive. Chris Goldscheider, a viola player, sued the Royal Opera House for ruining his hearing. In 2012 during rehearsals of Wagner's *Die Walkure*, brass instruments were placed directly behind him in the orchestra pit, with the sound peaking at 137 decibels, the same loudness as a jet engine. Goldscheider suffered from acoustic shock, which causes the brain to hugely amplify ordinary everyday sounds. This can make day-to-day living horrendous. The Royal Opera House denied responsibility and also refused to recognize acoustic shock as a condition. But in 2018, Goldscheider won his case—something with huge implications for the music industry.

Very loud music is certainly detrimental to hearing. The higher the decibel of sound, the more pressure we are subjected to. If 0 decibels is inaudible, and 180 is what is produced from a rocket launch pad, permanent damage can occur with prolonged exposure with anything above 85, or after just ten minutes with 110 decibels. Ears can feel damaged after exposure to loud music or other loud sounds; the hearing system protects itself by briefly going slightly deaf. The potential at a rock concert is 150.[18] It is incredibly annoying to hear the music escaping from the headphones of the person next to you on the subway, but while it is temporary and irritating for you, they are doing great damage to their ears; exposure to loud noise produces auditory damage, causing irreparable nerve and sensory organ damage in the inner ear. People who go to rock concerts have a temporary hearing loss; but if they go again and again, permanent damage is almost guaranteed. Due to the prevalence of headphones and loud music there is currently an epidemic of hearing loss, but oddly—bearing in mind the social isolation of deafness—a surprising amount of people who go to be treated for hearing loss are only pretending to be deaf. The World Health Organization (WHO) estimates that by 2050 around one in four people will be living with some kind of hearing loss.[19] The WHO website also stated in March 2022 that "Millions of teenagers and young people are at risk of hearing loss due to the unsafe use of personal audio devices and exposure to damaging sound levels at venues such as nightclubs, bars, concerts, and sporting events."[20]

Manowar, an American heavy metal band from Auburn, New York, is known for its loud and bombastic sound and is, according to *The Guinness Book of Records*, the loudest band in the world. What a claim! And what has their music done to their hearing? Gallows, a British punk band, claimed to be even louder. It seems that Guinness has stopped this particular "award" as too many people were competing for the title and going deaf in the process.

A 2019 article in *The Guardian* detailed a mysterious hum that millions of people in urban areas all over the world claim to hear. Known as "the Hum," it is experienced by many people as a consistent low-pitched noise sounding like a constant throbbing drone, something like the bass frequency of a heavy truck with its engine on idle. It was first noted in the UK in the 1970s, and Britain still has the most reported cases. It wasn't observed in the US until the 1990s, but now it effects people worldwide, with an estimated 4 percent of the population hearing it.[21] David Deming, a geoscientist from the University of Oklahoma who hears the Hum, wrote that it is not a form of tinnitus but can be felt throughout the body with symptoms that range from insomnia to headaches and dizziness. The only relief from it seems to be to apply some kind of masking noise, which could be something like an ordinary electric fan.

It is thought that those who hear it are possibly picking up on certain wavelengths from radio transmissions. Some sufferers are nearly driven to suicide. In 1992, one sufferer wrote, "Last year it [the Hum] almost drove me to suicide, it completely drains energy, causing stress and loss of sleep. I have been on tranquilizers and have lost count of the number of nights I have spent holding my head in my hands, crying and crying."[22] People in the small coastal town of Largs, Scotland, with a population of twelve thousand, have been hearing the Hum since the 1980s, whereas Glasgow—only about twenty miles away—has very few sufferers. Since most people don't hear it, the Hum is not thought to be an acoustical sound. However, its origins are still a mystery; it is not thought to be psychosomatic.

PUBLIC POLICIES

"Of all modern phenomena, the most monstrous and ominous, the most manifestly rotting with disease, the most grimly prophetic of destruction, the most clearly and unmistakably inspired by evil spirits, the most instantly and awfully overshadowed by the wrath of heaven, the most near-to-madness and moral chaos, the most vivid with devilry and despair, is the practice of having to listen to loud music while eating a meal in a restaurant."[23] So wrote the English author and philosopher G. K. Chesterton, and this was well before the kind of loud music that now plays in many restaurants. Restaurants seem to be magnets for noise with echoing rooms. I have often asked for music to be turned down in restaurants and the staff are mostly obliging, but there's little that can be done in shops. Many restaurants make themselves intentionally loud with their wooden floors, which make sound reverberate against a hard ceiling. A quick turnover and an increase in alcohol consumption is ensured when conversation is drowned out by loud music. In many bars and restaurants, the music gets louder as the evening progresses so that more drink is consumed, leading to more profit. Of course if restaurants are too quiet and the tables too close together, there'd be little privacy to be had. But privacy is not much use if there is so much noise you can't hear your companion speak. Unfortunate staff get very disturbed by the same music on a loop; this led one Starbucks supervisor to say that if she had to listen to "Hamilton one more time I'm getting a ladder and ripping out all of our speakers from the ceiling."[24]

Pipedown, the campaign for the freedom from piped music in shops and restaurants, has as its tagline "You can close your eyes but not your ears."[25] Among its illustrious patrons are the pianist Alfred Brendel, the writer Philip Pullman, the actor and novelist Tom Conti, the conductor Simon Rattle, and the actor and media personality Stephen Fry. The journalist Rachel Johnson told me that she is leaving a substantial legacy to Pipedown. Pipedown is concerned that throughout the last century and into this one, there has been a massive increase of background music, but they are also concerned about the noise from sirens, traffic, and planes. They claim that 50 percent of people leave or don't go into a shop that has piped music. I find this an odd statistic as I'm sure that the shops that have piped music have installed it for marketing purposes to encourage people to shop with them. Would they really be willing to let 50 percent of their customers leave? The fact that so many people wear headphones means that public announcements on trains and buses have to be louder than necessary in order to be heard through the headgear.

But as with everything, there is always another side. The author Marlon James said on the radio show *Desert Island Discs* that an absence of sound made him uneasy.[26] The former nun Lavinia Byrne, who is a friend, responded to my request about silence with the following: "D'you know: as a raging extrovert I absolutely hate silence.

I listen to Radio 4 all day long, with brief smatterings of Radio 3. I talk endlessly to Maud and Ottoline, my dogs . . ." She thinks that she probably overdosed on silence when she was a young nun, which might be the reason that she so loves sound now. "I've always loved music too and find huge comfort in it, though I'm distressed to think the tune my dogs hear most often is probably the theme to *The Archers!*"[27] There are others who balk at the idea of silence, reckoning that they'll get enough of it when they're dead. But who knows if that will be the case!?

An inevitable consequence of economic development is that it brings with it more roads, airports, bigger cities, tall buildings, and an increase in noise pollution. In New York City, city officials receive over a thousand complaints about noise daily.[28] In the twenty-four-hour society in which most of us now live, there is never a silent time. In 2006, Shanghai City Council authorized the right to twenty-four-hour construction, resulting in twenty-four-hour noise pollution.[29] Tall buildings both screech and whistle, and the CitySpire building in New York originally had sets of louvre shutters that made such a din that they had to be removed.[30]

In 1950, commuters at Grand Central Station demanded silence from Muzak, an American brand of background music, and the "right not to listen."[31] If you don't want to see something temporarily, you can always close your eyes, but the same does not apply to noise. Sound can therefore be an imposition. It can be very difficult to shut out other people's noise. Odysseus ordered his sailors to block their ears with beeswax as their ship approached the Sirens, as the Sirens' aim was to lure sailors with music and songs to eternal silence.[32] Somewhere I feel would benefit from silence is in the Sistine Chapel in Rome; it is difficult to appreciate Michelangelo's work with hordes of people talking, despite the regular pleas for silence from a loudspeaker, and I found that the loudspeaker was even more distracting than the hum of conversations.

A study from Denmark published in the *British Medical Journal* stated long-term residential exposure to traffic noise is detrimental to health: noise from road transport is linked to an increase in dementia.[33] The threshold for "serious annoyance" caused by environmental noise is 55 decibels, and a World Health Organization study found that 210 million European citizens are regularly exposed to 55 decibels or more from road and rail.[34] In America, the Occupational Safety and Health Administration (OSHA) states that over 30 million Americans are exposed to hazardous noise each year.[35] The frightening thing about this is that this kind of noise is the number one work-related health issue in the US. Helicopters are very noisy, and unmanned aerial vehicles (UAVs) looming above us, which will most certainly increase in numbers, are a new danger.[36] Technology will, of course, invent methods to silence things, we've already found ways to block or redirect sound waves. A device called Silenceair[37] cancels out noise waves, and this mechanism could be put outside air-conditioning units, thereby reducing the noise by up to 34 decibels.

Our noisy modern world has led to an increase in tinnitus, the perception of sound, or ringing in the ears when there is no external sound present. It can be caused by aging, and stress, and exposure to loud sounds over a prolonged period. There is no cure for tinnitus, but people who experience it use various strategies to help them deal with it, such as training themselves to ignore it, using "white noise," and practicing de-stress activities such as meditation and relaxation. There is a need to feel that you are controlling it rather than the other way round. It is a horrible condition—I have it mildly myself—because with tinnitus comes a total loss of silence. Perhaps one doesn't think too much about one's own silence until it no longer exists. A friend of mine who suffers from tinnitus feels that she has lost silence, realizing this one day in Wales as she "was lying back on the warm sheep nibbled grass with my eyes shut when it suddenly hit me that I could never be sure of silence again. Inside my head is a perpetual stream of rushing, whistling, and pulsing sounds." She manages to create a silence for herself by deciding whether she wants to listen to the sounds in her head: "Be still and find some silence. . . Be still and allow silence to find you. . ."[38]

The art historian David Fraser Jenkins described what it was like to work in a noisy part of London today and how many layers of silence are masked by noise. His office was high under the roof at Tate Britain, with a large electric fan just beneath his window already whirring noisily when he arrived in the morning and its noise only diminishing when it was turned off at 6 p.m. He writes, "I could then hear arrive an irresistible and crashing silence in the aural world where it used to live. This was a positive silence, like a pressure released." But then the usual London noises, which had been there all the time, took over: "So the silence turned out to be not silent at all, even if certainly so in comparison to the racket from the fan. Silence must be ever present, and only obscured by noise, like the coloured ground of a painting beneath its figures. I hear the tic toc of my clock, but I cannot concentrate enough to hear the gaps between them."[39]

None of this is new. People have seen the danger of noise for many years. In a letter to *The Times* in 1959, John Connell, a civil servant, wrote that we tend to forget that noise is a major pollutant. As a result of this, he founded the Noise Abatement Society, a society that was responsible for initiating both rubber dustbin lids and plastic milk crates.

It is not just humans who are adversely affected by noise. The journalist and editor Mary Wakefield wrote in *The Spectator* that British songbirds have started singing late at night since the daytime traffic drowns them out and they have an urgent need to be heard.[40]

The dawn chorus around airports now begins earlier, before airplane flights have begun, and whales sing louder in shipping lanes. During the COVID-19 lockdown, many people assumed that birds were singing louder than usual, when in fact the reverse was true. Since the birds were competing with less humanmade noise, they were in fact singing softer than normal.

FINDING A SILENT SPACE

The Rt. Rev. Dr. Michael Marshall gave a sermon at Holy Trinity Church in London's Sloane Street during Lent in March 2019 in which he recommended trying to make time to seek out a place in which to find silence and solitude. One need not go to a hermitage or meditation retreat, take a vow of silence, or construct sound-proof rooms to find a silent place. Nowadays we tend to look after our physical bodies by going to a gym or by jogging and the like, but Marshall stressed that our inner life and spiritual well-being also need exercising. He suggested that our churches should be "open, empty, and silent, offering sacred space" and that they should be there for those who want to step aside for a while in order to recover that inner silence "through which God may speak to the ears of our hearts." He suggested adopting Thomas Merton's fourfold formula: "Silence is a listening to the truth of things. If we do not listen, we do not come to truth. If we do not pray, we do not even get as far as listening. The four things go together: silence, listening, prayer, truth"—the truth about ourselves, others, and God.[41]

The Jungian analyst Anne Baring has described her feelings about silence and how she has made it intrinsic to her life. She wonders how many people in this frenetic world consciously make a time for silence by creating a sanctuary in both their home and their heart. According to her, by creating a space for the "agitated mind" to rest, it becomes possible to find somewhere to forget about daily worries and "the soul can enter the door you have opened and make itself known to you." All kinds of thoughts, feelings, and creative ideas can emerge and, as we know from the coronavirus lockdown, we are far more likely to hear the sounds of nature. Baring goes on to write, "You may even remember who you are in your soul-essence and why you have decided to live a life on this planet. You may find through the Silence you have allowed to exist that the visible world has been reconnected with the invisible one. None of this can happen without Silence."[42]

The journalist Rachel Johnson craves silence, often retreating to her house on Exmoor, a wild moorland area in the west of England. She explains, "I love and crave silence, which is why I am sitting in the depths of a river valley on Exmoor and all I can hear is a wood pigeon, a bumble bee thudding against a windowpane in another room, and the high twittering of birds I can't name, birdsong that sounds like conversation on a planet far sweeter and purer than ours. And the strokes of my fingers on the MacBook keyboard as I write this for you!"[43]

There are some people who find it easier to be silent while "doing" and creating. An artist friend, Liz Claridge, who loves and needs silence, relishes her days of silence when there are no calls on her attention: "I feel deprived of oxygen if I don't get enough silence. Living and working alone I can achieve silence easily," but she finds it easier to be active in her silence—whether it be gardening, making art, or washing up. "Silence enables me to 'do' mindfully, concentrated on the task." But this happy "doing" can be ruined by self-attacking thoughts—all beginning with the word *I*: "With no 'thou' around to bolster a benign sense of myself, or at least distract me, I am at their mercy." To gain peace of mind, she would like to banish *I* from her mental vocabulary.[44]

However much we can incorporate silence into our home lives, most of us still have to go out to work (although this has changed post-pandemic). Not only can places of work be noisy but there is also the getting there. The Bhagavad Gita encourages silent work, saying that if someone finds silence in their work and then discovers that silence is work, this person will find peace in their work.[45] These verses promote silent work but also state that silence can be found *in* work. In what kind of work can silence be found? I suspect that it can be found in any work that is truly absorbing and that this is a silence that needn't be thought about—it just rather wonderfully happens. If you work as an artist or a writer, you can choose to work in silence, but much work involves a certain amount of sound, which isn't all bad. The aim isn't to create a totally silent world but to be more mindful about both sound and soundlessness.

After Karen Armstrong had left her convent, left Oxford, left her teaching job, and embarked on writing her book *A History of God*,[46] she found herself alone with her books in a silent world. She would go for days without speaking to anybody. At first this silence had seemed a deprivation, since she had spent years resisting solitude, but she gradually began to see this silence as something positive, something "that seemed to hum, gently but melodiously, and orchestrate the ideas that I was contending with, until they started to sing too, to vibrate and reveal an unexpected resonance."[47] She felt almost able to listen to the silence, and it made her feel at home and alive; it had become her teacher. Although in the convent she had spent much of her time in silence, she recognized that it was a busy silence full of attention, anxiety, anger, and irritation; whereas her solitary silence felt like a "soft shawl." She felt this solitary silence seeping into her, allowing it to open up wide spaces in her head, and she became convinced that this was the only way to study religion. She taught herself theology and found herself "hour by silent hour, falling in love with my subject." She also found that the silence she lived in opened her ears and eyes to the suffering of the world, and she felt that she could hear the pain that is behind the anger and arrogance in social and political life: "Silence and solitude strip away a skin, they break down that protective shell of heartlessness which we cultivate in order to prevent ourselves from being overwhelmed by the suffering of the world that presses in upon us on all sides."[48]

Silence and solitude can, of course, also be found outside and in open spaces. If you lose yourself to wild places and can immerse yourself in the silence of woods, hills, the sea, or desert, Thomas Merton writes, "sit still while the sun comes up over that land and fills its silences with light." After an active day, "to sit still again in meditation in the evening when night falls upon that land and when the silence fills itself with darkness and with stars,"[49] the silence can be truly beneficial. Merton says that there are only a few who can belong completely to this silence (maybe because the majority of us don't give it time) and who can "let it soak into their bones, to breathe nothing but silence, to feed on silence, and to turn the very substance of their life into a living and vigilant silence."[50]

But before searching for a completely silent place—is there even such a thing?—it might be worth reflecting on Blaise Pascal's adage that "all of humanity's problems stem from man's inability to sit quietly in a room alone."[51] Pascal may have been happy to sit in his room, a confined area, alone, but as we have seen he found the "eternal silence of infinite spaces" frightening.[52] In *A Room of One's Own*, Virginia Woolf extols the importance for women to have a room with a lock on the door in order to be able to write.[53] I think it's important to try to find silent space for oneself, either inside or outside; this is obviously harder in a city but not impossible. It can be disillusioning to go somewhere specifically searching for silence only to find that the silence you had hoped for doesn't exist. When the journalist Rachel Johnson retreats to her cottage on Exmoor, she often hears dogs in a nearby cottage barking and barking with "the volleys reverberating around the valley."[54]

In his book *Science and Spiritual Practices*, Rupert Sheldrake wrote that since the modern world is full of noise and distractions, meditation is one way of being silent, but there are others. "Finding times and places to be silent is one of the simplest ways to expand our sensory and spiritual awareness."[55] When he is walking alone and in silence, he becomes far more observant, noticing birds and flowers in more detail. He finds the same in an art gallery; by chatting to someone in front of a painting he finds himself constrained by words. When sound draws one in, it can be rather overwhelming and one becomes less responsive to the visual. Silence encourages our inner thoughts as well as enhancing our other senses. Sheldrake wrote that "silence helps us to be more open to sights and sounds and smells, and to the world around us,"[56] and he observed that there have always been wild and silent places even within a city—the art today is in finding them. Many places of worship are open during the day, and when there is no service, they can provide oases of silence and stillness in the middle of a bustling city.

The poet and gardener Sean Swallow wrote to me about what silence means to him and how it has become something that has grown increasingly important in his life. In the same way that words are often necessary for teaching silence, he finds that it is the paradox that strikes him. If a blank page can be seen as the equivalent of silence, "then writing about silence fills the void. It could be in a sense interruptive or disruptive to write about it." He thinks of himself as naturally quite a noisy person who led a noisy and reckless childhood and says that he often writes noisy poems with conflicting voices. He questions why one would choose silence and describes how he came to it only in desperation, finding it healing after a breakdown: "I was addicted to a lot of things, and noise was part of drowning out the chaos. And numbing the negative outcome of that chaos. Active addiction is noisy. I could neither settle with myself nor sit in silence." Swallow was terrified of silence: "The television, radio, my mouth—something was always turned on, and turned up very loud!" But since addiction is treatable, there is also hope:

"The deep enriching flip side to my recovery is an increasing love of silence." He recommends trying to find the silence around thoughts and making friends with yourself, thereby finding a certain kind of spiritual peace. Finding silence and peace of mind in a garden is obviously easier than under the runway of a jet engine—but maybe the spiritually advanced don't have that problem; silence can be a state of mind or being and can be available anywhere. Swallow concludes that for words on silence to have a real impact, as in the poems of R. S. Thomas and W. S. Graham, "there must be some devotional practice prior to the written word." They "are effective because they extend from within silence and are not standing outside and commenting on it." Our brains devote a whole lot of energy to "extraneous, jumbled-up thoughts . . . So in another sense, silence is the attitude of relinquishing mental anxiety." The realization that life is painful and that one isn't in control and that one will die can inevitably lead to a cacophony of noisy thoughts, but if you can learn to sit with these thoughts, in silence, a deep sense of being can emerge: "'Be still and know that I am God.' Stillness—silence's sister."[57]

But silence has to be chosen, not imposed by social isolation, something that can make it seem bleak and disorientating. The silence forced on so many people by the 2020 pandemic has already had devastating results to many people's mental health. Silence, even when it is chosen, has an exacting aspect. Embracing it can be part of a spiritual journey, but there is inevitably a lack of connectedness with others—since as Liz Claridge said you are alone with yourself, there is no "other" to reinforce the sense of "I." For a follower of a theistic religion, God can be put into this space of "thou," and for Buddhists, the aim is toward an ego-free state of bliss. But there are many who do not have anything with which to fill this gap. As Andrew Harvey says, "The things that ignore us save us in the end. Their presence awakens silence in us; they refresh our courage with the purity of their detachment."[58]

Tragedies often galvanize us into holding silent vigils or occasions. Being silent in a group is very powerful, and it is this collective power that makes a silent gathering special.

The 2015 Wim Wenders film *Pope Francis: A Man of His Word* shows Pope Francis visiting the typhoon-ravaged Philippines. He tells the crowd, many of whom had lost members of their families as well as their homes, "I don't know what to tell you—I can only be silent. I accompany you silently in my heart."[59] That silence is more powerful than any words could have been.

The two-minute silence commemorating Armistice Day has become an established tradition. A year after the calamity of the devastating fire at Grenfell Tower in West London in 2017 in which seventy-two people died, survivors gathered for a silent walk, described by one participant as something that in its strength, compassion, and power they had never experienced before. Evidently only a slight prompt was necessary before the march began—silently. One of the participants on the march wrote on the Quaker website: "I've been learning lots about the collective power of silence since starting to work for Quakers. And the silence for Grenfell was held by the most incredible community supporting one another in grief, whilst searching for the three words that kept echoing in the signs people carried—love, truth, justice."[60] In the words of the community members who organized the silent walk: "Let them hear our silence. Let them know we want justice. Let them know we won't stop fighting. Let them know."[61]

In November 2010, I attended an annual event called Just This Day[62] at the Church of St. Martin-in-the-Fields in Trafalgar Square in London, described as a unique and quiet day of stillness and silence. It was a combination of discussions, talks, and music interspersed with times of silence. Since the church is located in one of the busiest and noisiest parts of London, the event made a welcome contrast to the racket outside.

In a different context, the power of silence was shown at the United Nations. In October 2015, Benjamin Netanyahu paused for forty-five seconds during a speech he was making to the UN General Assembly, highlighting what he felt was the "deafening" silence coming from the rest of the world over the nuclear deal with Iran. Regardless of his policies, this was an incredibly powerful thing to do, making his audience both uncomfortable and reflective.[63]

Refugees inevitably often feel lonely and isolated. In 2016, Amnesty International launched a short video, *Look Beyond Borders*,[64] to try to break down barriers between recently arrived refugees and Europeans. It was based on the theory that by sitting a refugee opposite a sympathetic local, a deep connection could be forged by each person looking another in the eye for an uninterrupted four minutes, mostly in silence. The experiment, filmed in Germany, was based on a theory developed in 1997 by the American psychologist Arthur Aron; it was used widely in Europe and other parts of the world and had overwhelmingly positive results, but bizarrely it only ran for a few months.

CONCLUSION

Silence can connect and link us to the past. The more reading that I've done about silence—its history, its benefits, and also its negatives—the more aware I am of what a powerful *link* silence can be. Both paintings and literature are a silent link to the creative minds of others, and nature is something we can enjoy in silence if we immerse ourselves in it.

As well as being this positive link to other times, silence is what we could certainly all do with more of in our increasingly noisy world. Of course, silence isn't really lost in the sense that it could never be found, but it has disappeared from the lives of many and is in danger of becoming even rarer as our twenty-four-hour world gains momentum. I hope that I have shown that through the exploration of silence through history, art, literature, nature, and music, for the open-minded and curious there are positive and beneficial links to the past that are of benefit to lives today. Inevitably there is a dark side to silence, but I would encourage people not to push silence away. Rather, embrace it and reap its benefits, which can bring peace, creativity, and positive connection to others.

Now that we insist on constant connectivity and feel bereft if we can't have it, there is never a need for us to be alone. There is always some kind of device at hand with which we can communicate with someone else. But there are all kinds of initiatives to help wean people away from this. In August 2018, London City Airport offered passengers what they called "dumb phones," which could only make and receive calls; the gesture was done in the hope that passengers would agree to an amnesty from their smartphones for at least forty-eight hours. Most British adults own a smartphone, and the average user checks it every twelve minutes. This effort by City Airport was to "help travelers reduce digital distraction and reclaim those quality moments with family and friends on holiday."[65] It's not clear whether the initiative worked, but it was certainly a creative attempt to try and silence our brains.

With so many diverse ways of bringing silence into our lives, it should be possible for anyone who wants to experience the healing powers of silence to do so. Of course, there are silent retreats and meditation, but it is also possible to incorporate silence into ordinary daily life. Whether this be by finding a space at home or in the garden to associate with silence or by discovering a quiet corner in a public park, cemetery, or church. And once in this quiet spot, just sitting or reading a poem can help bring you to a place of internal silence.

I have learned and thought so much about silence while writing this book, but I wonder whether it has made me a more silent person. I am objectively more aware of the benefits and importance of silence, but I haven't noticeably changed my life—though I have had some powerful experiences. It is perhaps the links to the artists, musicians, and meditators of previous generations that I have found most exciting; these connections, stretching over the centuries, emphasize our common humanity. Since much of the book was written during the pandemic lockdown, I was living in a more externally silent world than usual, but I think that my main realization is that true silence for me is dependent on my state of mind at any given time. However silent a place is, it is what is going on inside my head that keeps me from silence, and I keep going back to that charmed time in the Antarctic. That for me was the yardstick by which I've measured all subsequent silences, and nothing has matched up to it. Not the silent retreats nor the meditation nor the Quaker meetings; nothing matches that magic time in the Antarctic—yet. I think it was so profound because I wasn't searching for it; I was simply open to new experiences and was rewarded with something very special. I'm not suggesting that you'd need to go to the Antarctic to find silence. In fact, the challenge is to remain open and curious and to try to find it in unusual places and situations that can be close to home, but for me it was the beginning of a quest. Having had that experience, I know that it could happen again. However long it takes, it would be worth the wait.

NOTES

INTRODUCTION

1. Lao Tzu, *Tao Te Ching*, in Arthur Waley, *The Way and Its Power* (London: Allen and Unwin, 1934), 210.
2. *Ancrene Riwle*, quoted in E. D. Blodgett and H. G. Coward, eds., *Silence, the Word and the Sacred* (Ontario: Wilfred Laurier University Press, 1989), 17.
3. *Shorter Oxford English Dictionary on Historical Principles*, 3rd ed (Oxford: Oxford University Press, 1990).
4. Robert Macfarlane, *Underland: A Deep Time Journey* (London: Hamish Hamilton, 2019), 375.
5. Søren Kierkegaard, quoted in Max Picard, *The World of Silence* (London: Harvill Press, 1952), 231.
6. Mahatma Gandhi, *Young India: 1927–1928* (journal), India, 1927 (Madras, India: S. Ganesan, 1935).
7. Ludwig Wittgenstein, *Tractatus Logico-Philosophicus* quoted in Leslie Kane, *The Language of Silence: On the Unspoken and the Unspeakable in Modern Drama* (Plainsboro, NJ: Associated University Presses, 1984), 7.
8. Ram Dass, quoted in Anne D. LeClaire, *Listening Below the Noise: The Transformative Power of Silence* (New York: Harper Perennial, 2009), 44.
9. Socrates, quoted in Maggie Ross, *Silence: A User's Guide* (London: Darton, Longman & Todd, 2014), 128.

1. MY SILENCE

1. G. M. Trevelyan, *Walking*, quoted in David Vincent, *A History of Solitude* (Cambridge: Polity, 2020), 50.

2. Bruce Chatwin, *The Songlines* (London: Jonathan Cape, 1987), 21.

3. Roger Deakin, *Waterlog: A Swimmer's Journey through Britain* (London: Chatto & Windus, 1999).

4. Izaak Walton, *The Compleat Angler* (1665), quoted in David Vincent, *A History of Solitude* (Cambridge: Polity, 2020), 100–101.

5. Aidan Hart, letter to the author, November 2017.

6. Bernard Moitessier, *The Long Way* (New York: Doubleday, 1975).

7. Ronald Rolheiser, "The Language of Silence," *Catholic Herald*, February 2, 2007.

8. T. S. Eliot, *Four Quartets* (London: Faber & Faber, 1972), 15.

9. Richard Philp, letter to the author, June 2018.

10. Mike Boxhall, "Mike's Work," Stillness, accessed January 21, 2023, www.stillness.co.uk/mikes-work.

11. Augustus Hare, *Days Near Rome* (Philadelphia: Porter & Coates, 1875), 235.

2. SEEKING ELUSIVE SILENCE

1. Arthur Schopenhauer, "On Noise and Sounds," in *Parerga and Paralipomena*, vol. 2, ed. and trans. Adrian Del Caro, ed. Christopher Janaway (1851); published online by Cambridge University Press, November 5, 2015, www.cambridge.org/core/books/abs/schopenhauer-parerga-and -paralipomena/on-noise-and-sounds/4CE981B7477E3E1D5DE68915C 26B800C.

2. Jacques Lusseyran, *And There Was Light* (Boston: Little, Brown, 1963), 25.

3. Garrett Carr, "The Silence and the Scream," BBC Radio 4, July 23, 2018.

4. Charles Dickens, in Charles Babbage, *A Chapter on Street Nuisances* extracted from *Passages in the Life of a Philosopher* (London: John Murray, 1864).

5. John Leech, quoted in George Michelsen Foy, *Zero Decibels: The Quest for Absolute Silence* (New York: Scribners, 2010), 40.

6. Thomas Carlyle to Geraldine Dewsbury, June 15, 1840, The Carlyle Letters Online, https://carlyleletters.dukeupress.edu/search-results /Silence%20silence.

7. Thomas Carlyle to Margaret A. Carlyle, July 11, 1853, The Carlyle Letters Online, https://carlyleletters.dukeupress.edu/search-results/dandy%20carriages.

8. Thomas Carlyle to Jean Carlyle Aitken, August 11, 1853, The Carlyle Letters Online, https://carlyleletters.dukeupress.edu/search-results/artfully%20ventilated.

9. Thomas Carlyle to James [sic] Carlyle, May 11, 1854, The Carlyle Letters Online, https://carlyleletters.dukeupress.edu/volume/29/lt-18540511-TC-JC-01.

10. Orlando Figes, *The Europeans* (London: Penguin, 2020), 358.

11. George Prochnik, *In Pursuit of Silence: Listening for Meaning in a World of Noise* (New York: Random House, 2010), 206.

12. Winnie Hu, "New York Becomes the City That Nevers Shuts Up," *New York Times*, July 19, 2017.

13. William Whyte, "Octavia Hill: Her Life and Legacy," National Trust, accessed September 30, 2022, www.nationaltrust.org.uk/features/octavia-hill-her-life-and-legacy.

14. Stephen Batchelor, *The Art of Solitude* (London: Yale University Press, 2020), 133.

15. Stuart Kelly, review of *Silence: A Christian History*, by Diarmaid MacCulloch, *The Guardian*, March 30, 2013.

16. Sara Maitland, "Far from the Madding Crowd" *Guardian Review*, January 11, 2014.

17. Isabel Colegate, *A Pelican in the Wilderness* (London: HarperCollins, 2002), 28.

18. Henry David Thoreau, *Some Scraps from an Essay on "Sound and Silence"* from *The Writings December 1838* (Boston and New York: Houghton Mifflin & Co, 1906) quoted in Alain Corbin, *A History of Silence: From the Renaissance to the Present Day* (Cambridge: Polity, 2018), 19.

19. Thoreau quoted in Alain Corbin, *A History of Silence: From the Renaissance to the Present Day* (Cambridge: Polity, 2018), 19.

20. Jack Kerouac, *The Dharma Bums* (London: Andre Deutsch, 1959), 157.

21. Anne D. LeClaire, *Listening Below the Noise: The Transformative Power of Silence* (New York: Harper Perennial, 2009), 47.

22. Alexander Chancellor, "Long Life," *The Spectator*, December 8, 2012.

23. Chancellor, "Long Life."
24. Karin Paish in Sara Maitland, *A Book of Silence* (London: Granta, 2008), 274n and www.karinpaish.com.
25. "Not Speaking for a Week Changed My Life," BBC, January 8, 2018, www.bbc.co.uk/bbcthree/article/3bd877ea-6cb0-4d8a-826f-9467fad98d38.

3. NATURE

1. Robert Sardello, *Silence: The Mystery of Wholeness* (Berkeley, CA: North Atlantic Books, 2008), 1.
2. Luigi Russolo, *The Art of Noises* 1913; quoted in George Prochnik, *In Pursuit of Silence* (New York: Doubleday, 2010), 126.
3. Blaise Pascal, *Pensées: 392* (London: Harvill Press, 1962), 221 quoted in Alain Corbin, *A History of Silence: From the Renaissance to the Present Day* (Cambridge: Polity, 2018), 115.
4. John Gray, *The Silence of Animals: On Progress and Other Modern Myths* (London: Allen Lane, 2013), 162.
5. Annie Dillard, *Teaching a Stone to Talk* (Edinburgh: Canongate, 2016), 92.
6. One Square Inch: A Sanctuary for Silence at Olympic National Park, accessed September 30, 2022, https://onesquareinch.org.
7. Horatio Clare, *Icebreaker: A Voyage Far North* (London: Chatto & Windus, 2017).
8. Robert Kull, quoted in Stephen Batchelor, *The Art of Solitude* (London: Yale University Press, 2020), 78.
9. Neil Ansell, *The Last Wilderness: A Love Letter to Scotland* (London: Tinder Press, 2018).
10. Michael Finkel, *The Stranger in the Woods: The Extraordinary Story of the Last True Hermit* (New York: Simon & Schuster, 2017), 65.
11. Finkel, *Stranger in the Woods*, 113.
12. Imke Kirste, Zeina Nicola, Golo Kronenberg, Tara L. Walker, Robert C. Liu, and Gerd Kempermann, "Is Silence Golden? Effects of Auditory Stimuli and Their Absence on Adult Hippocampal Neurogenesis," *Brain Structure & Function* 220, no. 2 (December 1, 2013): 1221–28.
13. Richard E. Byrd, *Alone* (London: Neville Spearman, 1958), 5.
14. Byrd, *Alone*, vii.
15. Byrd, *Alone*, 85–86.

16. Byrd, *Alone*, 163.

17. Sarah Drury, "The Grandson of Scott's Deputy Makes Music in Antarctic," *The Spectator*, September 28, 2013.

18. The OWLS project is a collaborative academic investigation and writing initiative between the Sixth Form Academic Scholarship holders of Oxford High School and Wimbledon High School—the work is published in OWLS Quarterly journal. The initial edition took inspiration from real birds of prey: Edition 1, February 2018, https://oxfordhigh .gdst.net/sixth-form/the-360-programme/horizons/owls/.

19. Llewelyn Powys, *Earth Memories* (London: John Lane, 1934), quoted in John Gray, *The Silence of Animals* (London: Allen Lane, 2013), 176.

20. Beatrix Potter, *The Tale of Squirrel Nutkin* (London: Warne, 2002).

21. "A Wise Old Owl," originally published in April 1875 in *Punch Magazine*.

22. John Muir, quoted in Alain Corbin, *A History of Silence: From the Renaissance to the Present Day* (Cambridge: Polity, 2018), 29.

23. Nan Shepherd, *The Living Mountain* (Edinburgh: Canongate, 2011), 75.

24. Shepherd, *Living Mountain*, 75.

25. James Crowden, *The Frozen River: Seeking Silence in the Himalaya* (London: William Collins, 2020), 2.

26. Max Picard, *The World of Silence* (Chicago: Henry Regnery, 1952), 116.

27. Émile Zola, *A Love Story*, quoted in Alain Corbin, *A History of Silence: From the Renaissance to the Present Day* (Cambridge: Polity, 2018), 29–30.

28. James Russell Lowell, "The First Snowfall," in *The Complete Poetical Works of James Russell Lowell* (Boston: Houghton, Mifflin, 1896), 292.

29. Robert Perkins, personal correspondence with author, December 2017.

30. Gontran de Poncins, *Kabloona* (New York: Reynal, 1941).

31. De Poncins, *Kabloona*, quoted in Max Picard, *The World of Silence* (London: Harvill Press, 1952), 143–44.

32. Henry David Thoreau, *The Maine Woods* (1864), quoted in Alain Corbin, *A History of Silence: From the Renaissance to the Present Day* (Cambridge: Polity, 2018), 95.

33. Stéphane Mallarmé, "Azure," quoted in Alain Corbin, *A History of Silence: From the Renaissance to the Present Day* (Cambridge: Polity, 2018), 18.

34. Jacques Cousteau, *The Silent World* (New York: Ballantine Books, 1977), 217.

35. Adam Nicolson, *Sea Room: An Island Life* (London: HarperCollins, 2001), 174.

36. W. H. Auden, "Look, Stranger," quoted in Adam Nicolson, *Sea Room* (London: HarperCollins, 2001), 373.

4. CALL OF THE DESERT

1. Aldo Leopold, from *A Sand County Almanac: With Essays on Conservation from Round River* (New York: Oxford University Press, 1970), 294.

2. Percy Bysshe Shelley, "Ozymandias" (London, 1818), in *Desert Air*, ed. Barnaby Rogerson (London: Baring & Rogerson, 2001), 26.

3. Robert Byron, *The Road to Oxiana* (1937; London: Penguin, 2007).

4. John Charles Van Dyke, *The Desert* (New York: Charles Scribner, 1911), 19.

5. Aldous Huxley, *Complete Essays: Volume V 1939–1956* (Chicago: Ivan R. Dee, 2002), 294.

6. David King Dunaway, *Aldous Huxley Recollected: An Oral History*, ebook (Walnut Creek, CA: AltaMira Press, 1998).

7. Huxley, *Complete Essays*, 294.

8. Aldous Huxley, "The Desert Boundlessness and Emptiness," United Architects—Essays, accessed September 30, 2022, https://danassays .wordpress.com/collected-essays-by-aldous-huxley/aldous-huxley -essays-the-desert-boundlessness-and-emptiness/.

9. T. E. Lawrence, *Seven Pillars of Wisdom* (London: Jonathan Cape, 1935), 29.

10. Antoine de Saint-Exupéry, *Wind, Sand and Stars* (New York: Reynal & Hitchcock, 1939), 21.

11. Paul Bowles, "Baptism of Solitude," in *Their Heads Are Green* (London: Peter Owen, 1963), 131.

12. Bowles, "Baptism of Solitude," 131.

13. Bowles, 143.

14. Sven Lindqvist, *Desert Divers* (London: Granta, 2000), 4.

15. Eugène Fromentin, *Between Sea and Sahara* (London: Tauris Parke, 2004) quoted in Alain Corbin, *A History of Silence: From the Renais-*

sance to the Present Day (Cambridge: Polity, 2018), 26.

16. Alain Corbin, *A History of Silence: From the Renaissance to the Present Day* (Cambridge: Polity, 2018), 26.

17. Isabelle Eberhardt, *The Passionate Nomad* (Boston: Beacon Press, 1987), 10.

18. Martin Buckley, *Grains of Sand* (London: Hutchinson, 2000), 50.

19. Buckley, *Grains of Sand*, 49.

20. Buckley, 50.

21. Buckley, 192.

22. William Atkins, *The Immeasurable World: Journeys in Desert Places* (London: Faber & Faber, 2018), 49.

23. James Crowden, *The Frozen River* (London: William Collins, 2020), 23.

24. Uwe George, *In the Deserts of This Earth* (London: Hamish Hamilton, 1978), 5.

25. Janette Turner Hospital, *Oyster* (London: Virago, 1996), 135.

26. Turner Hospital, *Oyster*, 145.

27. Robyn Davidson, *Tracks* (London: Vintage, 1980).

28. John Cassian, quoted in *The Desert Fathers*, trans. Helen Waddell (New York: Henry Holt and Company, 1936), 226.

29. George Prochnik, *In Pursuit of Silence* (New York: Doubleday, 2010), 30–31.

30. Peter France, *Hermits: The Insights of Solitude* (London: Chatto & Windus, 1996), 1.

31. Geoffrey Moorhouse, *Sun Dancing* (London: Weidenfeld & Nicolson, 1997), 144.

32. Corbin, *History of Silence*, 50.

5. SEARCHING FOR SILENT BUILDINGS

1. Lord Byron, from *The Siege of Corinth: Poetical Works* (London: Oxford University Press, 1928), 308.

2. Richard Coles, "Winter Walks" BBC 4, December 27, 2022.

3. David Tas, "The Walnut Tree," May 2015.

4. Max Picard, *The World of Silence* (London: Harvill Press, 1952), 168–69.

5. J. K. Huysmans, *The Cathedral* (London: Dedalus, 2011), 46.

6. J. K. Huysmans, *Against Nature* (London: Penguin, 1959).

7. Alain Corbin, *A History of Silence: From the Renaissance to the Present Day,* (Cambridge: Polity, 2018), 7.
8. Mark Cazalet, conversations with the author, October 2017.
9. Malcom Lowry, quoted in Stuart Sim, *Manifesto for Silence* (Edinburgh: Edinburgh University Press, 2007), 22.
10. George Michelsen Foy, "I've Been to the Quietest Place on Earth," *The Guardian Weekend*, May 19, 2012.
11. George Michelsen Foy, *Zero Decibels: The Quest for Absolute Silence* (New York: Scribner, 2010), 76.

6. RELIGIOUS PERSPECTIVES

1. Ovid, *Metamorphosis*, trans. David Raeburn (London: Penguin, 2004), 374.
2. Homer, *The Iliad* (London: Penguin, 2003).
3. Homer, *The Odyssey* (London: Penguin, 2003).
4. Pat Barker, *The Silence of the Girls* (London: Penguin, 2019).
5. Tacita Muta was a naiad punished by Jupiter who ripped her tongue out for talking excessively.
6. Plutarch Quotes, BrainyQuote.com, accessed September 8, 2022, www.brainyquote.com/quotes/plutarch_117780.
7. Amber Hatch, *The Art of Silence* (London: Little, Brown, 2017), 120.
8. Anne Baring, letter to the author, September 2017.
9. Herodotus, *The Histories*, trans. Aubrey de Sélincourt (London: Penguin, 1972), 197.
10. Aldous Huxley, *Complete Essays: Volume V 1939–1956* (Chicago: Ivan R. Dee, 2002), 294.
11. This and all subsequent quotations from the Bible are taken from King James Bible.
12. "Something Strange Is Happening" quoted in the *Catholic Herald*, April 3, 2021.
13. Isabel Colegate, *A Pelican in the Wilderness: Hermits and Solitaries* (London: HarperCollins, 2002), 126.
14. Brother Alberic, quoted in George Prochnik, *In Pursuit of Silence* (New York: Random House, 2010), 27.
15. A Carthusian, *The Call of Silent Love* (London: Darton, Longman & Todd, 1995), 96–97.

16. Carthusian, *Call of Silent Love*, 97.
17. *Into the Great Silence*, directed by Philip Gröning, 2005.
18. Timothy Radcliffe, *Why Go to Church? The Drama of the Eucharist* (London: Bloomsbury, 2008), 30.
19. Meister Eckhart, quoted in Shirley Du Boulay, *A Silent Melody: An Experience of Contemporary Spiritual Life* (London: Darton Longman & Todd, 2014), 223.
20. William Langland, *Piers the Ploughman*, trans. J. Goodridge (London: Penguin, 2006).
21. Maggie Ross, *Silence: A User's Guide* (London: Darton, Longman & Todd, 2014), 46n.
22. Dante Alighieri, *The Divine Comedy*, trans. Robin Kirkpatrick (London: Penguin, 2012).
23. George R. Marek, *The Bed and the Throne: The Life of Isabella d'Este* (New York: Harper and Row, 1976), 12n.
24. Wikipedia, s.v. "Isabella D'Este," last modified December 5, 2022, 18:16, https://en.wikipedia.org/wiki/Isabella_d%27Este.
25. St. Ignatius Loyola, quoted in Alain Corbin, *A History of Silence: From the Renaissance to the Present Day* (Cambridge: Polity, 2018), 42–43.
26. Diarmaid MacCulloch, *Silence: A Christian History* (London: Allen Lane, 2013), 111.
27. Peter France, *Hermits: The Insights of Solitude* (London: Chatto & Windus, 1996), 30.
28. Robert Cardinal Sarah, *The Power of Silence: Against the Dictatorship of Noise* (San Francisco: Ignatius Press, 2017), 52.
29. Alberto Manguel, *A History of Reading* (New York: Viking, 1996), 49.
30. St. John Climacus, quoted in *Meditatio Newsletter* 40, no. 4 "A Letter from Laurence Freeman," OSB (December 2016): 4.
31. St. Teresa of Avila, quoted in Diarmaid MacCulloch, *Silence: A Christian History* (London: Allen Lane, 2013), 156.
32. Stuart Kelly, review of *Silence: A Christian History*, by Diarmaid MacCulloch, *The Guardian*, March 30, 2013.
33. Graham Speake, *Mount Athos: Renewal in Paradise* (New Haven: Yale University Press, 2002), 196.
34. Aidan Hart, letter to the author, November 2017.
35. St. Isaac the Syrian, quoted in Aidan Hart, letter to the author, November 2017.

36. Sister Teresa Keswick, letter to the author, November 2017.

37. Abbot Moses, quoted in George Prochnik, *In Pursuit of Silence* (New York: Doubleday, 2010), 31.

38. Diarmaid MacCulloch, *Silence: A Christian History* (London: Allen Lane, 2013).

39. Patrick Barkham, *Islander: A Journey around Our Archipelago* (London: Granta, 2017), 259.

40. Patrick Barkham, "Bardsey, My Pleasure Island," *The Oldie Magazine*, July 2020.

41. MacCulloch, *Silence*, 92.

42. MacCulloch, 97.

43. Miguel de Molinos, quoted in Jane Brox, *Silence: A Social History of One of the Least Understood Elements of Our Lives* (New York: Houghton Mifflin Harcourt, 2019), 20.

44. St. Francis de Sales, quoted in Diarmaid MacCulloch, *Silence: A Christian History* (London: Allen Lane, 2013), 83.

45. William Law, quoted in Stuart Sim, *Manifesto for Silence: Confronting the Politics of Culture and Noise* (Edinburgh: Edinburgh University Press, 2007), 41.

46. William Penn, quoted in Stuart Sim, *Manifesto for Silence: Confronting the Politics of Culture and Noise* (Edinburgh: Edinburgh University Press, 2007), 66.

47. George H. Gorman, quoted in Stuart Sim, *Manifesto for Silence: Confronting the Politics of Culture and Noise* (Edinburgh: Edinburgh University Press, 2007), 8.

48. Caroline Stephen, quoted in Jane Brox, *Silence: A Social History: One of the Least Understood Elements of Our Lives* (New York: Houghton Mifflin Harcourt, 2019), 20.

49. Eden Grace in "The Friend," *The Quaker Magazine*, November 16, 2018, 11.

50. Seneca, *Letters from a Stoic*, quoted in George Michelsen Foy, 37.

51. Plutarch, "On the Fortune of Alexander," in *Moralia*, vol. 4, Loeb Classical Library, trans. Frank Cole Babbit (Cambridge: Harvard University Press, 1936), 417.

52. Augustine, *Confessions* 6.3.3., quoted in Jeremy Norman, "Was Silent Reading Unusual in Augustine's Time?" History of Information.com,

accessed September 30, 2022, www.historyofinformation.com/detail
.php?entryid=4341.

53. Alberto Manguel, *A History of Reading* (London: HarperCollins, 1996), 49.
54. Isidore of Seville quoted in Alberto Manguel, *A History of Reading* (London: HarperCollins, 1996), 49.
55. E. M. Forster, *A Passage to India*, quoted in Timothy Radcliffe, *Why Go to Church?* (London: Bloomsbury, 2008), 29.
56. W. H. Vanstone, quoted in Diarmaid MacCulloch, *Silence: A Christian History* (London: Allen Lane, 2013), 224.
57. Jorge Luis Borges, *The Aleph and Other Stories* (1945), trans. Norman Thomas Di Giovanni (New York: Bantam Books, 1971), 13.
58. Elie Wiesel's reply to Ronald Eyre, BBC program *The Long Search*, 1977.
59. Sri Ramana Maharshi, *The Teachings of Ramana Maharshi*, ed. Arthur Osborne (London: Random House, 2014), 156.
60. Shirley Du Boulay, *The Cave of the Heart* (Maryknoll, NY: Orbis, 2005), 150.
61. W. Somerset Maugham, *Points of View* (London: Heinemann, 1958), 58.
62. W. Somerset Maugham, *The Razor's Edge* (1944; London: Vintage, 2000).
63. Marguerite Porete, *The Mirror of Simple Souls* (New York: Paulist Press, 1993).

7. MEDITATION

1. Aelred Graham, "On Meditation," in *Studies in Comparative Religion* 1, no. 1 (November 10, 1965), www.studiesincomparativereligion.com/public/articles/On_Meditation-by_Dom_Aelred_Graham.aspx.
2. Max Picard, *The World of Silence* (London: Harvill Press, 1952), 12.
3. Aelred Graham, *Contemplative Christianity* (London: Catholic Book Club 1975), 55.
4. Diarmaid MacCulloch, *Silence: A Christian History* (London: Allen Lane, 2013), 223–24.
5. Laurence Freeman, *Finding Oneself 1*, Meditatio Talks Series (Singapore: Medio Media, 2017).

6. John Main, *Moment of Christ: The Path of Meditation* (London: Darton, Longman & Todd, 1987), 97.

7. Thomas Merton, *Mystics and Zen Masters*, quoted in George Woodcock, *Thomas Merton: Monk and Poet* (Edinburgh: Canongate, 1978), 155.

8. William Johnston, *Arise, My Love: Mysticism For a New Era* (Maryknoll, NY: Orbis, 2000), 72.

9. Thich Nhat Hanh, *For a Future to Be Possible: Buddhist Ethics for Everyday Life* (Berkeley, CA: Parallax Press, 2007), 105.

10. William Johnston, *Christian Zen* (New York: Harper & Row, 1971), 44.

11. William Johnston, *Silent Music: The Science of Meditation* (London: Fontana, 1976), 56.

12. Vicki Mackenzie, *Cave in the Snow: A Western Woman's Quest for Enlightenment* (London: Bloomsbury, 1998).

13. Thomas Merton, *Thoughts on the East* (London: Burns & Oates, 1996), 15.

14. Richard Anthony Cashen, *Solitude in the Thought of Thomas Merton* (Collegeville, MN: Cistercian Publications, 1981), 102.

15. Ted Gioia, *Healing Songs* (Durham, NC: Duke University Press, 2006), 100.

16. Thomas Merton, *Thoughts in Solitude: Meditations on the Spiritual Life and Man's Solitude before God* (New York: Dell Pub. Co, 1961), 111, quoted in Jane Brox, *A Social History of One of the Least Understood Elements of Our Lives* (New York: Houghton Mifflin Harcourt, 2019), 211.

17. Johnston, *Arise, My Love*, 46.

18. Meher Baba, quoted in Shirley du Boulay, *A Silent Melody* (London: Darton, Longman & Todd, 2014), 43.

19. Hindu monk, quoted in Anne D. LeClaire, *Listening Below the Noise* (New York: Harper Perennial, 2009), 215.

20. Raimon Panikkar, quoted in Shirley du Boulay, *A Silent Melody* (London: Darton, Longman & Todd, 2014), 154.

21. Opus Dei, a controversial Catholic organization founded in 1928.

22. Raimon Panikkar, *The Silence of God* (Maryknoll, NY: Orbis, 1989), vi.

23. Main, *Moment of Christ*, 75.

24. Main, 77.

25. Thomas Merton, *Choosing to Love the World: On Contemplation* (Louisville, CO: Sounds True, 2008), 82.

26. Johnston, *Silent Music*, 117.

27. Johnston, *Silent Music* 21.

28. Johnston, *Christian Zen*, 21.

29. Bede Griffiths, *The Marriage of East and West* (London: Collins, 1982), 75.

30. Johnston, *Arise, My Love*, 101.

31. Sam Harris, *Waking Up: Searching for Spirituality Without Religion* (London: Black Swan, 2015).

32. Waking Up app, www.wakingup.com.

33. Rebecca Erwin Wells, Gloria Y. Yeh, Catherine E. Kerr, Jennifer Wolkin, Roger B. Davis, Ying Tan, Rosa Spaeth, Robert B. Wall, Jacquelyn Walsh, Ted J. Kaptchuk, Daniel Press, Russell S. Phillips, Jian Kong, "Meditation's Impact on Default Mode Network and Hippocampus in Mild Cognitive Impairment: A Pilot Study," *Neuroscience Letters* 556 (November 27, 2013), DOI:10.1016/j.neulet.2013.10.001.

34. James Roose-Evans, *Passages of the Soul: Ritual Today* (Shaftesbury, UK: Element, 1994), 108.

35. Sam Keen, *To a Dancing God* (London: Harper & Row, 1990), 43.

36. Étienne Gilson, *The Spirit of Mediaeval Philosophy*, trans. A. H. C. Downes (London: Sheed and Ward, 1936).

37. Aldous Huxley, *Ends and Means* (London: Chatto & Windus, 1941).

38. Cashen, *Solitude in the Thought of Thomas Merton*, 149.

39. Thomas Merton, *A Search for Solitude: The Journals of Thomas Merton, Volume Three 1952–1960*, ed. Lawrence S. Cunningham (New York: HarperSanFrancisco, 1997), 16.

40. Thomas Merton, quoted in Richard Anthony Cashen, *Solitude in the Thought of Thomas Merton* (Collegeville, MN: Cistercian Publications, 1981), 168.

41. Thomas Merton, quoted in Richard Anthony Cashen, *Solitude in the Thought of Thomas Merton* (Collegeville, MN: Cistercian Publications, 1981), 8.

42. Cashen, *Solitude in the Thought of Thomas Merton*, 50.

43. Cashen, 86.

44. Thomas Merton, *Elected Silence* (London: Burns & Oates, 1961), 220.

45. Ronald Rolheiser, "The Last Word: The Language of Silence," *Catholic Herald*, February 2, 2007.

46. Thomas Merton, *Contemplation in a World of Action* (London: George Allen & Unwin, 1971), 168–69.
47. Merton, *Elected Silence*, 218.
48. Thomas Keating, quoted in James Roberts, "Be Still and Know," *Tablet Magazine*, November 28, 2009.
49. Keating, quoted in Roberts, *Tablet Magazine*.
50. Patrick Leigh Fermor, *A Time to Keep Silence* (London: John Murray, 1957).
51. Leigh Fermor, *A Time to Keep Silence*, 9.
52. Leigh Fermor, 28.
53. Leigh Fermor, 29.
54. Leigh Fermor, 9.
55. Leigh Fermor, 37.
56. Pico Iyer, "Out of the Cell," September 25, 2017, http://granta.com/out-of-the-cell.
57. Tim Parks, "Try Something Quietly Profound," *The Guardian*, November 12, 2010.
58. Belden Lane, *The Solace of Fierce Landscapes: Exploring Mountain and Desert Spirituality* (New York: Oxford University Press, 2007), 224.
59. Kathleen Norris, *Amazing Grace: A Vocabulary of Faith* (New York: Riverhead Books 1998), 17.
60. "Pupils Banned from Talking while Walking Between Lessons Under Headteacher's Silence Policy," *The Telegraph*, July 19, 2018.
61. Kate Sapera, letter to the author, September 2019.

8. LITERATURE

1. George Steiner, *Language and Silence* (London: Faber & Faber, 1967), 56.
2. Hayden Carruth, "Fallacies of Silence," *Hudson Review* 26, no. 3 (1973): 464.
3. Wikipedia, s.v. "Beowulf," last edited February 5, 2023, https://en.wikipedia.org/wiki/Beowulf.
4. Wikipedia, s.v. "Edda," last edited December 19, 2022, https://en.wikipedia.org/wiki/Edda.
5. William Wordsworth, "Upon Westminster Bridge" (1802), in *The

Oxford Book of English Verse 1250–1918 (Oxford: Oxford University Press, 1966), 615.

6. John Keats, "Ode on a Grecian Urn" (1819), in *The Oxford Book of English Verse 1250–1918* (Oxford: Oxford University Press, 1966), 745–46.

7. Arthur Hugh Clough, "Review of Mr. Newman's 'The Soul,'" Poems and Prose Remains, Vol. 1, accessed September 30, 2022, www.telelib .com/authors/C/CloughArthurHugh/prose/poemsproseremainsv1 /newmansoul.html.

8. Arthur Hugh Clough, "Uranus," Poems and Prose Remains, Vol. 1, accessed September 30, 2022, www.telelib.com/authors/C/Clough ArthurHugh/verse/poemsproseremains/uranus.html.

9. Alfred, Lord Tennyson, "In Memoriam A. H. H.," canto 19, Poets.org, accessed September 30, 2022, https://poets.org/poem/memoriam -h-h.

10. D. H. Lawrence, "Silence," in *The Collected Poems of D. H. Lawrence* (London: Martin Secker, 1932), 130.

11. D. H. Lawrence, "Silence," in Daniel Mark Fogel, "The Sacred Poem to the Unknown in the Fiction of D. H. Lawrence," *D. H. Lawrence Review* 16, no. 1 (1983): 45–57.

12. D. H. Lawrence, "Snake," in *The Collected Poems of D. H. Lawrence* (London: Martin Secker, 1932), 445.

13. T. S. Eliot, "Ash Wednesday" (1930), in *T. S. Eliot Collected Poems* (London: Faber & Faber, 1963), 102.

14. Rainer Maria Rilke, *The Book of Hours*, trans. Susan Ranson (Rochester, NY: Camden House, 2008), 9.

15. Stuart Kelly, review of *Silence: A Christian History*, by Diarmaid MacCulloch, *The Guardian*, March 30, 2013.

16. Ludwig Wittgenstein, quoted in Erling Kagge, *Silence: In the Age of Noise* (London: Viking, 2017), 92.

17. Philip Gross, *A Bright Acoustic* (London: Bloodaxe Books, 2017).

18. Philip Gross, "Mind the Gap," *The Author* (Spring 2018): 11.

19. Gross, "Mind the Gap," 11.

20. Sean Swallow, letter to the author, January 2018.

21. R. S. Thomas, "The Untamed," in *Collected Poems 1945–1990* (London: Phoenix, 2000), 140.

22. Max Picard, *The World of Silence* (London: Harvill Press, 1952), 145.

23. H. C. Andersen, *The Little Mermaid* (1837), in *Fairy Tales of Hans Christian Andersen* (London: Reader's Digest, 2005).

24. Ralph Waldo Emerson, *Friendship and Other Essays* (Totnes, UK: Arcturus Classics, 2019), Kindle.

25. Ralph Waldo Emerson, *Complete Prose Works* (Digital Library of India, 2015), 472.

26. George Eliot, *Adam Bede* (London: Penguin, 1980), 202.

27. Stuart Sim, *Manifesto for Silence* (Edinburgh: Edinburgh University Press, 2007), 11.

28. Alain Corbin, *A History of Silence: From the Renaissance to the Present Day* (Cambridge: Polity, 2018), 7.

29. Lydia Davis, "The International Man Booker Winner on the Pleasurable Challenge of Translating Proust," *The Guardian*, November 11, 2017.

30. Marcel Proust, *Swann's Way*, vol. 1 of *Remembrance of Things Past*, trans. C. K. Scott Moncrieff (London: Chatto & Windus, 1966), 172.

31. Corbin, *History of Silence*, 80.

32. Joseph Conrad, "An Outpost of Progress," in *Tales of Unrest* (London: Penguin, 1977), 159.

33. Joseph Conrad, *The Shadow Line* (Oxford: Oxford University Press, 2003).

34. Virginia Woolf, *The Voyage Out*, quoted in Michael Mayne, *This Sunrise of Wonder* (London: Fount, 1995), 7.

35. Virginia Woolf, *To the Lighthouse* (London: Penguin, 2000), 69.

36. Robert Walser, *Jakob von Gunten*, quoted in Tim Parks, *Teach Us to Sit Still* (London: Harvill Secker, 2010), 244.

37. Jiddu Krishnamurti, Public Talk 7, Saanen, Switzerland, July 22, 1979.

38. Emma Brockes interview with Colm Tóibín, "There's a Certain Amount of Glee at the Sheer Foolishness of Brexit," *The Guardian*, March 30, 2018.

39. Tracy Chevalier, "The Rest Is Noise," *The Guardian*, March 16, 2013.

40. Tracy Chevalier, *The Last Runaway* (London: HarperCollins, 2013).

41. Chevalier, "The Rest Is Noise," *The Guardian*.

42. Chevalier, *The Last Runaway*, 261.

43. Chevalier, *The Last Runaway*, 261.

44. Halldór Laxness, *Under the Glacier* (New York: Vintage, 2005), 60–61.

45. Blaise Pascal, quoted in Alain Corbin, *A History of Silence: From the Renaissance to the Present Day* (Cambridge: Polity, 2018), 99.

46. Nicholas Sparks, *The Notebook* (New York: Warner Books, 1996), 180.

47. Wikipedia, s.v. "Index Librorum Prohibitorum," last modified January 5, 2023, 1:25, https://en.wikipedia.org/wiki/Index_Librorum_Prohibitorum.

48. Oliver Milman, "'Rapid Acceleration' in US School Book Censorship Leads to 2,500 Bans in a Year," *The Guardian*, September 19, 2022, www.theguardian.com/education/2022/sep/19/us-school-book-censorship-bans-pen-america.

49. Jonathan Friedman and Nadine Farid Johnson, "Banned in the US: The Growing Movement to Censor Books in Schools," PEN America, September 19, 2022, https://pen.org/report/banned-usa-growing-movement-to-censor-books-in-schools/.

50. Tillie Olsen, *Silences* (London: Virago, 1980), 6.

51. Gerard Manley Hopkins, "The Habit of Perfection," in *The Oxford Book of English Verse 1250–1918* (Oxford: Oxford University Press, 1966), 1011–12.

52. Gerard Manley Hopkins, "The Wreck of the Deutschland," in W. H. Gardner, *Gerard Manley Hopkins: A Selection of His Poems and Prose* (London: Penguin, 1963), 12.

53. Gerard Manley Hopkins, "Nondum," All Poetry, accessed February 2, 2023, https://allpoetry.com/poem/13534643-Nondum--Not-yet--by-Gerard-Manley-Hopkins.

54. Sergeanne Golon, *Angelique* (London: Heinemann, 1959).

55. "Nielsen BookData Report Cites a Decline in Audiobook Sales in the UK," Frontlist, November 23, 2022, www.frontlist.in/nielsen-bookdata-report-cites-a-decline-in-audiobook-sales-in-the-uk.

56. Zoe Wood, "Indie Bookshop Numbers Hit 10-year High in 2022 Defying Brutal UK Retail Year," *The Guardian*, January 6, 2023.

57. Katie Fitzgerald, "5 Reasons I Listen to Audiobooks at Double Speed," Read-At-Home, March 26, 2019, www.readathomemom.com/2019/03/5-reasons-i-listen-to-audiobooks-at.html.

58. Shakespeare, *King Lear*, act 1, sc. 1, line 61.

59. Shakespeare, *King Lear*, act 1, sc. 1, line 89.

60. Shakespeare, *Hamlet*, act 5, sc. 2, line 350.

61. Eugène Ionesco, *Fragments of a Journal* (New York: Grove Press, 1968), 72.

62. Samuel Beckett, *Dream of Fair to Middling Women* (London: Calder, 1993), 138.

63. Samuel Beckett, *Act Without Words I* and *Act Without Words II*, in *The Complete Dramatic Works of Samuel Beckett* (London: Faber, 2006).

64. Samuel Beckett, quoted in Belden Lane, *The Solace of Fierce Landscapes: Exploring Mountain and Desert Spirituality* (Oxford: Oxford University Press, 2007), 78.

65. Samuel Beckett, *Breath and Other Shorts* (London: Faber and Faber, 1975).

66. Nicholas Lezard, "Play Samuel Beckett's Mouth? Not I," *The Guardian*, July 8, 2009.

67. Leslie Kane, *The Language of Silence: The Unspoken and the Unspeakable in Modern Drama* (Plainsboro, NJ: Associated University Presses, 1984), 15.

68. Harold Pinter, from a speech made at the National Student Drama Festival in Bristol 1962, in Harold Pinter, *Various Voices: Prose, Poetry, Politics 1948–1998* (London: Faber, 1998), 25.

69. Harold Pinter, *Plays: 2* (London: Faber, 1996).

70. Harold Pinter, speech, National Student Drama Festival, 25.

71. Harold Pinter, quoted in Leslie Kane, *The Language of Silence* (Plainsboro, NJ: Associated University Presses, 1984), 132–33.

72. Harold Pinter, *Silence*, in *Plays: Three* (London: Eyre Methuen, 1978).

73. Harold Pinter, *The Caretaker and The Dumb Waiter: Two Plays by Harold Pinter* (New York: Grove Press, 1988).

74. Kane, *Language of Silence*, 77.

75. James Graham, *This House*, premier Royal National Theatre, London 2012.

76. *Cigarettes and Chocolate*, first broadcast on BBC radio in 1988.

77. Nicholas Lezard, "Philosophical Thoughts on the Art and Science of Film-Making from One of the Great Directors – Review of Robert Bresson *Notes on the Cinematograph*," *The Guardian*, January 14, 2017.

9. PAINTINGS

1. Hisham Matar, *A Month in Siena* (London: Viking, 2019).
2. Leonardo da Vinci, *Leonardo On Painting: An Anthology of Writings* (New Haven: Yale University Press, 1989), 28.
3. Geoffrey Chaucer, *The Canterbury Tales* (London: Penguin, 2003).
4. Max Picard, *The World of Silence* (London: Harvill Press, 1952), 170.
5. Paul Johnson, "When Silentiaries Whacked Their Pillar in Ancient Byzantium," *The Spectator*, June 21, 2003.
6. Stephen Batchelor, *The Art of Solitude* (London: Yale University Press, 2020), 28.
7. Alain Corbin, *A History of Silence: From the Renaissance to the Present Day* (Cambridge: Polity, 2018), 72.
8. Marcel Proust, *Remembrance of Things Past: The Captive*, pt. 1, trans. C. K. Scott Moncrieff (London: Chatto & Windus, 1966), 250.
9. Picard, *World of Silence*, 167.
10. Chardin, quoted in Paul Johnson, *Art: A New History* (London: Weidenfeld & Nicolson, 2003), 414.
11. Eugène Delacroix, quoted in Alain Corbin, *A History of Silence: From the Renaissance to the Present Day* (Cambridge: Polity, 2018), 72.
12. George Prochnik, *In Pursuit of Silence: Listening for Meaning in a World of Noise* (New York: Random House, 2010), 122.
13. Caspar David Friedrich, quoted in Julian Bell, "Caspar David Friedrich at the Edge of the Imaginable, *Times Literary Supplement*, October 26, 2012.
14. Wikipedia, s.v. "*Isle of the Dead* (painting)," last modified January 6, 2023, 18:44, https://en.wikipedia.org/wiki/Isle_of_the_Dead_(painting).
15. Salvador Dali, *The True Painting of the "Isle of the Dead" by Arnold Böcklin at the Hour of the Angelus* (Von der Heydt Museum, Wuppertal, Germany).
16. Harpocrates, *Emblem XI* in Mason Tung *The Variorum Edition of Alciato's Emblemata* (Moscow: University of Idaho Press 2014), www.emblems.arts.gla.ac.uk/alciato/facsimile.php?emb=A15a011.
17. Wikipedia, s.v. "*The Scream*," last modified December 17, 2022, 19:46, https://en.wikipedia.org/wiki/The_Scream.
18. Henri Matisse, *Chatting with Henri Matisse: The Lost 1941 Interview* (Los Angeles: Getty Research Institute, 2013), 7.

19. Morisot, *The Cradle*, Museé d'Orsay, Paris.

20. Edward Hopper, quoted in Robert Hughes, *American Visions: The Epic History of Art in America* (London: Harvill Press, 1997), 422.

21. Leslie Kane, *The Language of Silence: On the Unspoken and the Unspeakable in Modern Drama* (Plainsboro, NJ: Associated University Presses, 1984), 21–22.

22. "Piet Mondrian," Google Arts and Culture, accessed September 30, 2022, https://artsandculture.google.com/entity/piet-mondrian/mocrnb5?hl=en.

23. Isabel Colegate, *A Pelican in the Wilderness: Hermits, Solitaries, and Recluses* (London: HarperCollins, 2002), 15.

24. Jean Arp, *Arp on Arp: Poems, Essays, Memories* (London: Viking, 1972), 231.

25. Filippo Tommaso Marinetti, "Manifesto of Futurism," Art Theory, accessed September 30, 2022, https://theoria.art-zoo.com/futurism-manifesto-marinetti/.

26. Mark Rothko quoted in Josef Helfenstein, Laureen Schipsi, Suzanne Deal, *Art and Activism: Projects of John and Dominique de Menil* (Houston: Menil Collection, 2010), 249.

27. Dominique de Menil quoted in exhibition catalog, *Silence* by Toby Kamps, Steve Seid, Jenni Sorkin, Menil Collection (Houston, TX), Berkeley Art Museum and Pacific Film Archive (New Haven, CT: Yale University Press, 2012), 7.

28. Lot essay in Christie's exhibition catalog *Post-War & Contemporary Art*, October 2016.

29. Rowan Williams, *Silence and Honey Cakes: The Wisdom of the Desert* (Oxford: Lion, 2003), 69.

30. Andrew Marr, "Diary," *The Spectator*, June 23, 2018.

31. Jaume Plensa quoted in Kurt McVey, "Master Artist Jaume Plensa's Latest Exhibition, 'Silence,' Is a Dream," *Forbes Magazine*, February 14, 2017.

32. Susan Sontag, quoted in exhibition catalog, *Silence* by Toby Kamps, Steve Seid, Jenni Sorkin, Menil Collection (Houston, TX), Berkeley Art Museum and Pacific Film Archive (New Haven, CT: Yale University Press, 2012), 63.

33. Cities and Memory, www.citiesandmemory.com.

34. "Edmund de Waal: Making Silence," January 28, 2019, YouTube video, 44; 42, www.youtube.com/watch?v=4-VwUyK-hCQ.

10. MUSIC

1. Aldous Huxley, *The Rest Is Silence* in *Music at Night and Other Essays* (1931; London: Flamingo, 1994), 12.
2. Alfred Brendel, "An A-Z of the Piano: Alfred Brendel's Notes from the Concert Hall," *The Guardian*, August 31, 2013.
3. Paul Robertson, *Soundscapes: A Musician's Journey through Life* (London: Faber, 2016), 160.
4. Robertson, *Soundscapes*, 160.
5. Richard Kostelanetz, *Conversing with Cage* (London: Psychology Press, 2003), 70.
6. William Howard, conversations with the author, July 2019.
7. John Cage, *Silence* (Middletown, CT: Wesleyan University Press, 2011), 51.
8. Luigi Russolo, "The Art of Noises," Obelisk Art History 2022, accessed September 30, 2022, https://arthistoryproject.com/artists/luigi-russolo/the-art-of-noises/.
9. George Michelsen Foy, *Zero Decibels: The Quest for Absolute Silence* (New York: Scribners), 65.
10. Michelsen Foy, *Zero Decibels*, 65.
11. John Tavener, quoted in Stuart Sim, *Manifesto for Silence* (Edinburgh: Edinburgh University Press, 2007), 114.
12. John Rutter, quoted in Paula Marvelly, "John Tavener: Toward Silence," The Culturium, May 21, 2017, www.theculturium.com/john-tavener-towards-silence/.
13. Stuart Sim, *Manifesto for Silence: Confronting the Politics and Culture of Noise* (Edinburgh: Edinburgh University Press, 2007), 114.
14. William Butler Yeats, "Long-Legged Fly," All Poetry, accessed September 30, 2022, https://allpoetry.com/Long-Legged-Fly.
15. Ken Johnson, "George Brecht, 82, Fluxus Conceptual Artist, Is Dead," *New York Times,* December 15, 2008.
16. Michelsen Foy, *Zero Decibels*, 66.
17. Tom Johnson, *The Voice of New Music: Collection of Articles Originally*

Published in the Village Voice (Eindhoven, Netherlands: Het Apollo-huis, 1989).

18. Michael Pisaro, "Time's Underground," Edition Wandelweiser, June 1997, www.wandelweiser.de/_michael-pisaro/texts.html.

19. Rupert Sheldrake, *Science and Spiritual Practices: Transformative Experiences and Their Effects on Our Bodies, Brains, and Health* (London: Coronet, 2017), 160–61.

20. William Howard, conversations with the author, July 2019.

21. Thomas Merton, *No Man Is an Island* (London: Hollis & Carter, 1955), quoted in *Friends of Silence* 17, no. 6 (June 2004).

22. Diarmaid MacCulloch, *Silence: A Christian History* (London: Allen Lane, 2013), 48.

23. Valery Rees, *From Gabriel to Lucifer* (London: Bloomsbury, 2012), 21.

24. John Milton, *Paradise Lost*, bk. 7 (Oxford: Oxford University Press, 2008), line 215.

25. Paul Johnson, "When Silentiaries Whacked Their Pillar in Ancient Byzantium," *The Spectator*, June 21, 2003.

26. Shirley du Boulay, *A Silent Melody* (London: Darton, Longman & Todd, 2014), 222.

27. Michael Church, *Peter Maxwell Davies: Max of the Antarctic, Independent*, February 11, 2005.

28. Aldous Huxley, *The Perennial Philosophy* (New York: Harper Brothers, 1945), 218.

29. Max Picard, *The World of Silence* (London: Harvill Press, 1952), 198.

30. Picard, *World of Silence*, 209.

31. Picard, 19.

32. Kate Chisholm, "Sound of the Gods," *The Spectator*, December 2, 2017.

33. Kate Chisholm, "The Ties That Bound Us," *The Spectator*, October 28, 2017.

34. School siege that lasted three days in September 2004 in North Ossetia, Russia.

35. Rhidian Brook, "The Archbishop's Pause," *Thought for the Day*, BBC Radio 4, December 28, 2017.

36. Rowan Williams, "Silence in the Face of Mystery," The Christian Century, August 21, 2018, www.christiancentury.org/article/critical-essay/silence-face-mystery.

37. Robert Everett-Green, "Dame Evelyn Glennie, the Deaf Percussionist who Listens with Her Whole Body," The Globe and Mail, March 1, 2011, www.theglobeandmail.com/arts/music/dame-evelyn-glennie -the-deaf-percussionist-who-listens-with-her-whole-body/article 568725/.

11. WAR

1. Fred Ball, "Ordinary War on the Somme" in John Lewis, *True World War 1 Stories: Gripping Eye-Witness Accounts from the Days of Conflict and Pain* (London: Robinson, 1999), 85.

2. Wilfred Owen, "Anthem for Doomed Youth," in *The Penguin Book of First World War Poetry*, ed. Jon Silkin (London: Penguin, 1979), 178.

3. David Jones, *In Parenthesis* (1937; London: Faber & Faber, 1961), 24.

4. Siegfried Sassoon, "Repression of War Experience, in *The Penguin Book of First World War Poetry*, ed. Jon Silkin (London: Penguin, 1979), 128–29.

5. George Michelsen Foy, *Zero Decibels: The Quest for Absolute Silence* (New York: Scribners), 42.

6. B. Neyland, "A Wireless Operator" in John Lewis, *True World War 1 Stories: Gripping Eye-Witness Accounts from the Days of Conflict and Pain* (London: Robinson, 1999), 109.

7. Neyland, "A Wireless Operator," *True World War 1 Stories*, 111.

8. Neyland, "A Wireless Operator," *True World War 1 Stories*, 113.

9. Shakespeare, *Henry V*, act 4, sc. 1. in *The Tudor Edition of William Shakespeare: The Complete Works* (London: Collins, 1959), 571.

10. Ivor Gurney, "That Centre of Old," in P. J. Kavanagh, *Ivor Gurney Selected Poems* (Oxford: Oxford University Press, 1990), 22.

11. Siegfried Sassoon, "The Death Bed," in *The Penguin Book of First World War Poetry*, ed. Jon Silkin (London: Penguin, 1979), 122–23.

12. Frank Gardner, *Blood and Sand* (London: Bantam, 2006), 13.

13. Wilfred Owen, "Exposure," in *The Penguin Book of First World War Poetry*, ed. Jon Silkin (London: Penguin, 1979), 175–76.

14. Wilfred Owen, "Strange Meeting," in *The Penguin Book of First World War Poetry*, ed. Jon Silkin (London: Penguin, 1979), 191–93.

15. Paul Fussell, *The Great War and Modern Memory* (Oxford: Oxford University Press, 1977), 87.

16. Ralph Waldo Emerson, "Intellect," *Essays* (Chicago: Cuneo Press, 1936), 232, referred to by Pico Iyer in "Where Silence Is Sacred," UTNE, accessed January 30, 2023, www.utne.com/mind-and-body/where-silence-is-sacred-chapels/.

17. Chris Agee, "Poetic Silence," *Poetry Ireland Review*, no. 40 (Winter 1993–1994): 88.

18. George Steiner, "Silence and the Poet," in *Language and Silence: Essays 1958–1966* (London: Faber, 1967), 74.

19. Isaac Rosenberg, letter to Laurence Binyon, Autumn 1916, "The Isaac Rosenberg Collection," First World War Poetry Digital Archive, accessed September 30, 2022, https://oxford.omeka.net/s/ww1lit/page/rosenberg-letters.

20. Steiner, "Silence and the Poet," 74.

21. Leslie Kane, *The Language of Silence: On the Unspoken and the Unspeakable in Modern Drama* (Plainsboro, NJ: Associated University Presses, 1984), 102.

22. Hayden Carruth, "Fallacies of Silence" *Hudson Review* 26, no. 3 (1973): 462.

23. Kate Chisholm, "Switch Off," *The Spectator*, February 28, 2009.

24. Chisholm, "Switch Off," *The Spectator*.

25. Chris Agee, "Poetic Silence," 88.

26. Paul Fussell, *Great War and Modern Memory*, 174.

27. Stuart Sim, *Manifesto for Silence* (Edinburgh: Edinburgh University Press, 2007), 2–3.

28. Sim, *Manifesto for Silence*, 31.

29. Janine di Giovanni, letter to the author, September 2017.

12. PRISON AND SOLITARY CONFINEMENT

1. John Howard, quoted in Jane Brox, *Silence: A Social History of One of the Least Understood Elements of Our Lives* (New York: Houghton Mifflin Harcourt, 2019), 32.

2. Oliver Sacks, from Robert B. Silvers (lecture, New York Public Library, New York City, September 21, 2009).

3. Charles Dickens, *American Notes* (London: Penguin, 2004), 111.

4. Dickens, *American Notes*, 111.

5. Charles Dickens, *David Copperfield* (1849; London: Oxford University Press, 2008).

6. Charles Dickens, *Little Dorrit* (1855–57; London: Oxford University Press, 1999).

7. Eugenia Ginzburg, quoted in Jane Brox, *Silence: A Social History of One of the Least Understood Elements of Our Lives* (New York: Houghton Mifflin Harcourt, 2019), 117.

8. Arthur Koestler, *Dialogue with Death* (1937; New York: Macmillan, 1942), 217.

9. Arthur Koestler, *Darkness at Noon* (London: Macmillan, 1940).

10. Christopher Burney, *Solitary Confinement* (London: Clerke & Cockeran, 1952), 150.

11. Vera Figner, *Memoirs of a Revolutionist* (Ithaca, NY: Cornell University Press, 1927).

12. Edith Bone, *Seven Years Solitary* (London: Hamish Hamilton, 1957), 90.

13. Anthony Grey, *Hostage in Peking* (London: Michael Joseph, 1970).

14. Chris Wood, "The Beijing-Born British Translator Who Survived Solitary Confinement during the Cultural Revolution" *Post Magazine*, January 18, 2019.

15. Roger Cooper, *Death Plus Ten Years* (London: HarperCollins, 1993).

16. Terry Waite, *Taken on Trust* (London: Hodder & Stoughton, 2016).

17. Albert Woodfox, epilogue, *Solitary: Unbroken by Four Decades in Solitary Confinement—My Story of Transformation and Hope* (New York: Grove Press, 2019), 395, Kindle.

18. "Mystical Experience of Loss of Freedom," *Network Review: Journal of the Scientific and Medical Network*, no. 112 (2016/3).

19. "Mystical Experience of Loss of Freedom," *Network Review.*

20. "Mystical Experience of Loss of Freedom," *Network Review.*

21. Dimitri Panin, *The Notebooks of Sologdin* (New York: Harcourt Brace Jovanovich, 1976), 145.

22. "Mystical Experience of Loss of Freedom," *Network Review.*

23. "Mystical Experience of Loss of Freedom," *Network Review.*

24. "Mystical Experience of Loss of Freedom," *Network Review.*

25. Aleksandr Solzhenitsyn, *Gulag Archipelago* (New York: Harper & Row, 1974), 484.

26. Wikipedia, s.v. "John Mirk," last modified June 16, 2022, 19:55, https://en.wikipedia.org/wiki/John_Mirk.

27. Quoted in Jane Brox, *Silence: A Social History of One of the Least Understood Elements of Our Lives* (New York: Houghton Mifflin Harcourt, 2019), 171.

28. Daryl Austin "What You're Saying When You Give Someone the Silent Treatment," *The Atlantic*, March 26, 2021, www.theatlantic.com/family /archive/2021/03/psychology-of-silent-treatment-abuse/618411/.

29. David Thomas, letter to the editor, *The Spectator*, October 2017.

30. Thomas Merton, *Seeds of Contemplation* (1949; Cambridge, MA: New Directions, 1987).

31. "The International Thomas Merton Society," http://merton.org/ITMS/.

32. Anthony Storr, *Solitude* (London: Ballantine Books, 1988), 60.

13. CONSCIOUS LISTENING

1. Washakie, in Maggie Ross, *Silence: A User's Guide* (London: Darton, Longman & Todd, 2014), 126.

2. Douglas Adams, *The Hitchhikers Guide to the Galaxy* (London: Pan Books, 2009).

3. Karen Armstrong, writer and presenter of six-part documentary series *The First Christian*, commissioned by John Ranelagh, first screened January 1984, Channel 4.

4. Karen Armstrong, *The Spiral Staircase: A Memoir* (London: Harper-Collins, 2004), 271.

5. Horatio Clare, *Icebreaker: A Voyage Far North* (London: Chatto & Windus, 2017), 49–50.

6. Sara Wheeler, "The Ice Was All Around," *The Spectator*, November 18, 2017.

7. Erling Kagge, *Silence: In the Age of Noise* (London: Viking, 2017), 102.

8. Nicholas Pearson, letter to the author, January 2018.

9. Douglas Harding, *On Having No Head* (London: Arkana, 1986).

10. Nicholas Pearson, letter to the author, January 2018.

11. Aldous Huxley, *The Doors of Perception* (London: Chatto & Windus, 1954).

12. Stephen Batchelor, *The Art of Solitude* (London: Yale University Press, 2020), 25.

13. Batchelor, *Art of Solitude*, 26.

14. Bella Bathurst, *Sound* (London: Wellcome Collection, 2017), 202.

15. Wikiwand, s.v. "The History of Sign Language," accessed September 30, 2022, www.wikiwand.com/en/History_of_sign_language.

16. Jean-Dominique Bauby, *The Diving-Bell and the Butterfly* (London: Fourth Estate, 1997), 97.

17. Jonathan Bryan, *Eye Can Write: A Memoir of a Child's Silent Soul Emerging* (London: Lagom, 2018).

18. Stuart Sim, *Manifesto for Silence* (Edinburgh: Edinburgh University Press, 2007), 20.

19. "WHO: 1 in 4 People Projected to Have Hearing Problems by 2050," World Health Organization, March 2, 2021, www.who.int/news /item/02-03-2021-who-1-in-4-people-projected-to-have-hearing -problems-by-2050.

20. "Over One Billion People at Risk of Hearing Loss: WHO," UN News, March 2, 20222, https://news.un.org/en/story/2022/03/1113182.

21. Philip Jaekl, "What Is the Mysterious 'Global Hum' – and Is It Simply Noise Pollution?" *The Guardian*, March 13, 2019.

22. David Deming, "The Hum: An Anomalous Sound Heard Around the World," *Journal of Scientific Exploration* 18, no. 4 (2004): 571–95.

23. G. K. Chesterton, "On Popular Music and Modern Jazz," *Illustrated London News*, April 22, 1933

24. Posted by Supervisor dangerouspraline Reddit, 2019, www.reddit. com/r/starbucks/comments/ah2m1d/if_i_have_to_hear_hamilton _one_more_time_im/.

25. Pipedown, www.pipedown.org.uk.

26. *Desert Island Discs*, BBC Radio 4, March 17, 2019.

27. Lavinia Byrne, letter to the author, April 2019.

28. Sim, *Manifesto for Silence*, 44.

29. Sim, 1.

30. Sim, 24.

31. George Prochnik, *In Pursuit of Silence* (New York: Random House, 2010), 113.

32. Homer, *The Odyssey*, translated by Emily Wilson (New York: W. W. Norton & Company, Inc., 2018), 302.

33. Manuella Lech Cantuaria, Frans Boch Waldorff, Lene Wermuth, Ellen Raben Pedersen, Aslak Harbo Poulsen, Jesse Daniel Thacher, Ole

Raaschou-Nielsen, Matthias Ketzel, Jibran Khan, Victor H. Valencia, Jesper Hvass Schmidt and Mette Sørensen, "Residential Exposure to Transportation Noise in Denmark and Incidence of Dementia: National Cohort Study," *British Medical Journal*, September 9, 2021, BMJ 2021; 374: n1954, doi: 10.1136/bmj.n1954.

34. "Environmental Noise Guidelines for the European Region," World Health Organization, Regional Office for Europe, January 30, 2019, www.who.int/europe/publications/i/item/9789289053563.

35. "What Is Occupational Noise Exposure?" Safety Culture, December 16, 2022, https://safetyculture.com/topics/occupational-noise-exposure/.

36. Sim, *Manifesto for Silence*, 27.

37. Sim, 23.

38. Johanna Roeber, letter to the author, January 2018.

39. David Fraser Jenkins, letter to the author, March 2018.

40. Mary Wakefield, "We're Living amid a Rising Tide of Background Noise," *The Spectator*, March 23, 2019.

41. Rt. Rev. Dr. Michael Marshall, "Sermon on 1st Sunday of Lent at Holy Trinity," Sloane Square, March 10, 2019.

42. Anne Baring, letter to the author, September 2017.

43. Rachel Johnson, letter to the author, 2018.

44. Liz Claridge, letter to the author, November 2017.

45. Bhagavad Gita 4:18, translator Juan Mascaro (London: Penguin, 1962), 62.

46. Karen Armstrong, *A History of God* (London: Penguin, 1993).

47. Karen Armstrong, *The Spiral Staircase: My Climb Out of Darkness* (New York: HarperCollins, 2004), 318.

48. Armstrong, *Spiral Staircase*, 333.

49. Thomas Merton, *Thoughts in Solitude* (Boston: Shambhala Publications, 1993), 113.

50. Merton, *Thoughts in Solitude*, 113.

51. Blaise Pascal, *Pensées*, quoted in Alain Corbin, *A History of Silence: From the Renaissance to the Present Day* (London: Polity, 2018), 115.

52. Blaise Pascal, *Pensées: 392* (London: Harvill Press, 1962), 221.

53. Virginia Woolf, *A Room of One's Own* (London: Hogarth Press, 1929).

54. Rachel Johnson, letter to the author, 2018.

55. Rupert Sheldrake, *Science and Spiritual Practices: Reconnecting through Direct Experience* (London: Coronet, 2017), 49.

56. Sheldrake, *Science and Spiritual Practices*, 48.

57. Sean Swallow, letter to the author, January 2018.

58. Andrew Harvey, *A Journey in Ladakh* (London: Picador, 1993), 93.

59. Tom Shone, "Film Reviews: Pope Francis; The Negotiator," *The Sunday Times*, August 12, 2018.

60. Liz Cumming, "'Let Them Hear Our Silence:' Experiencing the Silent Walk for Grenfell," Quakers in Britain, July 2, 2018, www.quaker.org .uk/blog/experiencing-the-silent-walk-for-grenfell.

61. Cumming, "'Let Them Hear Our Silence.'"

62. Just This Day, www.contemplativeoutreach.org.uk.

63. BBC News, October 2, 2015.

64. "Look Beyond Borders: A 4 Minute Experiment," Amnesty International, YouTube video, 00:05, May 26, 2016, www.youtube.com/watch ?v=9Z68P9Gc77A.

65. Mark Blunden, "Airport Offers 'Dumb Phone' to Travellers," *London Evening Standard,* August 16, 2018.

BIBLIOGRAPHY

Ansell, Neil. *The Last Wilderness: A Journey into Silence.* London: Tinder Press, 2018.

Armstrong, Karen. *The Spiral Staircase: A Memoir.* London: HarperCollins, 2004.

Atkins, William. *The Immeasurable World: Journeys in Desert Places.* London: Faber & Faber, 2018.

Attlee, James. *Nocturne: A Journey in Search of Moonlight.* London: Hamish Hamilton, 2011.

Barkham, Patrick. *Islander: A Journey Around Our Archipelago.* London: Granta, 2017.

Batchelor, Stephen. *The Art of Solitude: A Meditation on Being Alone with Others in This World.* London: Yale University Press, 2020.

Bathhurst, Bella. *Sound: A Story of Hearing Lost and Found.* London: Wellcome Collection, 2017.

Bauby, Jean-Dominique. *The Diving-Bell and the Butterfly.* London: Fourth Estate, 1997.

Bhagavad Gita. Translated by Juan Mascaró. London: Penguin, 1962.

Blodgett, E. D., and H. G. Coward, eds. *Silence, the Word and the Sacred.* Waterloo, Ontario: Wilfrid Laurier University Press, 1989.

Bone, Edith. *Seven Years Solitary.* London: Hamish Hamilton, 1959.

Bowles, Paul. *Their Heads Are Green.* London: Peter Owen, 1963.

Brox, Jane. *Silence: A Social History of One of the Least Understood Elements of Our Lives.* Boston: Houghton Mifflin Harcourt, 2019.

Bryan, Jonathan. *Eye Can Write: A Memoir of a Child's Silent Soul Emerging.* Lerum, Sweden: Lagom, 2018.

Buckley, Martin. *Grains of Sand.* London: Hutchinson, 2000.

Bucklow, Spike. *The Anatomy of Riches: Sir Robert Paston's Treasure.* London: Reaktion, 2018.

Burney, Christopher. *Solitary Confinement.* London: Clerke & Cockeran, 1952.

Byrd, Richard. *Alone.* London: Neville Spearman, 1958.

Byron, Robert. *The Road to Oxiana.* London: Macmillan, 1937.

Cadby, Alex. "Silence and War." PhD diss., University of Exeter, 2010.

Cage, John. *Silence: Lectures and Writings.* Middletown, CT: Wesleyan University Press, 1961.

Cain, Susan. *Quiet: The Power of Introverts in a World That Can't Stop Talking.* London: Viking, 2012.

Campbell, Nancy. *The Library of Ice: Readings from a Cold Climate.* New York: Scribner, 2018.

Campbell-Culver, Maggie. *A Passion for Trees: The Legacy of John Evelyn.* Cornwall: Eden Project, 2006.

Camus, Albert. *The Plague.* London: Penguin, 2013.

Capps, Walter, ed. *Thomas Merton. Preview of an Asian Journey.* New York: Crossroad, 1989.

Carthusian, A. *The Call of Silent Love.* London: Darton, Longman & Todd, 1995.

Carruth, Hayden. "Fallacies of Silence." *Hudson Review* 26, no. 3 (1973): 462–70.

Cashen, Richard Anthony. *Solitude in the Thought of Thomas Merton.* Collegeville, MN: Cistercian Publications, 1981.

Chatwin, Bruce. *The Songlines.* London: Jonathan Cape, 1987.

Chevalier, Tracy. *The Last Runaway.* London: HarperCollins, 2013.

Clare, Horatio. *Icebreaker: A Voyage Far North.* London: Chatto & Windus, 2017.

Claxton, Guy (Swami Anand Ageha). *Wholly Human: Western and Eastern Visions of the Self and Its Perfection.* London: Routledge & Kegan Paul, 1981.

Colegate, Isabel. *A Pelican in the Wilderness: Hermits, Solitaries, and Recluses.* London: HarperCollins, 2002.

Conrad, Joseph. *An Outpost of Progress.* London: Penguin, 2015.

Cooper, Roger. *Death Plus Ten Years: My Life as the Ayatollah's Prisoner by "Notorious British Spy."* London: HarperCollins, 1993.

Corbin, Alain. *A History of Silence: From the Renaissance to the Present Day.* Cambridge: Polity, 2018.

Cousteau, J. Y. *The Silent World: A Story of Undersea Discovery and Adventure Unfolding Wonders Never Before Seen by Man.* London: Hamish Hamilton, 1953.

Crowden, James. *The Frozen River: Seeking Silence in the Himalaya.* London: William Collins, 2020.

Davidson, Robyn. *Tracks: One Woman's Journey Across 1,700 Miles of Australian Outback.* London: Cape, 1980.

Deakin, Roger. *Waterlog: A Swimmer's Journey through Britain.* London: Chatto & Windus, 1999.

de Poncins, Gontran. *Kabloona.* New York: Reynal, 1941.

de Saint-Exupéry, Antoine. *Wind, Sand and Stars.* London: Penguin, 2000.

Dillard, Annie. *Teaching a Stone to Talk: Expeditions and Encounters.* Edinburgh: Canongate, 2017.

Du Boulay, Shirley. *A Silent Melody: An Experience of Contemporary Spiritual Life.* London: Darton, Longman & Todd, 2014.

Edwards, Nina. *Darkness: A Cultural History.* London: Reaktion, 2018.

Epstein, Hugh. *Hardy, Conrad and the Senses.* Edinburgh: Edinburgh University Press, 2020.

Fergusson, Maggie. "How Does It Really Feel to Be Lonely?" 1843 Magazine, *The Economist,* January 22, 2018.

Figes, Orlando. *The Europeans: Three Lives and the Making of a Cosmopolitan Culture.* London: Penguin, 2020.

Finkel, Michael. *The Stranger in the Woods: The Extraordinary Story of the Last True Hermit.* London: Simon & Schuster, 2017.

Fontana, David. *Psychology, Religion, and Spirituality.* Oxford: Wiley-Blackwell, 2003.

Foy, George Michelsen. *Zero Decibels: The Quest for Absolute Silence.* New York: Scribner, 2010.

France, Peter. *Hermits: The Insights of Solitude.* London: Chatto & Windus, 1996.

Freeman, Laurence. *Light Within: The Inner Path of Meditation.* London: Darton, Longman & Todd, 1995.

———. *The Selfless Self: Meditation and the Opening of the Heart.* London: Darton, Longman & Todd, 1996.

Fromentin, Eugène. *Between Sea & Sahara*: *An Algerian Journal*. London: Tauris Parke, 2004.

Fussell, Paul. *The Great War and Modern Memory*. Oxford: Oxford University Press, 1977.

Gardner, Frank. *Blood and Sand*. London: Bantam, 2006.

Gemmell, Nikki. *On Quiet*. Melbourne: Melbourne University Press, 2018.

George, Uwe. *In the Deserts of This Earth*. London: Hamish Hamilton, 1978.

Ginzburg, Eugenia. *Within the Whirlwind*. London: Collins, 1981.

Gray, John. *The Silence of Animals*: *On Progress and Other Modern Myths*. London: Allen Lane, 2013.

Grey, Anthony. *Hostage in Peking*: *A Correspondent's Story of Despair, Ingenuity, and Fortitude in Solitary Confinement*. London: Michael Joseph, 1970.

Griffiths, Bede. *A New Vision of Reality*: *Western Science, Eastern Mysticism and Christian Faith*. London: Collins, 1989.

Haggerty, Donald. *Contemplative Provocations*: *Brief, Concentrated Observations on Aspects of Life with God*. San Francisco: Ignatius Press, 2013.

Hanh, Thich Nhat. *For a Future to Be Possible*: *Buddhist Ethics for Everyday Life*. Berkeley, CA: Parallax Press, 1993.

Harding, D. E. *On Having No Head*: *Zen and the Rediscovery of the Obvious*. London Arkana, 1986.

Hatch, Amber. *The Art of Silence*. London: Piatkus, 2017.

Haynes, Roslynn D. *Seeking the Centre*: *The Australian Desert in Literature, Art and Film*. Cambridge: Cambridge University Press, 1998.

Hempton, Gordon, and John Grossman. *One Square Inch of Silence*: *One Man's Quest to Preserve Quiet*. New York: Atria Books, 2010.

Hospital, Janette Turner. *Oyster*. London: Virago, 1996.

Huxley, Aldous. *Complete Essays*: *Volume V 1939–1956*. Chicago: Ivan R. Dee, 2002.

———. *The Perennial Philosophy*: *An Interpretation of the Great Mystics, East and West*. London: Chatto & Windus, 1946.

Jefferies, Richard. *The Story of My Heart*. London: Penguin, 1938.

Johnston, William. *Arise, My Love*: *Mysticism for a New Era*. Maryknoll, New York: Orbis Books, 2000.

———. *Silent Music*: *The Science of Meditation*. New York: Fordham University Press, 1997.

Kagge, Erling. *Silence in the Age of Noise*. London: Viking, 2017.

Kamps, Toby; Seid, Steve; Sorkin, Jenni. *Silence* exhibition catalogue, Menil Collection (Houston, TX), Berkeley Art Museum and Pacific Film Archive. New Haven, CT: Yale University Press, 2012.

Kane, Leslie. *The Language of Silence: On the Unspoken and the Unspeakable in Modern Drama*. Plainsboro, NJ: Associated University Presses, 1984.

Keen, Sam. *To a Dancing God: Notes of a Spiritual Traveler*. New York: Harper & Row, 1990.

Kerouac, Jack. *The Dharma Bums*. New York: Viking, 1958.

Kirste, Imke; Nicola, Zeina; Kronenberg, Golo; Walker Tara L.; Liu, Robert C; and Kempermann, Gerd. "Is Silence Golden? Effects of Auditory Stimuli and Their Absence on Adult Hippocampal Neurogenesis," *Brain Structure & Function* 220, no. 2 (December 1, 2013): 1221–28.

Knox-Johnston, Robin, A. *A World of My Own: The First Ever Non-Stop Solo Round the World Voyage*. London: Cassell, 1969.

Koestler, Arthur. *Kaleidoscope: Essays from "Drinkers of Infinity" and "The Heel of Achilles" and Later Pieces and Stories*. London: Hutchinson, 1981.

Kornfield, Jack. *After the Ecstasy, the Laundry: How the Heart Grows Wise on the Spiritual Path*. New York: Bantam Books, 2001.

Krakauer, Jon. *Into the Wild*. London: Macmillan, 1998.

Laird, Martin. *Into the Silent Land: The Practice of Contemplation*. London: Darton, Longman & Todd, 2006.

Lane, Belden C. *The Solace of Fierce Landscapes: Exploring Desert and Mountain Spirituality*. Oxford: Oxford University Press, 1998.

Lawrence, T. E. *Seven Pillars of Wisdom: A Triumph*. London: Cape, 1935.

Laxness, Halldór. *Under the Glacier*. London: Vintage, 2022.

LeClaire, Anne D. *Listening Below the Noise: A Meditation on the Practice of Silence*. New York: Harper Perennial, 2009.

Leigh Fermor, Patrick. *A Time to Keep Silence*. London: John Murray, 1957.

Leopold, Aldo. *A Sand County Almanac and Sketches Here and There*. Oxford: Oxford University Press, 1949.

Lindqvist, Sven. *Desert Divers*. London: Granta, 2000.

Lusseyran, Jacques. *And There Was Light: The Extraordinary Memoir of a Blind Hero in the Resistance in World War II*. Novato, CA: New World Library, 2014.

MacCulloch, Diarmaid. *Silence: A Christian History*. London: Penguin, 2014.

Macfarlane, Robert. *Underland: A Deep Time Journey*. London: Hamish Hamilton, 2019.

Mackenzie, Vicki. *Cave in the Snow: A Western Woman's Quest for Enlightenment*. London: Bloomsbury, 1998.

McGahern, John. *Memoir*. London: Faber & Faber, 2005.

McGilchrist, Iain. *The Master and His Emissary: The Divided Brain and the Making of the Western World*. London: Yale University Press, 2009.

Maguire, Nancy Klein. *An Infinity of Little Hours: Five Young Men and Their Trial of Faith in the Western World's Most Austere Monastic Order*. New York: PublicAffairs, 2006.

Main, John. *Moment of Christ: The Path of Meditation*. London: Darton, Longman & Todd, 1987.

Maitland, Sara. *A Book of Silence*: *A Journey in Search of the Pleasures and Powers of Silence*. London: Granta, 2008.

Malraux, André. *The Voices of Silence: Man and His Art*. London: Secker, 1956.

Manguel, Alberto. *A History of Reading*. London: HarperCollins, 1996.

Martineau, Robert. *Waypoints: A Journey on Foot*. London: Cape, 2021.

Maugham, W. Somerset. *Points of View*. London: Heinemann, 1958.

———. *The Razor's Edge*. London: Vintage, 2000

Mayne, Michael. *This Sunrise of Wonder: Letters for the Journey*. London: Fount, 1995.

McGrath, Sandra, and John Olsen. *The Artist and the Desert*. Sydney: HarperCollins 1981.

Merton, Thomas. *The Asian Journal*. New York: New Directions, 1975.

———. *Contemplation in a World of Action*. London: George Allen & Unwin, 1971.

———. *Elected Silence: The Autobiography of Thomas Merton*. London: Burns & Oates, 1961.

———. *Mystics and Zen Masters*. New York: Farrar, Straus and Giroux, 1999.

———. *Waters of Silence*. London: Hollis & Carter, 1950.

Meynell, Alice. "Solitude" in *Essays*. Westport, CT: Greenwood Press, 1970.

Moorhouse, Geoffrey. *Sun Dancing: A Medieval Vision*. London: Weidenfeld & Nicolson 1997.

Nicolson, Adam. *Sea Room: My Love Affair with the Islands*. London: HarperCollins, 2001.

Norris, Kathleen. *The Cloister Walk*. New York: Riverhead Books, 1997.

Olsen, Tillie. *Silences*. London: Virago, 1980.

"OWLS—Oxford and Wimbledon Leading Scholars," Oxford High School GDST, https://oxfordhigh.gdst.net/owls-oxford-and-wimbledon-leading-scholars/.

Parks, Tim. *Teach Us to Sit Still: A Sceptic's Search for Health and Healing*. London: Harvill Secker, 2010.

Picard, Max. *The World of Silence*. London: Harvill Press, 1952.

Pinter, Harold. *Landscape and Silence*. London: Methuen, 1970.

Prochnik, George. *In Pursuit of Silence: Listening for Meaning in a World of Noise*. New York: Doubleday, 2010.

Radcliffe, Timothy. *Why Go to Church?: The Drama of the Eucharist*. London: Bloomsbury, 2008.

Ramana Maharshi. *The Teachings of Ramana Maharshi: In His Own Words*. Edited by Arthur Osborne. London: Random House, 2014.

Rees, Valery. *From Gabriel to Lucifer: A Cultural History of Angels*. London: Bloomsbury, 2012.

Robertson, Paul. *Soundscapes: A Musician's Journey Through Life and Death*. London: Faber, 2016.

Rogerson, Barnaby and Alexander Monro. *Desert Air: A Collection of the Poetry of Place—of Arabia, Deserts and the Orient of the Imagination*. London: Baring & Rogerson Books, 2001.

Roose-Evans, James. *Finding Silence: 52 Meditations for Daily Living*. Cheltenham, UK: History Press, 2009.

———. *Inner Journey, Outer Journey: Finding a Spiritual Centre in Everyday Life*. London: Rider & Company, 1987.

Rosen, William. *Justinian's Flea: Plague, Empire and the Birth of Europe*. London: Cape, 2007.

Ross, Maggie. *Silence: A User's Guide*. London: Darton, Longman & Todd, 2014.

Sands, Sarah. *The Interior Silence: 10 Lessons from Monastic Life*. London: Short Books, 2021.

Sarah, Robert Cardinal. *The Power of Silence: Against the Dictatorship of Noise*. San Francisco: Ignatius Press, 2017.

Sardello, Robert. *Silence: The Mystery of Wholeness*. Berkeley, CA: North Atlantic Books, 2008.

Shapiro, James. *1606: William Shakespeare and the Year of Lear*. London: Faber, 2015.

Shawcross, Harriet. *Unspeakable: The Things We Cannot Say*. Edinburgh: Canongate, 2019.

Sheldrake, Rupert. *Science and Spiritual Practices: Reconnecting Through Direct Experience*. London: Coronet, 2017.

Shepherd, Nan. *The Living Mountain: A Celebration of the Cairngorm Mountains of Scotland*. Edinburgh: Canongate, 2011.

Sim, Stuart. *Manifesto for Silence: Confronting the Politics and Culture of Noise*. Edinburgh: Edinburgh University Press, 2007.

Solnit, Rebecca. *The Mother of All Questions: Further Feminisms*. London: Granta, 2017.

Sontag, Susan. "The Aesthetics of Silence." In *Essays of the 1960s and 70s*. 292–320. New York: Library of America, 2013.

Steiner, George. "Silence and the Poet." In *Language and Silence: Essays 1958–1966*. 36–54. London: Faber, 1967.

Storr, Anthony. *Solitude: A Return to the Self*. London: Flamingo, 1988.

Taylor, Barbara Brown. *When God Is Silent*. Norwich, UK: Canterbury Press, 2013.

Tuchman, Barbara. *A Distant Mirror: The Calamitous 14th Century*. New York: Alfred A. Knopf, 1978.

Van Dyke, John C. *The Desert*. New York: Charles Scribner, 1911.

Vincent, David. *A History of Solitude*. Cambridge: Polity, 2020.

Wales, H. R. H, with Ian Skelly and Tony Juniper. *Harmony: A New Way of Looking at Our World*. London: HarperCollins, 2010.

Wallace, Marjorie. *The Silent Twins: The Harrowing True Story of Sisters Locked in a Shocking Childhood Pact*. London: Chatto & Windus, 1986.

Walser, Robert. *Jakob von Gunten*. New York: New York Review of Books, 1999.

Whistler, Laurence. *Audible Silence*. London: Rupert Hart-Davis, 1961.

Williams, Rowan. *Silence and Honey Cakes: The Wisdom of the Desert*. Oxford: Lion Books, 2003.

INDEX

Merton, Thomas, 94, 159
  biographical information, 112–14
  on Eastern spiritual traditions, 101
  fame and influence, 98, 112, 114–15
  fourfold formula of, 220
  on God, contemplating, 102
  on music, 171
  Seeds of Contemplation, 201
  on silence, 103, 104, 106, 223
Messiaen, Olivier, 168
Mexico, "Silence Zone," 62
Michaela Community School, 121
Millet, Jean-François, 154, 156
Milton, John, *Paradise Lost*, 172, 173
mindfulness, 108, 118, 120, 205
Mingaladon monastery, 118
Minghella, Anthony, *Cigarettes and
  Chocolate* (radio play), 144
Mirk, John, *Mirk's Festial*, 198
misophonia, 212–13
Mithraism, 77
Moitessier, Bernard, *The Long Way*,
  10
Mojave Desert, 54–55
Molinos, Miguel de, 89
Mompou, Frederic, 167
monasteries and abbeys, 11, 64–68,
  79, 80, 101–2, 118, 161. *See also*
  Abbey of Gethsemani
monasticism, 78
  Christian, 86, 88, 93–94, 96
  meditation in, 102–4, 116–17
  silence in, 12, 106, 118
  Thai Forest tradition, 27
Mondrian, Piet, 158
Montaigne, Michel de, 25
Moore, Henry, 162
Morandi, Giorgio, 157, 160–61,
  163–64

mountains, 10, 45–46, 223
Muir, John, 36, 45
Munch, Edvard, 156
Murphy, Robert, 77
museums, 75, 147, 156–57, 160–61,
  185. *See also* National Gallery
  (London)
music, 165–66
  composers, 166–69
  experimental, 169–70
  hearing damage from, 213–14
  paintings and, 150, 155
  in public, 215–16
  and silence, interplay between, 83
  silent, 87
music of the spheres, 28, 87, 94–95,
  172, 173
Muta, 74, 238n5
mutism, xii, 3, 131–32, 184
Myanmar (formerly Burma), 118–19
mystery religions, 76–77
mysticism, 54, 81–82, 112, 158
  Christian, 83–84, 85–86, 87–88,
    96–97, 103, 118, 159
  Jewish, 95

Naga (Serpent God), 75
National Gallery (London), 146, 147,
  148, 149, 151, 152
National Gallery of Art (Washington
  D. C.), 157
natural disasters, 65
nature, 28, 227. *See also* deserts;
  forests; mountains; oceans and
  seas
Netanyahu, Benjamin, 227
neuroscience, 166. *See also* brain
  functions
Neuroscience Letters, 108–9

religious and spiritual traditions
drug use in, 209
meditation in, 98, 99–100
and psychology, link between, 107
silence in, 11, 81
Remembrance Sunday, 183
retreats, 102
author's, 10–13, 117–18
solitary/silent, 119, 120
Rice, Julia Barnett, 24
Rievaulx, 64–65
Rilke, Rainer Maria, *The Book of Hours*, 129
Roberts, Sophy, *The Lost Pianos of Siberia*, 170–71
Rolheiser, Ronald, OMI, 12–13
Roman Empire, 74
Roose-Evans, James, 109
Rosa, Salvator, 151
Rosenberg, Isaac, 184
Rothko, Mark, 159–60
Rothko Chapel, 159–60, 161
Royal Academy of Painting, 153
ruins, 63–65
Russian Orthodox Church, 27
Russolo, Luigi, 35, 159, 167
Rutter, John, 168

Sacks, Jonathan, 185
Sacks, Oliver, 189
Sahara, 55–56
sailing, 8, 10
Saint-Exupéry, Antoine de, *Wind, Sand and Stars*, 55
Samye Ling Monastery, 101–2
Santa Maria de Montserrat Abbey, 11, 161
Sapera, Kate, 122
Sappho, 163

Sassoon, Siegfried, 180, 181
Satyananda Saraswati, 105
Schnabel, Artur, 165, 171
Schopenhauer, Arthur, 18, 19, 133
Schubert, Franz, 171
science, 109, 110–11, 130. *See also* neuroscience
scold's bridle, 199
Scotland, 101–2, 180, 199, 215
Scotus, John Duns, "Nondum," 138
Scully, Sean, 160
sculpture, 161, 162
self
desert and, 57
East and West distinctions on, 100
meditation and, 99
rising sense of, 92
silence and, 90, 91
true, harmony with, 114
understanding, 102
self-reflection, 55, 121
Selfridges department store, 68
Seneca, 91–92
senses, 129, 166, 224
shadow side, 116
Shakespeare, 137
Hamlet, 141
Henry V, 181
King Lear, 141
Sheldrake, Rupert, 109, 170, 223–24
Shelley, Percy Bysshe, 53, 125
Shepherd, Nan, *The Living Mountain*, 46
Shiant Isles, 51
Siberia, 44, 170–71
sign language, 75, 88, 89, 145, 160, 210–11
silence
absolute/total, 58–59, 134

ABOUT THE AUTHOR

Sarah Anderson founded the Travel Bookshop in Notting Hill in 1979, the shop that later featured in the film *Notting Hill*. Her books include *Heaven's Face Thinly Veiled: A Book of Spiritual Writing by Women*, *Anderson's Travel Companion*, *Inside Notting Hill*, and *Halfway to Venus: A One-Armed Journey*. She lives in London and travels and paints.